the **Art** of Knotting and Splicing

the Art of Knotting & Splicing

by
CYRUS LAWRENCE DAY

FOURTH EDITION

Edited by
Ray O. Beard, Jr.
and M. Lee Hoffman, Jr.

NAVAL INSTITUTE PRESS
ANNAPOLIS, MARYLAND

Copyright © 1947
by
Dodd, Mead and Company, Inc.
New York, New York

Second printing, 1988

Copyright © 1955, 1970, 1986
by
The United States Naval Institute
Annapolis, Maryland

Library of Congress Cataloging-in-Publication Data

Day, Cyrus Lawrence, 1900–1968.
    The art of knotting and splicing.

    Bibliography: p.
    Includes index.
    1. Knots and splices.   I. Beard, Ray O.   II. Hoffman,
M. Lee.   III. Title.
VM533.D295   1986   623.88′82   86-16299
ISBN 0-87021-062-9

Printed in the United States of America

Preface to the First Edition

The Art of Knotting and Splicing has grown by gradual degrees out of my former book, *Sailors' Knots*, which was published in 1935. During the twelve years that have elapsed since that date, I have given a good deal of thought to the subject of knots, and I have learned a good deal that I did not know then, not only about knots themselves, but also about the best ways to describe and picture them.

The following devices aim to make the present book convenient and easy to use:

(1) Illustrations and text always face each other, so that the reader, in studying the one, is not obliged to thumb the pages in order to consult the other.

(2) Illustrations and text are often further coordinated by means of separate expository paragraphs numbered to correspond with the individual photographs.

(3) Successive stages in the tying of the knots are fully illustrated whenever necessary.

(4) The ends of the rope are clearly distinguished from the standing parts. To achieve this result I have sometimes sacrificed realism and pictured the ends as shorter than they ought to be, for otherwise they would not always appear within the limits of the photographs. The reader is therefore cautioned, when following the directions, to leave the ends long enough so that the successive stages in the tying of the knots will be possible, and so that the ends will not slip out when the knots are completed and in use.

In preparing this book, I have profited by the advice and assistance of many friends and correspondents. I am particularly indebted, for a variety of suggestions, to Professor Malcolm Agnew, Professor Gerald Brace, Professor R. R. Cawley, Mr. L. W. Case, Professor Daniel Coogan, Professor J. M. Drew, Mr. Alan Gray, Miss Marjorie Hurd, Mr. Clifford Lynam, Mr. Hal McKail, Mr. F. L. R. Murray, Mr. David Poffenberger, Mr. Edward Ross, Mr. Guy H. B. Smith, the late Mr. G. H. Taber, Mr. Lloyd Teitsworth, and Mr. David Upson.

I owe much, also, to Professor H. K. Preston, Professor T. D. Mylrea, and the late Dean R. L. Spencer for aid and instruction in the use of the testing machines in the materials-testing laboratory at the University of Delaware; and to Mr. L. G. Miller for permission to publish his identifications of the knots described by Oribasius. Mr. Miller, in addition, has furnished me with many items of miscellaneous information from his vast store of knot knowledge.

The books that I have found most helpful in my study of knots are David Steel's *Elements and Practice of Rigging and Seamanship* (2 volumes, London, 1794), D'Arcy Lever's *Sheet Anchor* (second edition, London, 1819), Hjalmar Öhrvall's *Om Knutar* (second edition, Stockholm, 1916), George Russell Shaw's *Knots Useful and Ornamental* (second edition, Boston, 1933), and *The Ashley Book of Knots* by Clifford Ashley (New York, 1944). This last will always remain, I feel sure, the definitive encyclopedia of knots, for unlike most knot books it is based on actual usage and does not rely uncritically on previous authorities. It is a pleasure to acknowledge the help that I have received from this book and from its author.

Additional debts to friends and to books are acknowledged at relevant places in the text. A bibliography of knot books is included.

CYRUS DAY

Newark, Delaware
August 1947

Preface to the Fourth Edition

This edition's sections on the characteristics of rope and rope construction contain additional information on synthetic fibers. Our effort was greatly assisted by Charles Tobin, Ray Wong, and G. P. Foster of Samson Ocean Systems, Inc. Thanks are also extended to P. A. LeMaistre of Yale Cordage for the many samples of synthetic fiber lines and pamphlets he provided.

Two new sections describe the hot knife and liquid vinyl methods of sealing synthetic lines. The halter hitch, a knot often used by sailboaters, is described in this edition. Another new section details the swage (mechanical eye) splice in wire rope. We appreciate the helpful advice of Pat Jinks of Bay Rigging, Annapolis. Thanks also to Carl R. Moser of Universal Wire Products, Inc., for providing information on Nicropress measurements.

New splices with double-braid synthetic lines compose the largest addition. Descriptions of the basic eye-splice, the back splice, the end-for-end splice, the Brummel splice, and the double-braided rope-to-wire splice are included. Bob Halley, Steve Perez, and Jim Mumper of the Naval Station Small Craft Facilities Rigging Shop, Annapolis, provided valuable advice, for which we are grateful.

Quick-reference line and knot usage tables, as well as a discussion of hardware, have been added to this edition. Thanks to Gay Gemmill and Paul McCoy of Fawcett Boat Supplies, Inc., Annapolis, for allowing us to photograph their inventory to illustrate the hardware section.

The bibliography contains a new section composed of currently available knot and splicing books. Special thanks are extended to Bert Wyldes of the Naval Academy Seamanship Department for his advice and assistance throughout this project.

Contents

MISCELLANEOUS OPERATIONS

SPLICING

END KNOTS AND MULTISTRAND KNOTS

TURK'S-HEADS

the Art of Knotting and Splicing

Knots in Folklore and in History

The antiquity of knots is usually taken for granted in knot monographs, or asserted perfunctorily, with merely a show of conviction. This used to be my own attitude, as expressed in *Sailors' Knots* (1935). Only gradually have I come to realize how tremendously old the art of knot tying is. As a matter of fact, with the possible exception of sticks and stones for striking, prodding, and scratching, knots may be mankind's oldest tool. Certainly they are one of the oldest, for gorillas use them to hold creepers and saplings down in making their nests. Ivan Sanderson once counted two dozen knots in a single nest, most of them grannies, but three of them square knots, "which had undoubtedly resulted merely by chance."[1] Now it can hardly be doubted that the most primitive humans were able to do what gorillas can do. Indeed, the first conscious use of knots as a tool must go back not just a few thousand years to, say, neolithic times, but tens or perhaps hundreds of thousands of years, to the savage and even animal beginnings of the race. The wheel, fire, the cultivation of the soil, and other great prehistoric discoveries undoubtedly postdate the knot by countless eons.

Since primitive people associate all their possessions and experiences with their religion, it is not surprising to find that knots play a basic role not only in primitive religion, but also in the superstitions and folklore that everywhere have grown out of primitive religion. The Latin word *religio* is related to the word *religare*, which means *to tie* or *to bind*, and tying implies, or at least suggests, knots. The common assumption used to be that the primitive or ur-Roman worshiper considered himself to be tied by his god, but Westermarck argues persuasively that it must have been the other way around—that the god was tied by the worshiper.[2] In support of this view, he cites

a custom of the unsophisticated folk of Morocco, who tie rags to a saint's grave, or to a place where a saint camped or sat, in the belief that they are binding the saint to grant their petitions. If later they get what they want, they return to the shrine, untie the rag, and release the saint. Westermarck once saw many such rags tied to a pole in a cairn dedicated to the saint Mulai 'Abd-ŭl-Kâdu. "A Berber servant of mine," he writes, "invoked Lälla Răhma Yusf, a great female saint . . . and tied his turban, saying, 'I am tying thee, Lälla Răhma Yusf, and I am not going to open the knot till thou hast helped me.'" On another occasion a person in distress knotted the leaves of a palmetto near the grave of Lälla Răhma Yusf, saying, "I tied thee here, O Saint, and I shall not release thee unless thou releasest me from the toils in which I am at present." We call this sort of thing magic; the ancient Romans would have called it religion.

Folklore confirms the intimate association of knots and early religion or magic. For example, in many parts of the world, wizards and witches (or people regarded as such) used to claim the power of tying up the wind with charmed knots; and mariners, who are notoriously superstitious, bought these charmed knots and untied them when they were becalmed. Usually there were three knots; when they were untied in order, they were supposed to release, first, a moderate wind, then half a gale, and, finally, a hurricane.[3] This superstition was once common in Finland, Lapland, Shetland, Lewis, the Isle of Man, and other northern communities, and in fact it persisted well into the present century in Shetland, Lerwick, and, probably, elsewhere. Perhaps it is still held in outlying ports and fishing villages. That similar beliefs were common in ancient Greece is shown by

---

[1] *Animal Treasure* (1937), p. 187.

[2] *The Origin and Development of the Moral Ideas*, vol. 2 (1908), pp. 584–85.

[3] Professor R. R. Cawley has furnished me with two early references to this superstition: Richard Eden, *Of the Northeast Frostie Sea* (1555), printed in part in *Notes upon Russia*, Hakluyt Society, vol. 2 (1852), p. 225; and Olaus Magnus, *Compendious History of the Goths, Swedes, and Vandals, and Other Northern Nations* (London, 1658), p. 47 (originally published in Latin in 1555).

the fact that Ulysses, in Homer's epic, was presented by Aeolus, king of the winds, with all the winds tied up in a leather bag.

Another widespread belief is that knots, by the principle of what is called homeopathic or imitative magic, have the power of binding up and restricting men and women in the performance of certain tasks. Thus, among the Germans of Transylvania, the Lapps, the aborigines of Borneo, and many other primitive peoples, pregnant women have been forbidden to wear any knots or knotted garments, lest their delivery be restricted. In some cases these taboos were extended to the husbands of pregnant women, and in others to the wearing of rings, to the locking of locks, or to sitting cross-legged.[4] The superstition has many variations. Throughout Scandinavia in former times it was pressed into service as a primitive birth-control method. When two parents had all the children they wanted, they would give the name *Knut* (English *Canute,* meaning *knot*) to the latest-born boy, hoping thereby to prevent the conception of another child.

A similar belief, common in Europe until the end of the eighteenth century, was that magic knots could bewitch a bridegroom and prevent the consummation of a marriage. Anyone who locked a lock or tied a knot during a marriage ceremony and then threw the lock or the knot into water would cast a spell that could not be broken until the lock or knot was found and unlocked or untied. As late as 1705 in Scotland two people were condemned to death for concealing nine magic knots that had been tied for the purpose of marring the wedded happiness of one Spalding of Ashintilly. In 1718 the parliament of Bordeaux sentenced someone to be burned alive for thus bewitching a whole family with knotted cords. Robert Burns refers to the superstition in a stanza of his well-known *Address to the Deil:*

> Thence mystic knots mak great abuse
> On young guidmen, fond, keen, an' crouse;
> When the best wark-lume i' the house
>   By cantrip wit,
> Is instant made no worth a louse,
>   Just at the bit.

People also used to believe that magic knots could inflict diseases and other misfortunes. Westermarck quotes a relevant passage from Plato's *Laws,*[5] which he translates as follows: "He who seems to be the sort of man who injures others by magic knots or enchantments or incantations or any of the like practices, if he be a prophet or a divine, let him die."[6] In ancient Babylon, according to Frazer, it was thought that a witch or wizard could strangle a victim, wrack his limbs, and tear his entrails merely by tying knots in a cord and uttering certain magic words. Fortunately, the injury could be undone by untying the knots. An Arab commentator explains a reference to magic knots in the Koran by telling a story about a wicked Jew who bewitched Mohammed himself with nine knots. The archangel Gabriel came to the rescue and told Mohammed where the knots were hidden, and when they were brought to him he uttered some powerful countercharms, at each verse of which a knot untied itself and relieved the prophet of some of his pain.

Knots can cure illness as well as cause it, or so it used to be believed. Pliny writes as follows in his *Natural History:* "As for greene wounds, it is wonderfull how soon they will be healed, in case they be bound up and tied with a Hercules knot: and verily it is thought that to knit our girdles which we weare about us every day with such a knot, hath a great vertue in it, by reason that Hercules first devised the same."[7] And in another passage he tells how diseases of the groin can be cured by tying seven or nine knots in a thread, naming a widow as each knot is tied, and tying the knotted thread to the patient's groin.[8] A favorite way to get rid of warts in Germany used to be to tie some knots in a string, one for each wart, and then to leave the string under a stone. The first person to step on the stone would get the warts, and the original sufferer would be cured. Or if a person had a fever, he would go to a willow tree and tie knots in the branches, one for each day of the fever. Then, if the proper spells were uttered and some other conditions observed, the tree would acquire the fever, and the patient would be cured.

Zulu hunters tie a knot in the tail of every animal they kill, as a charm against getting a stomachache from eating the meat of the animal. An ancient Hindu recipe for a successful journey called for a number of knots to be tied in the skirts of the traveler's garments. A traveler among the Caffre tribes of Natal often takes the precaution of knotting a few blades of grass together to assure himself of a safe journey.

---

[4]Most of the examples in this and the next five paragraphs are from Sir J. G. Frazer, *The Golden Bough,* vol. 3 (1911), pp. 293–317.

[5]11.933.

[6]Westermarck, *Origin and Development,* vol. 2 (1908), p. 652. See p. 585, n.2, for a statement of his reasons for translating the word *katadesis* as he does. Other translators of Plato assign the word a more general meaning.

[7]28.6 (Holland's translation, 1634).

[8]28.48.

And all over the world—in Russia, Bulgaria, Armenia, Ceylon, England, Scotland, Germany, and elsewhere—knots and locks have traditionally been used as protective amulets against all sorts of dangers and evils. Frazer cites numerous other examples of these and similar superstitions in his great work *The Golden Bough.*

The love knot or true-love knot is probably the most familiar magic knot among educated people today, not because the efficacy of love knots is still credited, but because so many allusions to them are found in literature. Virgil's *Eighth Eclogue,* in which a lovesick maiden seeks by magic charms to regain her lover, Daphnis, is a typical example:

> Around his waxen image first I wind
> Three woolen fillets, of three colors join'd;
> Thrice bind about his thrice-devoted head,
> Which round the sacred altar thrice is led.
> Unequal numbers please the gods.—My charms,
> Restore my Daphnis to my longing arms.
> Knit with three knots the fillets; knit 'em straight;
> And say: "These knots to love I consecrate."[9]

Although this sounds like a mere literary exercise, it probably reflects beliefs actually held in Virgil's day, though perhaps not by Virgil himself. In modern times the love knot has been used as a sort of game, without serious expectation of results, as in the following lines from Shakespeare's *Two Gentlemen of Verona:*

> *Luc.* Why then, your ladyship must cut your hair.
> *Jul.* No, girl; I'll knit it up in silken strings
> With twenty odd-conceited true-love knots.[10]

John Gay's *Shepherd's Week* (1714) contains the following lines:

> As Lubberkin once slept beneath a tree,
> I twitch'd his dangling garter from his knee;
> He wist not when the hempen string I drew.
> Now mine I quickly doff of inkle blue;
> Together fast I tie the garters twain,
> And while I knit the knot repeat this strain,
> *Three times a true-love's knot I tie secure.*
> *Firm be the knot, firm may his love endure.*

Goldsmith, in *The Vicar of Wakefield* (1766), says of the farmers of the neighborhood that they "kept up the Christmas carol, sent true love-knots on Valentine morning, ate pancakes on Shrovetide,—showed their wit on the first of April, and religiously cracked

nuts on Michaelmas eve." And here is the "pathetic" conclusion to the old ballad of "Fair Margaret and Sweet William," written, probably, in the fifteenth century:

> Margaret was buried in the lower chancel,
>   Sweet William in the higher;
> Out of her breast there sprung a rose;
>   And out of his a brier.

> They grew as high as the church top,
>   Till they could grow no higher,
> And then they grew in a true lover's knot,
>   Which made all people admire.

Let us turn now from magic knots to real knots, from folklore to archaeology and history. By neolithic times, humans in many parts of the world had discovered how to weave cloth, make nets, and twist plant fibers into cords and ropes. The materials used in these arts are perishable, and therefore the remains that have been discovered do not by any means represent mankind's earliest endeavors in the manufacture of textiles and cordage. Occasionally, however, a favorable environment, chemically speaking, has resulted in the preservation of extremely ancient specimens. For example, the vestiges of a fishnet, thought to date from as early as 7800 to 5000 B.C., were unearthed about 1920 near Viborg, in Finland.[11] The net had sink stones and 18 pine-bark floats, and it was made of double-threaded cord of coarse-fibered plant, but the chemical changes it had suffered made identification of the mesh knots impossible.

The lake dwellers of Switzerland, a late Stone Age folk, were excellent weavers and rope makers. One of their settlements on Lake Zürich was exposed in the nineteenth century, and it yielded "a great many specimens of flax, yarn ropes, balls of thread, bits of ribbon and variously-woven cloth, fishing and hair nets, plaited borders, fringes, and mats."[12] These remarkable relics survived because they had been carbonized but not destroyed by a conflagration, and so they did not decay when they sank into the ooze at the bottom of the lake. The lake dwellers used flax for their best cloth and nets, but they also used coarser materials, such as rushes, reeds, straw, and bast (of the lime tree). Their best rope measured about half an inch in diameter and was twisted or laid up with professional skill. They used the sheet bend to hold

---

[9]Dryden's translation.
[10]2.7.44–46.

[11]J. G. D. Clark, *The Mesolithic Settlement of Northern Europe* (1936), p. 109.
[12]Robert Munro, *The Lake Dwellings of Europe* (1890), p. 114.

the meshes of their nets in place.[13] It is clear that, even then, rope making and knotting were ancient arts.

The Incas of Peru, another prehistoric people, were even more proficient than the lake dwellers in the textile arts and in the use of cordage. Some specimens of their textiles in the American Museum of Natural History are considered to be at least four thousand years old. These textiles are considered by archaeologists to be some of the finest examples of the weaver's art produced by any age or race. Incan ropes were made of the fibers of the maguey, among other material, and were strong enough to support primitive suspension bridges such as Thornton Wilder describes in *The Bridge of San Luis Rey*. They used the sheet bend and the square knot in their nets.

Among the most remarkable relics of the Incan civilization are the so-called *quipus,* or knot records. The Incas never discovered the art of writing, but they developed a decimal system of numbers and were able to handle rather large mathematical sums and other calculations. The quipu, as described by L. L. Locke,[14] has the following characteristics:

1. There is a main or horizontal cord varying in length from a few centimeters to a meter or more.

2. Vertical cords, from one or two to more than a hundred in number, and seldom longer than half a meter, are suspended to the main cord.

3. Knots are tied in the vertical cords. The lowest knots, near the ends of the cords, represent the digits from 1 to 9; the next higher knots, a little farther from the ends, represent the tens; the next higher, the hundreds; and so on. The largest number noted by Nordenskiöld in any quipu is 37,076.[15] Numbers from 2 to 9 are represented by multiple overhand knots, higher numbers by groups of single overhand knots. The number 1 is generally represented by a figure-eight knot. The number 456, for example, would be represented by a six-fold overhand knot near the end of the cord, a group of five overhands farther up the cord, and a group of four overhands still farther from the end.

4. Subsidiary cords, also with knots in them, are often attached to the vertical cords, and complicate the interpretation of the quipus.

5. The cords are made of wool or cotton and are often dyed; the significance of the colors remains obscure.

It is said that quipus are still used by the aboriginal shepherds of Peru to record the number of sheep in their flocks. Probably they were used for similar practical purposes by the Incas. However, the ancient quipus that happen to have been preserved were all found in graves, and for this reason Nordenskiöld believes that these quipus were associated somehow with the religious superstitions of the Incas and had significance other than practical for the people in whose graves they were deposited. The number 7, he says, occurs in the quipus in as many combinations as possible, and 7 is a magic number in many parts of the world. Astronomical numbers repeatedly occur in various combinations, such as multiples of 365 (the number of days in the year), 397 (their calculation, presumably, of the synodical revolution of Jupiter), and 116 (the synodical revolution of Mercury). The Incas probably knew something about astronomy, but they likely put their knowledge to astrological use.

The Indians of North America also knew how to make twisted fiber cordage, and they used knots for calculating dates, but in a more elementary manner. For example, if two or more tribes or individuals wished to meet on a specified future date, they would tie the same number of knots in each of two cords. Then each tribe or individual would untie or cut off one knot each day. When all the knots were gone, the time of the meeting was at hand.

Some interesting specimens of Indian rope come from the Nootka and other tribes of the Pacific Northwest. These tribes learned how to hunt whales with harpoons in log canoes about 35 or 40 feet long. Each canoe carried six paddlers, a helmsman, and a harpooner. Although their canoes carried no sails and were not decked over, these tribes often pursued their quarry far out of sight of land. Their whaling lines were made of small cedar limbs, twisted into three-strand rope about 4 or 5 inches in circumference which was very regular in appearance. This material is supposed to be almost as strong as manila hemp and to last four or five times as long in water. One of their whaling lines is known to have been 1,200 feet long. For their harpoon lanyards, they used the sinews of the whale, twisted into three-strand rope. A completely equipped Pacific Coast whaling canoe, more than one hundred years old, is on exhibit in the Museum of the American Indian in New York.

The ancient Egyptians and Phoenicians were skillful seamen and rope makers. When Xerxes crossed with his army from Asia to Europe in 492 B.C., he employed Phoenicians and Egyptians to supply the rope that held together the bridge of boats he built across the Hellespont. Herodotus gives a detailed account of the operation. "Beginning then from Abydos they whose business it was made bridges across to

[13]Ferdinand Keller, *The Lake Dwellings of Switzerland*, vol. 1 (1878), pp. 506–10.
[14]*The Ancient Quipu* (1923).
[15]*Calculations with Years and Months in the Peruvian Quipus* (1925).

that headland, the Phoenicians one of flaxen cables, and the Egyptians the second, which was of papyrus. From Abydos to the opposite shore it is a distance of seven furlongs." When a storm broke the cables and scattered the ships, Xerxes ordered the waters of the Hellespont to be punished with three hundred lashes, and he had the overseers beheaded. Under new overseers, two pontoon bridges were built, one of 360 boats, the other of 314. This time the workmen "stretched cables from the land, twisting them taut with wooden windlasses, and they did not as before keep the two kinds apart, but assigned for each two cables of flax and four of papyrus. All these were of the same thickness and fair appearance, but the flaxen were heavier in their proportion, a cubit thereof weighing a talent."[16]

Several difficulties in the interpretation of Herodotus's account arise. The ropes are said to have been made of *sparto* and *byblos,* which may mean *flax* and *papyrus* respectively, but which Macan thinks mean *grass* and *papyrus.* If the cubit was the Greek cubit (1½ feet), and if the talent was the *emporic* talent (82 pounds), then according to Macan the *sparto* rope must have weighed 54⅔ pounds per linear foot.[17] It has been calculated, I do not know by whom, that the ropes must have been 28 inches in circumference. They must have been about a mile (8 *stades*) long. This is pretty competent rope work.

All the rope made by the Phoenicians has probably long since rotted and decayed, but many specimens of Egyptian rope have been found in the dry, sealed tombs of Egyptian kings and princes. Some good specimens dating from about 3000 B.C. (25 centuries before the time of Xerxes) may be seen in the Metropolitan Museum of Art in New York. The Metropolitan Museum has several Egyptian boat models from the tomb of Prince Mehenkwetre, who died about 2000 B.C., but the rigging appears to be modern. The door leading into the third shrine of Tutankhamen's tomb was tied shut with rope, and the end is secured with what appears to be, in one of the photographs I have seen of it, a clove hitch. A *New York Times* report of the excavation of Cheops's solar ship mentions a "curiously intricate knot on a piece of rigging that appeared to be basically akin to a bowline knot."[18]

Egyptian art furnishes little information about the knots of ancient Egypt. Cordage, and even the process of manufacturing cordage, are often depicted, but seldom any knots. M. A. Murray studied this subject in 1922 and found a few square knots, chiefly

in jewelry, but nothing else.[19] Ordinarily, according to Murray, knots were represented in Egyptian art by meaningless curves, and accuracy was intentionally avoided. It is slightly possible that this was due to a tendency among Egyptian artists to conventionalize what they portrayed; more likely it had some connection with the universal fear of knots among superstitious people. If the latter explanation is correct, then the square knot may have been permitted because in Egypt, as later in Greece and Rome, it was perhaps regarded as magically beneficent rather than harmful.

In ancient Greece, the most celebrated knot was the Gordian knot. Plutarch, among other writers, tells how Alexander the Great conquered Phrygia, and at Gordium, the chief city, "saw the famous chariot fastened with cords made of the rind of the cornel tree [the dogwood], which whosoever should untie, the inhabitants had a tradition, that for him was reserved the empire of the world. Most authors tell the story that Alexander finding himself unable to untie the knot, the ends of which were secretly twisted round and folded up within it, cut it asunder with his sword. But Aristobulus tells us it was easy for him to undo it, by only pulling the pin out of the pole, to which the yoke was tied, and afterwards drawing off the yoke itself from below."[20] The writings of Aristobulus have been lost, but since he was a friend of Alexander's, his version of the story may well be the true one. Ever since that time, "to cut the Gordian knot" has meant "to dispose of a difficult matter by summary, daring measures."

The square knot was well known in ancient Greece and Rome and may be seen in numerous works of classical art. It is often worked into the handles of vases; Mercury's staff sometimes shows it; and in several pieces of sculpture the girdles of Roman women are tied with it. The Romans called it the Hercules knot (*nodus Herculis, Herculeus,* or *Herculaneus*), perhaps because Hercules was supposed to have invented it, perhaps because it was used to tie the forelegs of the lion's skin that was thrown over Hercules' shoulders, or perhaps for some other reason. It was supposed to exercise beneficent magical power. Paulus Diaconus says that it was the custom for a Roman bride to wear a girdle tied with a Hercules knot, which the husband untied on the marriage night as an omen of fecundity. Pliny's opinion of the healing qualities of the Hercules knot have already been quoted.

The only actual descriptions of knots before the

[16]7.34–36 (Godley's translation).
[17]R. W. Macan, *Herodotus,* vol. 1 (1908), pp. 53–54.
[18]12 Dec. 1954.

[19]*Ancient Egypt,* pt. 1 (1922), pp. 14–19.
[20]Dryden's translation.

eighteenth century are found in the *Iatrikon Synagogos,* a medical treatise compiled by Oribasius of Pergamum in the fourth century A.D. Oribasius, a Greek, was court physician to the Emperor Julian, who died in 386 A.D. His material on knots, however, is considerably older than that, for he expressly states that he derived it from Heraklas. Nothing definite is known about Heraklas, but on the basis of stylistic evidence he is believed to have been a contemporary or pupil of Heliodorus, a physician who flourished about 100 A.D.

The knots he describes were used by physicians as slings, or as elements in slings, during operations and in the treatment of fractures. Nine different knots can be identified: the overhand knot, the lark's head, the clove hitch, the overhand noose, the square knot, the fisherman's loop knot, the jug sling, the Tom Fool knot, and a cat's cradle. These were variously utilized in forming sixteen different slings.

Some of Heraklas's terms are difficult to translate. The word *brokhos,* according to Liddell and Scott, means *noose, slip knot, snare, mesh,* or *halter.* A more precise translation, as Heraklas uses the term, would seem to be *sling.* Compare the verb *brokhizo,* which means to *hang,* to *strangle,* or, as used by Galen in the passive, to be *ligatured. Plinthios* is not recognized by Liddell and Scott. A *plinthos,* however, is a brick or a brick-shaped object, and since the *plinthios,* when interpreted, turns out to be a rectangular cat's cradle, the general signification of the term is clear.

The word *karkhesios* is more elusive. Liddell and Scott define it, in the plural, as the *halyards of a ship* or the *cords used in surgical operations.* The related word *karkhesion* denotes a *drinking cup* with two handles, the *masthead* of a ship, or a *crane* for unloading ships. Since the *simple karkhesios* is a fisherman's loop knot, the name may be due to a fancied resemblance between the handles of a drinking vessel and the two overhand knots that make up a fisherman's knot. On the other hand, the *double karkhesios* is our hackamore, which can be used either as a masthead knot or as a jug sling. Either function could be implied in the word *karkhesios.*

The *Herakleotikon hamma* presents difficulties, not because Heraklas's description is ambiguous, but because several authorities[21] deny that it is the *nodus Herculis* or square knot. The word *Herakleotikon,* it

is true, usually means *of Heraclea* (a city). However, Athenaeus (ca. 200 A.D.) and other late Greek writers occasionally use it as an adjective meaning *of Hercules,* and that is the way Heraklas uses it, apparently, in the medical collections of Oribasius. For a complete demonstration of the identity of the *Herakleotikon hamma,* the *nodus Herculis,* and the square knot, see Öhrvall's *Om Knutar* (1916) and his article on knots in *Eranos.*[22]

The following abridged version of Heraklas is based on the French translation of Bussemaker and Daremberg,[23] and on an English translation prepared for me by Professor Daniel Coogan. The knots are identified in square brackets after the chapter headings, with cross references to the photographs herein that illustrate them.[24] These identifications were kindly supplied by L. G. Miller for the first edition of this book. Confirmation of their accuracy has now come to light in Öhrvall's article in *Eranos.*[25] I had not seen this article in 1947.

THE FIRST EIGHTEEN CHAPTERS OF THE FORTY-EIGHTH BOOK OF THE MEDICAL COLLECTIONS OF ORIBASIUS OF PERGAMUM FROM [THE BOOKS OF] HERAKLAS

1. THE CONTINUOUS SLING [Lark's Head. See no. 108.]

Hold the ends of a doubled cord with the left hand. With the right hand place the loop on the ends. The ends, then, are held together by the middle of the loop, and the knotted part of the sling is on one side and the ends on the other.

This is a sling of unequal tension. It is useful in exerting traction, in supporting a limb that is being set, and in holding the body in position during an operation. It is suitable for exerting traction on a limb with two bones when one of the bones is fractured, the loop being put on the injured bone and the ends

[21]Pauly-Wissowa, *Realencyclopädie der Altertumswissenschaft,* s.v. "Hercules," by Haug, and s.v. "nodus," by Keyssner. Haug and Keyssner may have been misled by the illustrative plate in the Bussemaker and Daremberg edition of Oribasius (1862), in which only nos. 1 and 9 are correctly identified and pictured.

[22]Öhrvall, *Om Knutar* (1916), pp. 204–11, and idem, "Något om knutar i antiken, särskildt hos Oreibasios," *Eranos* 16 (1916): 64–71.

[23]*Oeuvres d'Oribase,* vol. 4 (Paris, 1862), pp. 253–70, 691 (plate).

[24]See especially figs. A–J, p. 8. In figs. A and B, note that *A* fits back of the heel, *B* under the sole, and *C* over the instep. In fig. E, note that the *skhasteriae,* or relaxing cords, are attached at *A* and *B.* And finally, note that Heraklas is ambiguous in chap. 12. The directions, if carefully followed, seem to produce a *simple karkhesios,* tied as in figs. 80G and 80H. Miller therefore suggests a lacuna in the manuscript and offers the method of tying the knot that is shown in fig. F.

[25]"Något om knutar i antiken," pp. 51–81. Öhrvall agrees substantially with Miller, except in his interpretation of chaps. 3, 4, and 16.

6

on the sound bone. The loop, being in contact with the skin, pulls the injured parts hard, while the ends stand away from the skin and exert little or no pull on the sound parts.

This sling is used to support the arm in the three kinds of elbow dislocations (inside, outside, and posterior) when the arm is bent and cannot be straightened. Place the loop round the forearm near the wrist; then bring the ends up and tie them to a fixed object. It is also useful in holding the body during operations. In the treatment of injuries to the buttocks, put the patient's forearms under his thighs, place *continuous slings* on his forearms near the wrists, bring the ends up behind the neck, and tie them together.

Not only can the *continuous sling* be prepared in advance, but it can also be tied at the time it is put on the limb. Double the cord, pass the loop around the limb, and thrust the ends through the loop. By this method the sling is tied as it is applied.

2. THE NAUTICAL SLING [Clove Hitch. See no. 112.]

Make two loops in the middle of a cord and place them together, the inside one outside, the outside one inside. Thus the knotted part of the sling is on one side and the ends on the other.

The sling is used to exert unequal traction and to hold the splints in fracture cases. After bandaging, hold the cord in the left hand and place two loose loops successively from the standing part round the injured limb. Pass the opposite end through the middle of the loops, going from the near to the far side, and hold it in the left hand. The sling being arranged, put splints on the limb inside the loops, pull the ends taut, and knot them to hold the splints.

In addition to exerting traction and holding splints, this sling is good for suspending the forearm. When the bandage itself is not big enough for the purpose, use the *nautical sling* on the forearm, with the loops separated, one near the elbow and one near the wrist, and tie the ends round the patient's neck.

3. THE DIAGONAL SLING [Overhand Noose. See no. 88.]

Hold the ends of a double cord in the left hand and the loop in the right hand. Twist the loop so that the ends cross (hence the name *khiestos*), and, this done, place the loop over the cross, and pull another loop from the lower end up through the first loop. The knotted part of the sling will then be in the middle, with a loop on one side and the two ends on the other.

This also is a sling of unequal tension.

4. THE HERDSMAN SLING OR SANDAL [Barton's Handkerchief or Cravat of the Heel. See figs. A and B, p. 8; H. R. Wharton, *Minor Surgery and Bandaging* (1896), p. 40; and n. 24 herein.]

First tie a *diagonal sling* (chapter 3). Then pull the upper part of the central knot up through the loop that is opposite the ends. The knotted part of the sling will then be on one side, the ends on the other, and three loops will be seen, two on each side and the third in the middle.

The sling is useful for applying traction when setting the ankle, one loop being placed round the Achilles tendon behind the ankle, the second in front over the instep, and the third (or middle loop) under the sole. The ends are then tied to the means of traction.

It is also used in reducing a dislocated lower jaw. Place one loop on the forehead, the second on the back of the neck, the third (or middle loop) in the mouth under the upper jaw. Then bring the ends up along the temples and over the patient's head, and use them either for support or for traction.

5. THE SLING CALLED THE DRAGON [Gerdy's Extension Knot. See E. L. Eliason, *Practical Bandaging* (1924), pp. 79–80.]

Place the middle of the cord back of the ankle on the Achilles tendon. Bring the ends forward along the sides of the ankle, cross them over the instep, pass them under the sole, and cross them again. Then bring the ends up and pass them (either upwards or downwards) under the part of the cord that is wrapped round the ankle. Then tie them to the means of traction. This sling is useful for exerting traction when setting the ankle bone.

6. THE SLING CALLED THE SIMPLE KNOT [Nameless Construction. See figs. C and D, p. 8.]

Tie a *haploun hamma* [i.e., an overhand knot] in a cord. Draw the loops up and let the ends hang free. Place the limb to be set between the upper loops, pass one of the loops through the other, lead it toward the ends, and tie it to the means of traction with a knot that also secures the ends.

This is a sling of unequal tension.

7. THE SLING CALLED THE WOLF [Nameless Construction Similar to the Square Knot. See fig. E, p. 8, and n. 24 herein.]

Double two cords; place the ends together and the bights opposite each other. Pull the ends of one cord up, and the ends of the other cord down, so that the

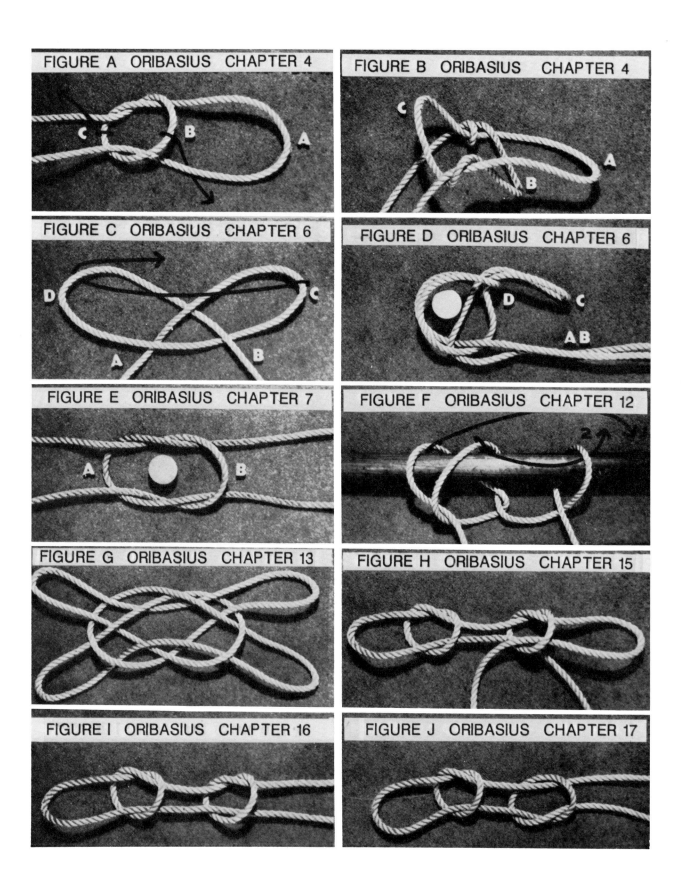

FIGURE A ORIBASIUS CHAPTER 4

FIGURE B ORIBASIUS CHAPTER 4

FIGURE C ORIBASIUS CHAPTER 6

FIGURE D ORIBASIUS CHAPTER 6

FIGURE E ORIBASIUS CHAPTER 7

FIGURE F ORIBASIUS CHAPTER 12

FIGURE G ORIBASIUS CHAPTER 13

FIGURE H ORIBASIUS CHAPTER 15

FIGURE I ORIBASIUS CHAPTER 16

FIGURE J ORIBASIUS CHAPTER 17

knotted part of the sling will be in the middle, and two ends on each side.

This is a sling of equal tension. It is convenient not only for exerting traction on a bone that is to be set, but also for binding the peritoneum in reducing intestinal hernia, and for binding hemorrhaging organs.

It is customary to tie linen cords, which doctors call *skhasteriae*, to the loops of this sling. These, rather than the ends of the sling, are used to relax constriction at will.

8. THE HERCULES KNOT [Square Knot. See no. 24.]

Take a cord and tie two knots in it a little distance apart. The *Herakleotikon hamma* is thus produced: a loop on one side, the two ends on the other.

It is a sling of equal tension. If the loop is cut, a *wolf sling* (chapter 7) is produced.

9. THE SIMPLE KARKHESIOS SLING [Fisherman's Loop Knot. See no. 80, fig. 80C.]

This is a sling of equal tension. Hold the ends of a doubled cord in the left hand. With the right hand, fold the loop over the ends. Lay the slack parts that are in the middle across each other. Then pull the loop that was folded over the ends down through the center of the crossed parts. A single loop is then on one side of the knotted part of the sling, and the two ends on the other.

10. THE DOUBLE KARKHESIOS SLING [Jug Sling. See no. 148, figs. 148A, 148B, 148C.]

This is a sling of equal tension, stronger than the *simple karkhesios*. Hold the ends of a doubled cord with the left hand, and let the loop hang free. Make a small loop in the opposite hanging part, and place it in the left hand. Pull the other hanging part through the center of this loop. Turn the knot by means of the loops, and place it in the left hand. Make another small loop with the opposite hanging part, and place it on the knot. Finally, draw the hanging loop up through the middle of the knot. The knotted part of the sling is then in the middle, with a loop on one side and the ends on the other.

11. THE DOUBLE KARKHESIOS MADE FROM A SIMPLE KARKHESIOS [Jug Sling. See no. 148, figs. 148F and 148G.]

The *double karkhesios* is tied in several ways: alone, with a *simple karkhesios,* or round the limb itself. We have shown the first method, and shall now show the second. Tie a *simple karkhesios* and separate the loops. Place the lower loop on the upper loop, separate the loops, and pull the loop opposite the ends through the center between the two other loops. The knotted part of the sling is in the middle, with the ends on one side and a loop on the other.

12. THE DOUBLE KARKHESIOS MADE IN ITS APPLICATION [Jug Sling. See fig. F, p. 8, and n. 24 herein.]

Sometimes the ends break because of excessive tension before they are adjusted. Therefore the *double karkhesios* can be tied at the time it is applied, without the ends being slackened. Hold the end of the cord with the left hand and make three loops round the limb, some distance apart. Place the first loop over the last, and pull the middle loop up between the other two, twisting it once or twice. In this way the knot of the sling is formed round the limb itself, with the two ends on one side and the loop on the other.

13. THE SLING CALLED THE FOUR-LOOP PLINTHIOS [Cat's Cradle. See fig. G, p. 8. This is the same as the Queensland string figure called "The Sun Clouded Over" in W. E. Roth's *North Queensland Ethnography* (1902), plate 10.]

Take a cord that is formed like a ring (that is, a cord without ends), and form small loops on the thumb and the little finger, and then on the forefinger, of each hand—three loops for each hand. Transfer the thumb loops to the ring fingers, and the little-finger loops to the forefingers. Then, with the thumbs, draw down the loops that are on the forefinger through the spaces between the first fingers. The resulting formation is a rhombus with two loops on each side. It is a sling of equal tension, useful to exert traction and to reduce chin fractures. In the latter case, the knot of the sling is placed round the chin, and the four loops are placed over the cheeks and tied above the head.

14. THE THONGED SLING [Tom Fool Knot. See no. 150, fig. 150E.]

Place the end of a cord on the [left] hand, between thumb and forefinger. Then wrap it round the back of the hand, then over the palm, after passing it over the thumbs [thumb?], and hold it between the little finger and the ring finger. Pull one part with the right hand, the other part with the little finger and ring finger [of the left hand]. In this way two loops will appear, with a knot between them.

This sling is used to hold the body in position during operations. Put the patient's hands in the loops, and secure his body with the ends.

15. THE SLING CALLED THE EARS [Nameless Construction. See fig. H, p. 8.]

First tie a *thonged sling* (chapter 14). Enlarge one of the loops and tie a *diagonal sling* (chapter 3) in it. There will then be two loops with two cords hanging between them.

This sling is useful in reducing dislocations of the lower jaw, and in putting back into articulation the epiphysis of the head in condylus occipitalis, the loops being placed over the patient's temples, the two ends on his forehead. The bandage called the rabbit (chapters 26, 27) is then used, and the ends carried above the patient's head and tied to the agent that holds them or exerts traction.

16. THE DOUBLE LOOPED SLING SOMETIMES INCORRECTLY CALLED THE STRANGLING SLING [Nameless Construction. See fig. I, p. 8.]

This sling is made with two *diagonal slings* (chapter 3), which are separated from each other. It is useful in giving the proper position to the body when treating the buttocks. Place the patient's forearms under his hams, and hold them with the *diagonal slings*. Lift the ends up to the patient's neck, and in this way give the body the desired position.

17. THE GENUINE STRANGLING SLING [Fisherman's Loop Knot with Overhands Separated. See fig. J, p. 8.]

Tie a *simple karkhesios* (chapter 9) and separate the knots. This sling is useful under the same circumstances as the *strangling sling* (chapter 16). Put the patient's forearms in the loops and draw taut. Round the sinews [of the neck], tie the part of the double cord that is hanging and that is in the middle of the loops.

18. THE INVERTED SLING [Clove Hitch Arranged as in no. 129. Compare the Collins Cinch, E. L. Eliason, *Practical Bandaging* (1924), pp. 79–80.]

This is made with a *nautical sling* (chapter 2). Place a *nautical sling* on the forearm, separate the loops, and tie the ends together behind the sinews [of the neck].

These are the knots that seem to be most useful in medical practice.

Between the time of Oribasius and the eighteenth century, the history of knots is nearly blank. In medieval England several common knots were used as heraldic "badges"—the carrick bend, for example, by the Anglo-Saxon leader Hereward the Wake in the eleventh century, as well as later by the Ormonde family. The carrick bend is known in heraldry as the Wake knot. The badge of the Staffords is the overhand knot; that of the Bourchiers, the granny. Other badges consist of complicated interlacings that can be called knots only by courtesy.

The true-love knot, true-lover's knot, or true love (as it was often called for short) began to be mentioned in English literature in the fourteenth century, the earliest instance recorded by the *New English Dictionary* being in *Sir Gawaine and the Greene Knight* (ca. 1350). It is not certain, however, what particular knot, if any, the medieval true-love knot was. Richard Huloet, in 1552, speaks of a "Knotte which runneth to, called a rydynge knot," and this may be the overhand running knot. In 1627, Captain John Smith, in his *Sea Grammar,* asserts that the three knots used by the seamen of his day are the wall knot, the bowline, and the sheepshank. Writers later in the seventeenth century copied Smith. Outside of these meager references, we have little precise information and can only surmise that most of the knots with which we are familiar today were also familiar to the sailors of medieval and Renaissance Europe, and probably to the ancient Egyptians, Phoenicians, Greeks, and Romans.

In the eighteenth century, knots began to be listed, pictured, and described in nautical dictionaries and manuals of seamanship. An early illustration of some two dozen knots is plate 2 in Nicola Zabaglia's *Castelli e Ponti* (Rome, 1743), a handsome folio volume first called to my attention by L. G. Miller. Daniel Lescallier's *Traité Pratique du Gréement des Vaisseaux* (Paris, 1791) has two plates that were later copied in part by David Steel in his *Elements and Practice of Rigging and Seamanship* (2 volumes, London, 1794), which in turn was often copied in the nineteenth century. Such publications as these illuminate the final phases of a development that occurred over many thousands of years. In the nineteenth century, during the heyday of the clipper ships, the art of knot tying reached its zenith and then rapidly declined. Steel, coal, and oil brought the era to a close, in knotting as in many other activities.

Characteristics of Rope

The terms rope and line are almost synonymous. To mariners, however, there is a difference. *Rope* is a general word for cordage that has no specific use, whereas *line* is a rope that has a definite purpose—as a mooring line, guy line, dock line, etc. On board all vessels, it is customary to refer to cordage as *line*.

Until the 1950s, the only types of rope available to

the public were made of natural fibers, of which there are six general types:

1. Manila
2. Sisal
3. Cotton
4. Hemp
5. Linen
6. Jute

Manila is the most important of the natural fibers. It is manufactured from the leaf of the Abaca plant, which is native to the Philippine Islands and some areas of Central America. Although it is more expensive than other ropes, manila is stronger and wears longer. Until the advent of synthetic rope, manila was the only rope considered suitable for all-around marine use.

Sisal is not customarily used in the marine field, except in the making of boat fenders. It is manufactured from the leaf of the Agave plant, which comes from the West and East Indies and parts of Africa. It has only about 80 percent of the strength of manila and has a greater tendency to mildew and rot.

Cotton rope has long been used for marine purposes where strength is not essential and where its special qualities, such as a white color and a soft feel, are required. For instance, cotton has been used for flag halyards, lashings, and leech cord on sails. Compared with manila, most cotton ropes are of relatively small diameter.

Italian hemp and linen were highly regarded years ago as sheets on yachts because of their flexibility and ease of handling. One form of Italian hemp was tarred and used as marline. However, untreated hemp and linen ropes rot quickly, and their service lives are relatively short. In fact, when these ropes were in vogue, it was not unusual for the yacht owner to remove the sheets made of these fibers and stow them below deck when the yacht was not in use. This prolonged their usability and kept them cleaner.

Jute has many of the characteristics of Italian hemp and is usually tarred and used as marline for whippings and servings. It is manufactured from the leaves of the Jute plant, common to India, Pakistan, and parts of the Orient. Both Italian hemp and jute have approximately 50 percent of the strength of good manila rope.

By the 1950s synthetic rope began to take the place of manila. One of the first used synthetic ropes was made from polyamide, commonly known as nylon. For certain purposes, nylon is superior to any other rope. For example, nylon is very elastic and will absorb seven times the shock load of manila, which makes it ideal for mooring and towing lines. It is also highly resistant to abrasion and will not rot, even when subjected to prolonged wetness. Size-for-size, nylon is at least twice as strong as manila. A half-inch manila line has a breaking strength of 2,650 pounds, whereas a nylon line of the same diameter has a breaking strength of 6,600 pounds. Nylon also has a high melting point, 480°F, and does not begin to lose strength until its temperature is above 350°F, whereas manila has a burning point of 350°F and loses strength rapidly above 180°F. Although nylon costs more initially than manila, nylon is less expensive in the long run because it wears so much better. For this reason, towing companies are willing to pay several thousand dollars for a single piece of nylon rope to be used for towing ocean-going vessels. Nylon's main drawback as a towing line is the very same elasticity that makes it so popular. When a nylon towline breaks, it snaps with such force that anyone within striking distance is in extreme danger.

Where elasticity is not desirable, the most popular synthetic yacht rope is polyester. Dacron by Du Pont, A.C.E. by Allied, Fortrel by Celanese, and Kodel by Eastman are all trade names for the generic family of polyester fibers. Dacron is the name most commonly used to identify polyester line. Polyester has many of the desirable qualities of nylon and about the same stretch characteristics as manila. For this reason, polyester rope is used for halyards, sheets, lifts, and guys. Like nylon ropes, polyester ropes are not weakened by rot, mildew, or salt water, and they do not deteriorate in storage.

Another advantage of polyester is its relatively light weight. A ¾-inch-diameter manila line has a breaking strength of 5,400 pounds and weighs 16 pounds per 100 feet. A ⁹⁄₁₆-inch-diameter polyester line has a breaking strength of 5,600 pounds and weighs only 9.8 pounds per 100 feet. Many yachtsmen use polyester halyards to reduce weight aloft.

Another type of synthetic rope is made of polyethylene, which is more flexible and resists abrasion better than manila. It is not affected by water and is available in colors. Polyethylene makes a superior line for towing water skiers because its slipperyness helps reduce the incidence of rope burns. Of minimum elasticity, polyethylene rope is not as strong as polyester, but it is somewhat stronger than manila of equal size.

Polypropylene rope, made in monofilament, multifilament, and film form, is similar to polyethylene rope but slightly stronger. Its strength is approximately 50 percent that of nylon and polyester. Polypropylene is actually stronger wet than dry. Its working elasticity is slightly greater than that of manila.

Like polyethylene, polypropylene is appropriate for dinghy painters, since its specific gravity is only 90 percent, which causes it to float and prevents it from wrapping around propellers. It is also useful for rigging life lines at bathing beaches and for other applications where floatability is desirable. Polypropylene is not as slippery as polyethylene, which makes it less suitable as a towline for skiers. Its greatest disadvantage is that it does not resist abrasion very well.

A newer synthetic fiber that has gained wide acceptance where high strength, low stretch, and light weight are essential is Kevlar. Kevlar is a special Du Pont fiber of the aramid fiber family and is comparable in strength and stretch characteristics to wire, yet much lighter. It has a very high safe working temperature, 423°F, and does not fully decompose until its temperature exceeds 800°F. Kevlar's use in lines for sailboat halyards and sheets has become standard for those who demand not only high strength and low stretch, but also reduced topside weight. Because of Kevlar's poor abrasion resistance and requirements for special blocks and sheaves, rope manufacturers such as Samson and Yale should be consulted for use guidelines.

Synthetic ropes tend to unlay when cut, so it is best to clap a seizing over the end of the line before it's cut. However, if the knife blade is heated almost red hot, it will cut through synthetic lines (with the exception of lines made of Du Pont's aramid fibers) like butter, leaving the ends sealed.

Lines of synthetic fibers can be spliced in the same manner as those of natural fibers, but because they are more slippery than manila, it is advisable to take at least one or two extra tucks. If a tapered splice is desired, it is possible to reduce the diameter of the strands after the first several tucks. To be sure that the splice will not unlay, it is a good practice to clap a seizing of sail twine over the last two or three tucks. To assure maximum strength, thimbles should be used in eye splices whenever possible.

Because some synthetic ropes are very elastic, an extra two or three turns should be taken around a cleat or bitt when making fast before securing with the customary figure eight. When paying out synthetic lines, which tend to soften when overheated, care must be exercised not to exert too much pressure. Pressure causes friction, which causes the lines to heat, soften, and, possibly, stick. This applies particularly to ropes made of polypropylene, which has a low melting point (330°F). This makes polypropylene ropes unsuitable for heavy work.

Table 1 lists the ways yachtsmen commonly use synthetic fibers. The characteristics of frequently

Table 1. Common Yachting Uses for Synthetic Fibers

Fiber	Use
Polyamide (nylon)	Anchor rodes Mooring lines Tow lines
Polyester	Main sheets Jib sheets Halyards Boom vangs Control lines
Polyethylene	Ski ropes Man-overboard ropes Rescue lines
Polypropylene	Dinghy painters
Kevlar	Main sheets Jib sheets Halyards Control lines

used ropes are delineated in table 2. Table 3 is intended as a ready reference to various knots and their uses. It does not contain all of the knots in this book, but it does present uses for the most common knots.

Terminology

The word *knot*, in its most general sense, denotes any fastening made by interweaving cordage. The principal varieties of knots are (1) the *hitch,* (2) the *bend,* and (3) the *knot* (in the limited, specific senses of the word). These may be defined as follows:

(1) HITCH. A knot used to secure a rope to another object or to another rope or to form a loop or a noose in a rope.

(2) BEND. A knot used to secure a rope to another object or to tie the ends of two ropes together.

(3) KNOT. A knot (in the general sense of the word) used to form a knob or a stopper in a rope; to enclose or bind an object; to form a loop or a noose; to tie a (small) cord to an object; to tie the ends of two (small) cords together.

The distinctions between hitches, bends, and knots are largely connotative rather than explicit. Hitches, for example, are generally easy to tie and untie, and they are generally better adapted for use in rope than in small cords like thread or twine. The word *hitch* suggests a temporary rather than a permanent fastening. (Compare Falconer's eighteenth-century definition: "a noose or knot . . . by which a rope is temporarily made fast to an object.")

The word *bend* is almost obsolete as a noun except in names like *carrick bend* and *sheet bend.* It is still used, though not extensively, as a verb (e.g., to bend a sail or a cable). Now primarily a nautical word, it

Table 2. Characteristics of Frequently Used Ropes

	Three-Strand Manila	Three-Strand Nylon	Three-Strand Polyester	Three-Strand Polyethylene	Three-Strand Polypropylene	Nylon Double Braid	Polyester Double Braid	Kevlar Single Braid
Strength								
Tensile strength dry	9,000 lbs	25,000 lbs	22,000 lbs	12,600 lbs	14,000 lbs	33,600 lbs	31,400 lbs	70,000 lbs
Wet strength compared to dry strength	Up to 120%	90–95%	100%	100%	102–105%	88%	100%	100%
Weight and density								
Pounds per 100 feet	27.0	26.0	30.5	18.5	18.0	26.0	32.0	30.0
Specific gravity of fiber	1.38	1.14	1.38	0.95	0.91	1.14	1.38	1.44
Ability to float	No	No	No	Yes	Yes	No	No	No
Elasticity and stretch (approximate)								
Permanent elongation at working loads (20% of tensile strength)	5%	14% dry 14% wet	9%	6%	4%	7% dry 13% wet	5%	2%
Working elasticity (temporary stretch under load) at working loads (20% of tensile strength)	5%	9% dry 13% wet	2–4%	6%	9%	9% dry 13% wet	2%	0.8%
Elongation at 100% load (at break) for broken-in ropes	13%	35%	20–22%	22%	24%	24%	17%	6%
Surface characteristics								
Coefficient of friction, new ropes on steel; ability to ease out smoothly under load over bitts	Poor	Poor	Good	Good (but requires extra wraps)	Poor	Good (requires fewer wraps)	Good	Good
Feeling of rope to the touch	Some harshness due to hairs; after use becomes very harsh due to broken fiber ends	Smooth; after use becomes fuzzy with a softer feel	Smooth and hard; not slippery; after use becomes fuzzy with a softer feel	Smooth; very slippery; after use becomes slightly harsh due to broken fiber ends	Smooth; not slippery; after use becomes harsh due to broken fiber ends	Smooth; after use becomes fuzzy with a softer feel	Smooth; not slippery; after use becomes fuzzy with a softer feel	Smooth
Water absorption of fiber (Some water will be held between fibers of all ropes)	Up to 100% of weight of rope	5–6%	Less than 1%	Zero	Zero	5–6%	Less than 1%	Zero
Resistance to rot, mildew, and attack by marine organisms (Some marine organisms will attach themselves to any submerged object, including synthetic ropes)	Poor	100% resistant	100% resistant	100% resistant	100% resistant	100% resistant	100% resistant	100% resistant
Deterioration								
Due to aging (stored ropes, ideal conditions)	About 1% per year	Zero	Zero	Zero	Zero	Zero	Zero	Zero
Due to exposure to sunlight	Slight	Slight	Almost none	White, some; black resists best	White, some; black resists best	Slight	Almost none	Slight
Resistance to chemicals								
To acids	Very poor	Fair, except to concentrated sulfuric and hydrochloric acids	Very good to excellent	Excellent, except to concentrated sulfuric acid	Excellent	Fair, except to concentrated sulfuric and hydrochloric acids	Very good to excellent	Very poor
To alkalis	Very poor	Excellent	Very good, except to concentrated sodium hydroxide at high temperatures	Good	Good	Excellent	Very good, except to concentrated sodium hydroxide at high temperatures	Fair
To solvents	Good	Good	Very good to excellent	Good	Good	Good	Very good to excellent	Good
Wear								
Resistance to surface abrasion	Good	Very good	Excellent	Good	Good	Excellent	Excellent	Fair
Resistance to internal wear from flexing	Good	Excellent	Very good to excellent	Very good	Very good	Excellent	Very good to excellent	Fair
Resistance to cutting (toughness)	Good	Excellent	Very good to excellent	Good	Good	Excellent	Very good to excellent	Good
Performance in extreme temperatures								
Melting point	Loses strength rapidly above 180°F; chars at 350°F	480°F; progressive strength loss above 350°F	480°F; progressive strength loss above 350°F	280°F; softens above 250°F	330°F; softens above 300°F	480°F; progressive strength loss above 350°F	480°F; progressive strength loss above 350°F	Chars at 800°F; begins to lose strength above 423°F
Low-temperature properties	No change	No change	No change	Brittle below minus 150°F	No change	No change	No change	Brittle below minus 50°F
Flammability	Burns like wood	Burns with difficulty	Burns with difficulty	Burns with difficulty	Burns with difficulty	Burns with difficulty	Burns with difficulty	Does not burn

NOTES: Ratings are based on published literature and/or new tests under laboratory conditions. All ropes are 1 inch in diameter.

Table courtesy of Samson Ocean Systems, Inc.

Table 3. Uses for Common Knots

Knot Name	Knot Number	Use
Figure-Eight	20	A stopper knot, to prevent a line from running through an opening A temporary knot, to prevent a line from fraying until a proper whip or seizure is applied
Square Knot (Reef Knot)	24	To tie two lines together under tension
Draw Knot (Half-Bowknot)	25	To tie reef points
Bowknot	26	To tie shoes or to decorate a parcel
Sheet Bend (Weaver's Knot)	31	To tie two lines of different sizes or materials together
Bowline Bend	56	A common way to tie two hawsers or lines together
Bowline on the Bight	62	Used as a boatswain's chair or sling
Hangman's Noose	97	To remove unwanted guests illegally
Two Half-Hitches	98	To tie a line temporarily to a ring, spar, post, or other object
Timber Hitch	107	To haul or tow large convex objects
Clove Hitch (Ratline Hitch)	112	A multipurpose knot, used for such tasks as tying one line to a main line, meshing ropes to form a net, etc.
Catspaw (2)	122	Used when the bight of a rope is to be hitched to a hook
Belaying	174	To secure halyards, sheets, and running rigging in general
Monkey's Fist	201	To hold weight at the end of a heaving line
Turk's-Head	222	A decorative knot
Square Sennit	231	A decorative knot, frequently used for lanyards

was once familiar to landsmen as well as to seamen. To *bend* a bow meant to *tie (bind, bend)* a bow string to a bow. By transference, the word acquired its modern meaning to *curve* or to *crook*.

Ashley tried to reestablish the word *bend* as a noun; he wanted, on the one hand, to limit its application to knots whose function is to join the ends of two cords or ropes, and, on the other, to call every such knot a *bend.* This system of nomenclature, however, cannot be justified on the grounds of traditional usage. The sheet bend, for instance, is so named because it was formerly used to bend the sheet to the clew of the sail, not to the end of another line. The fisherman's bend is not a bend at all according to Ashley's definition. And the fisherman's knot, though classified by Ashley as a *bend,* happens, perversely, to be called a *knot.*

The word *knot* lacks the nautical connotations of the word *bend.* It is apt to be used instead of *hitch* or *bend* in the names of knots that are customarily tied in small cords like thread or twine, knots that tend to jam when under strain. Thus, when the sheet bend is tied in rope by sailors, it is called a *bend;* when it is tied in yarns of wool or cotton by weavers, it is called a *knot* (the weaver's knot). This difference in nomenclature may also be due to the difference between nautical and nonnautical usage.

The word *knot,* finally, is apt to be used when the fastening is made in a single rope or its strands and does not involve another rope or object (e.g., the wall knot, the bowline knot). This distinction is probably as definite as any in knot nomenclature; yet—and this will surprise many readers—we find Luce calling the bowline a *bowline hitch* on page 193 of the second edition of his *Seamanship* (1863).

In brief, knot nomenclature is not, and never has been, entirely consistent, for knots, bends, and hitches have never been systematically differentiated in the minds of the people who have used them.

Further comment on nomenclature is provided in the discussions of individual knots. See especially nos. 9 to 13, 16, 17, 23, 79, 90, 108, 134, and 142. See the Glossary for definitions of terms.

The Strength and Security of Knots

Few people have precise notions regarding the security and breaking strength of knots. Indeed, the subject has been so systematically neglected by scientific investigators that little precise information about how knots work is presently available.

The relative breaking strength of a knot (usually expressed as a percentage) may be defined as the load required to break the knotted rope, divided by the load required to break the unknotted rope. Thus, if the unknotted rope breaks at 1,000 pounds, and the same rope with a knot in it breaks at 500 pounds, the relative strength of the knot is said to be 50 percent.

Bends seem to be weaker, on the average, than loops and nooses, and loops and nooses seem to be weaker than hitches. The figure usually given for the sheet bend, for example, is about 50 percent; for the bowline, about 60 percent; and for the timber hitch, about 75 percent or 80 percent of the strength of the unknotted rope. However, many variables must be reckoned with, as will be explained later, so that the percentages arrived at by different investigators vary considerably and are not applicable under all circumstances. Before considering these variables further, it seems advisable to say something about knot testing in general.

The procedure is roughly as follows. Eyes are spliced in the ends of the specimens and fitted over two steel bars, one at a fixed point, the other on the movable head of the testing machine. Long specimens (5½ to 8 feet for ¾-inch-diameter rope) give the best results. Electric power moves the head of the machine at a constant rate of speed, and a scale beam with a poise measures the tension in pounds. When the specimen breaks, the operator notes the tension that is recorded on the gauge.

When unknotted rope is tested, the eye-splices in the ends of the specimens are sometimes first soaked in water, the rope itself being kept perfectly dry. This is done because a wet splice or rope has a higher breaking strength than a dry one, and failure is thus more likely to occur in the center of the specimen than in the splice. The danger, of course, is that the moisture may penetrate beyond the splice and affect the rope itself. When knots are tested, the eye-splices need not be soaked, for knots are always weaker than splices.

The speed of the testing machine is usually set at four inches a minute, but experiments have shown that the strength of manila rope one inch in diameter is virtually unaffected by changes in speed between one inch and four inches a minute. At speeds of less than one inch a minute, the strength of rope lessens rapidly as the speed is reduced. Tests also indicate that variations in temperature between 67.8° and 76°F, and in humidity between 56 and 73, have little or no effect on the strength of rope. At least one researcher goes further, denying that there is a relationship at all between rope strength and either temperature or *absolute* humidity, though *relative* humidity affects rope strength significantly. In 38 tests made with ¾-inch-diameter manila rope, the breaking strength of the rope increased steadily from 4,900 pounds to 6,600 pounds as the relative humidity rose from 38 percent to 100 percent.

The author tested knots with ⅜- and ⅝-inch-di-ameter manila yacht rope. He found (1) that the bowline is 50 percent stronger after it has been soaked in water than when it is dry; (2) that the square knot, the sheet bend, and the fisherman's knot jam so hard under extreme tension that they are difficult or impossible to untie; (3) that the carrick bend, the fisherman's bend, and the timber hitch neither slip nor jam; (4) that reverse half-hitches (fig. 98D) tend to slip; (5) that the left-handed sheet bend (figs. 31F and 31J) tends to slip; (6) that the sheet bend is equally strong and secure whether tied *with* the lay (fig. 31C) or *against* the lay (fig. 31H); and that the fisherman's knot (no. 40) is 20 percent stronger when the overhands are tied *against* the lay (fig. 16B) than it is when they are tied *with* the lay (fig. 16A).

Two limitations of the knot tests undertaken to date should be mentioned. First, laboratory tests do not approximate conditions of actual service. Knots are rarely (if ever) subjected to the relentlessly increasing tension that is applied to them in a testing machine. In actual service the tension is apt to come unevenly and jerkily, or else to remain constant for a long time. Second, laboratory tests are usually made with new manila rope, between ⅜ inch and 1 inch in diameter, that has never been broken in and weathered. The objectives in knot testing should not be merely to ascertain the breaking strength of particular knots, but to compare the qualities of different knots; to find out the best ways to tie those knots that can be tied in different ways; to experiment with different rates and methods of applying the load; and to study the effect of knots on rope of different sorts, sizes, materials, qualities, conditions, and lays.

Table 4 lists the efficiency or relative breaking strength normally to be expected of twelve common knots when they are tied in manila rope up to 1 inch in diameter. The percentages are based on tests by Scovell, Miller, Dent, Trumpler, and myself. They are round numbers only—approximations. Anything more precise would be meaningless in view of the many variables that enter into knot testing and knot performance.

It is sometimes asserted that the breaking strength of a knot depends on the radius of the sharpest curve

Table 4. Breaking Strength of Common Knots

Overhand Knot	45%	Fisherman's Knot	65%
Figure-Eight Knot	45%	Fisherman's Bend	65%
Reef Knot	50%	Two Half-Hitches	65%
Sheet Bend	50%	Timber Hitch	70%
Carrick Bend	55%	Short Splice	90%
Bowline Knot	60%	Eye-Splice	95%

within the knot. When rope is bent under tension, the outside fibers are supposed to be the first to give way. From this it is inferred that the outside fibers of the sharpest curve within the knot—the curve with the smallest radius—will be the first to break. As a matter of fact, however, a knot seldom breaks internally; the break usually occurs in the standing part of the rope, at the point where it enters the knot. The curve at this point is seldom very sharp, especially as compared with some of the curves within the knot itself, yet it is here that failure occurs, perhaps because the complex stresses and strains that operate on the rope where it enters the knot are amplified by the rigidity with which the rope is held in place at that point by the knot itself.

The force that makes knots hold is friction. Hence, a knot that is secure in coarse material like hemp may be insecure in slippery material like nylon. The principle set forth in numerous knot books (including, I regret to say, both *Sailors' Knots* and the first edition of this book) that adjacent parts within a knot should tend to move in opposite directions when tension is applied, has little validity. The square knot seems to exemplify this principle, but few other knots, if any, do. More significant, probably, is another alleged principle: that the greater the tension, the more tightly the adjacent parts should be held or nipped together. Thus, in the bowline, the hitch called the cuckold's neck closes round the other parts and prevents them from moving—or at least it does so when the knot is tied in coarse enough material.

Because synthetic ropes are slippery and tend to stretch under tension, knots tied in them will sometimes pull down so tightly that they become almost impossible to untie, especially if the rope is subjected to a severe strain. For this reason, the only knots and hitches that should be used in synthetic rope are those that can be untied with ease.

Little is known about the mechanics of knots, and friction itself is still a scientific mystery. Under the circumstances, it behooves the layman to speak skeptically rather than dogmatically about why knots behave the way they do.

1. Useful Tools and Hardware.

Figs. 1A and 1B illustrate the tools that are used in knotting and splicing lines.

Fig. 1A: marlinespike, thimbles (pear-shaped and round), shackle, two types of pricker, fid.

Fig. 1B: palm, sail twine, netting needles (wood and plastic), beeswax, sail needles, scissors, knife.

Figs. 1C to 1N illustrate some of the many types of hardware that lines can be temporarily attached to, run through, or fitted with. The hardware in the figures is discussed left to right.

Fig. 1C: 5½-inch stainless steel four-hole cleat; 8-inch aluminum four-hole cleat; 8-inch anodized aluminum two-hole cleat; 7-inch anodized aluminum four-hole, open-based cleat; 8-inch bronze two-hole, hollow cleat; 10-inch bronze four-hole, hollow cleat.

Fig. 1D: 1¼-inch sliding midships cleat; 6-inch anodized aluminum two-hole jam cleat; 6-inch bronze coaming cleat; stainless steel folding neat cleat; nylon jam cleat.

Fig. 1E: 5/16- to ½-inch plastic line clam cleat; 3/8- to ¾-inch aluminum line clam cleat; 5/16- to ½-inch plastic line clam cleat with integral fairlead; 5/16- to 15/16-inch plastic Commodore line clam cleat; ¼- to 3/8-inch plastic clam bollard.

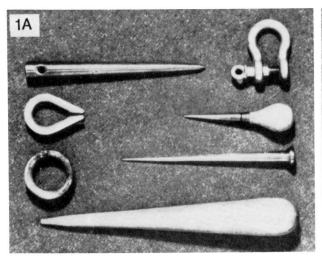

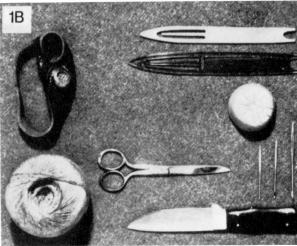

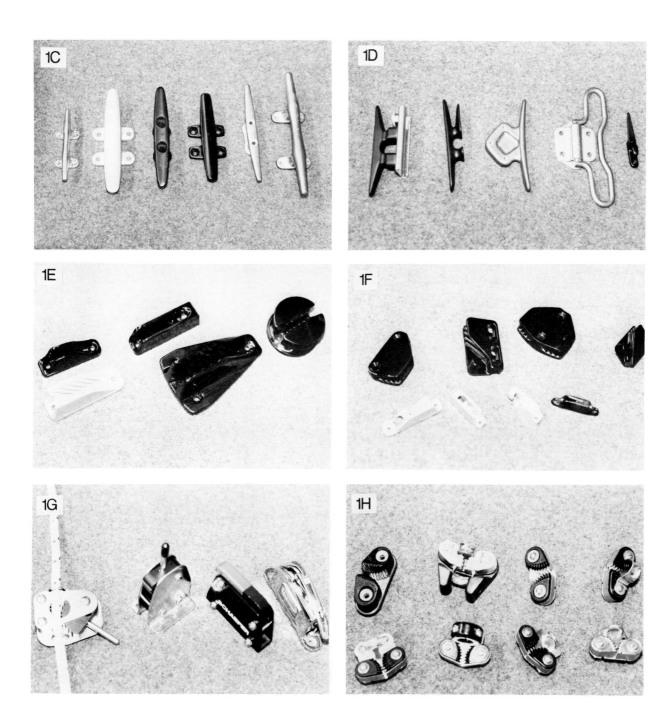

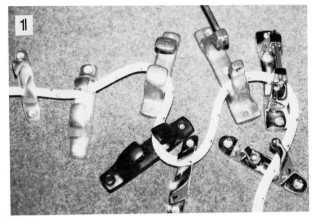

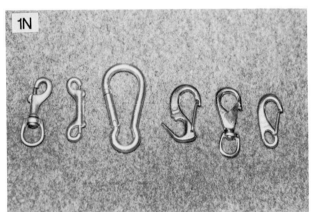

Fig. 1F: (*top*) ¼- to ⅜-inch plastic lateral port clam cleat; ¼- to ½-inch plastic horizontal large loop clam cleat; ¼- to ⅜-inch plastic horizontal clam cleat; ⅛- to ¼-inch plastic vertical loop clam cleat; (*bottom*) ⅛- to ¼-inch aluminum starboard vertical loop clam cleat; ⅛- to ¼-inch aluminum vertical clam cleat with integral fairlead; ⅛- to ¼-inch aluminum starboard vertical loop clam cleat; plastic jam cleat.

Fig. 1G: right-hand halyard stopper; sheet stopper; ⅝-inch single halyard stopper; clutch halyard stopper.

Fig. 1H: (*top*) ¾-inch cam cleat; trigger cam cleat; starboard cam cleat; starboard cam cleat with fairlead; (*bottom*) starboard cam cleat with rolling fairlead; starboard cam cleat with bull's-eye fairlead; starboard cam cleat with fairlead; starboard cam cleat with fairlead.

Fig. 1I: (*top*) aluminum starboard bow chock: aluminum straight chock; bronze straight chock; 7-inch bronze locking chock; 7-inch chrome-plated bronze locking chock; (*bottom*) anodized aluminum straight chock; 5¾-inch chrome-plated bronze starboard bow chock; chrome-plated bronze stern chock.

Fig. 1J: clew hook shackle; latch shackle; snap shackle with clevis pin; trunion shackle with clevis pin; fixed bail snap shackle.

Fig. 1K: snap shackle with D-bail; snap shackle with flared D-bail; trunion shackle with flared D-bail; snap shackle with D-bail and ring.

Fig. 1L: anodized aluminum headboard shackle for thimble with clevis pin; anodized aluminum headboard shackle for thimble; headboard shackle for rope; headboard shackle for rope with key slot pin.

Fig. 1M: bow shackle; D shackle; galvanized bow shackle; elongated D shackle; twist shackle.

Fig. 1N: swivel eye snap hook; double snap hook; safety snap hook; springless snap hook with bending arm; boat snap hook; springless snap hook.

2. Rope Construction. Laid rope is manufactured by twisting fibers together into yarns, yarns into strands, and strands into rope. The lay of the rope is the spiral twist of the strands.

Plain-laid rope has three strands laid up right-handed. See fig. 2A. For many years, manila made in this manner was the most common type of rope.

Shroud-laid rope has four strands laid up right-handed around a heart, or core, as shown in fig. 2B.

Cable-laid rope has three strands, each of which is a plain-laid rope, laid up left-handed, as in fig. 2C.

Plaited or eight-strand rope is made up of four right-hand and four left-hand turned strands, laid in pairs. This type of construction resists rotation and is used for flag halyards, clotheslines, etc.

The strands of right-laid rope are composed of yarns laid up left-handed, and the yarns are composed of fibers laid up right-handed. The terms *right-handed, left-handed, right-laid,* and *left-laid* have reference to the rope when the end is pointing forward, away from the observer, as in figs. 2A to 2C. As the eye of the observer moves toward the end of the rope (i.e., from the bottom to the top of the photographs), the lay or twist seems to be to the right in figs. 2A and 2B, and to the left in fig. 2C. The first two, accordingly, are said to be laid up right-handed, and the third to be laid up left-handed. These terms make sense only when the rope is viewed as described. When the rope is pointing toward, instead of away from, the observer, the terms are meaningless.

Theoretical cross-sections of three-strand and four-strand rope are shown in fig. 2D. Three tangent circles encompass a rather small space in the center, four tangent circles a rather large space. Hence, four-strand rope usually has a small strand called a *heart* or a *core* in the center. Query: Assuming that the rope is right-laid, do the arrows in fig. 2D point *with* or *against the lay?* Answer: The arrows are ambiguous in a diagram of this sort, for it is impossible to tell which way the rope points with respect to the observer.

Fig. 2E shows how to lay up the strands of right-laid rope when for any reason they have become unlaid. Grasp the rope with the left hand, and twist the nearest strand with the right hand until it is tight and compact. When twisted sufficiently it will tend to fall into place, especially if the natural kinks have not been entirely lost. In like manner twist the next strand (i.e., the one at the top in the photograph), then the next, then the first again, and so on. Do not allow the rope as a whole to rotate on its axis while the work is in progress, but hold it firmly in the left hand while the right hand moves from strand to strand. Hold each strand, as it is twisted, firmly in place with the thumb of the left hand. These directions apply to rope that is light enough to be held in the hands. Similar principles, but different mechanical expedients, are used when laying up the strands of large hawsers.

After the strands are laid up, seize the end of the rope by one of the methods described on pages 24 through 32.

Braided rope resembles plaited rope in construction except that it is made up of a great number of yarns instead of strands. The braids include single or hollow braids, solid braids, and double braids. Braided ropes are balanced because they have an equal number of left-hand and right-hand turns. See fig. 2F. For this reason, braided ropes resist twisting, kinking, and hockling, but they are not as elastic as other types of ropes. Braided rope is slightly stronger than conventional three-strand rope of the same diameter.

Three-strand, four-strand, and cable-laid "twisted" ropes are held together by a comparatively tight twist of yarns and strands. Braided ropes are held together by their interlocking construction, which allows a looser lay, resulting in greater strength and less elongation.

Because of its smoother outside surface, braided rope seems to grip the surface of a winch better than laid rope, so rope burns are a hazard with braided ropes. If properly handled when being coiled down, braided rope will not kink. The coil should be made in the form of a series of figure eights, each turn laid down in the opposite direction of the one preceding it. See fig. 2G.

Single or hollow braids are preferably of 12-strand, hexagonal construction. See fig. 2H. A common form of a hollow braid is an 8-strand diamond braid that is used for water-ski tow ropes. See fig. 2I. More conventional marine single-braided ropes are made up of 16, 20, 28, or 32 strands. As the number of strands increase, single-braid ropes are more likely to flatten. See fig. 2J. Single braids resist rotation, cannot be hockled, and are generally easy to splice.

In solid braided ropes, strands cross and fill the center of the rope. The center can also be reinforced with strands of synthetic fiber for increased strength and durability. See fig. 2K. Solid braided rope is normally only made in smaller sizes. Solid braids resist rotation and cannot be hockled, but they are more difficult to splice than hollow braids.

Double-braided ropes consist of a braided cover over a braided core, each being hollow braids. See fig. 2L. The braided cover will have between 16 and 32 strands, in pairs or singly. See fig. 2M. Double-braided ropes are nonrotating and cannot be hockled. They are also easy to splice and wear exceptionally

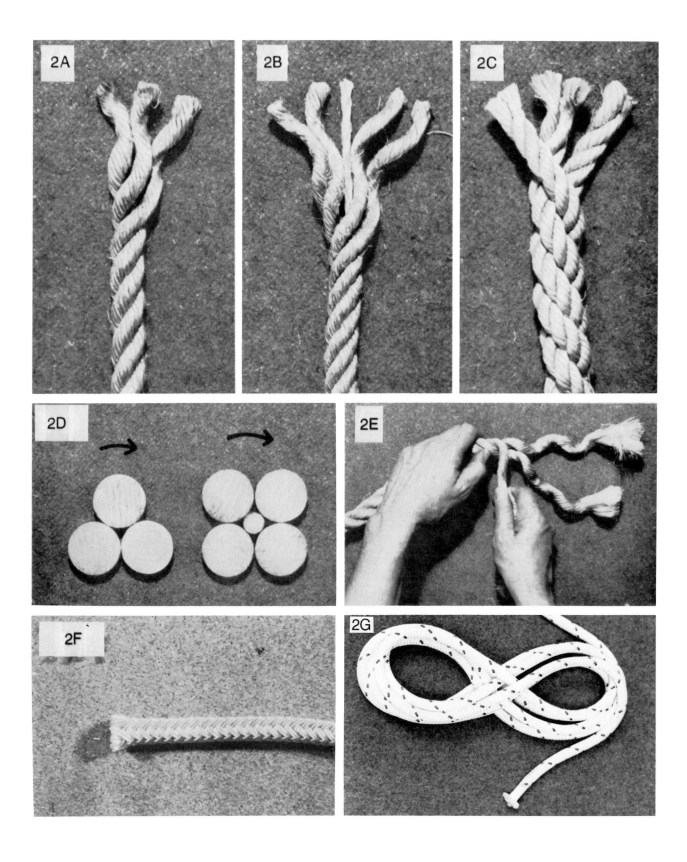

well. In balanced construction, the cover and the core share the load equally. For special applications, double braids can be constructed of a strong core, which can carry up to 90 percent of the load, and a cover designed for abrasion protection.

Recently, various fibers have been combined, forming a new category of ropes called composite or plied. An example of composite construction is the 12-strand braided rope shown in fig. 2N. Each strand is made up of polypropylene fibers surrounded by polyester fibers. Combining low-specific-gravity polypropylene fibers and strong, relatively inelastic, and abrasion- and ultra violet–resistant polyester fibers produces a durable rope with a high strength-to-weight ratio and low snap-back. Composite constructions are also being used to produce three-strand and eight-strand plaited and double-braided ropes with special properties.

No-lay rope is constructed of a core of pre-stretched polyester yarns laid parallel with minimum twist and covered with a jacket of extruded polyvinyl chloride. The terminal ends of such ropes can be fitted with common wire rope sockets and filled with epoxy. No-lay rope can be used for standing rigging and other special applications.

Another specialized rope is made of mylar, a polyester filament, which has been slit, twisted, and stretched. It is laid up in a three-, four-, or six-strand rope.

Rope six inches in circumference (two inches in diameter) and larger is put up in coils of 90, 100, 120, and 200 fathoms. Rope smaller than six inches in circumference is usually put up in full coils (200 fathoms) and half coils (100 fathoms). Lengths greater than 200 fathoms must be specially ordered. Manila rope is usually shipped in burlap-wrapped coils, while synthetics come on wooden reels.

Rope must be removed from a coil in the proper manner to prevent kinking. Lay the coil on its flat side so the outside end of the rope is pointing in a counterclockwise direction. After removing the cords that bind the coil, reach down into the center and pull the inside end of the rope upward, taking whatever footage is desired from the inside of the coil.

Rope can be removed from a reel by laying the reel on its side and rolling it along a smooth, clean surface. However, a better method is to support the reel on a suitable length of pipe. A synthetic rope should not be taken off a reel by flipping it off the head of the reel. This puts a turn in the rope and is likely to cause kinks or hockles.

In the manufacturing process, both natural and synthetic ropes are impregnated with a solution that acts as a preservative and a lubricant to prevent inter-nal friction. Additional lubricant is not necessary and is likely to do more harm than good.

The construction of wire rope is similar to that of twisted rope, except that the strands are made up of individual wires laid together. The strands are then laid together to form the wire rope. Wire rope is designated by the number of strands and the number of wires in each strand. A 6 × 19 wire rope would have 6 strands, 19 wires per strand.

Wire ropes can also be constructed with a fiber core, an independent wire rope core, or a wire strand core. The purpose of the core is to support the wire strands under tension.

Wire rope should be regularly inspected for corrosion, worn areas, kinks, and fish-hooks (broken wires). Wire rope failures are most commonly caused by:

1. Using wire that is undersized for the job
2. Improper lubrication
3. Chafing
4. Under- or oversized sheaves or drums
5. Misaligned sheaves or drums
6. Worn, broken, or improper grooves on sheaves
7. Jumping of sheaves
8. Exposure to corrosive material and/or atmosphere
9. Improper fittings
10. Infrequent inspections

As wire rope is turned or bent, each wire in each strand moves against other wires in the strand, causing wear. To prevent wear, wire rope should be cleaned and then dipped in hot chain lubricant, medium graphite grease, or even motor oil. Heated lubricant penetrates the strands better. Lubrication will also help prevent corrosion, which quickly decreases the strength of wire rope.

Care should be taken to avoid kinks in wire rope. Wire rope should be unrolled in the same way that synthetic rope is uncoiled. If a kink develops in a wire rope, place the kink on a firm object and push down on it until the kink straightens out somewhat. Lay the wire rope on a flat surface and pound it with a wooden mallet until it is smooth. A kinked wire rope that has had a heavy strain put on it can no longer be trusted; the kink should be cut out and the rope spliced.

Fish-hooks develop from abrasion, sharp bends, or kinks. The safe working load of wire rope is greatly reduced by fish-hooks. Wire rope is unsafe when 4 percent of the total number of wires in it are broken within the length of one wire rope lay. For example, a 6 × 7 wire rope with three broken wires in one strand, or a 6 × 19 wire rope with six broken wires in one strand, would be considered unsafe.

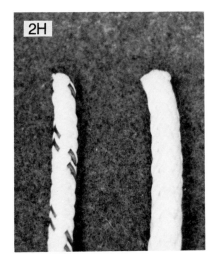

2H

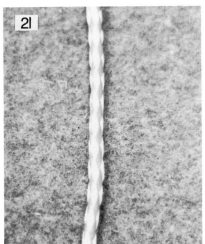

2I

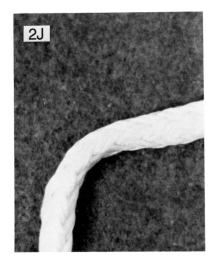

2J

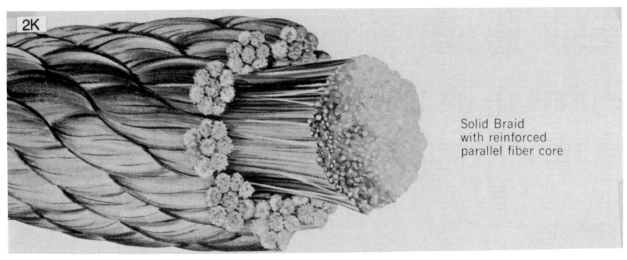

2K

Solid Braid
with reinforced
parallel fiber core

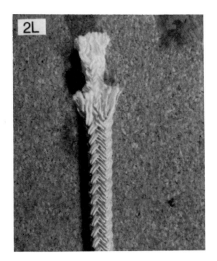

2L

2M

2N

Polypropylene center strands

Polyester
jacket strands

3. Plain Whipping. A whipping is a small lashing put on the end of a rope to prevent the strands from fraying and becoming unlaid. The material most commonly used is sail twine and (for large rope) marline. (For the sake of clarity, a heavier cord is used in the illustrations.)

First Method

Fig. 3A: Lay the inert end of the twine along the rope, pointing to the *right.* (The inert end should be longer than is shown in figs. 3A to 3D, for it will have to be pulled taut later.) Take two or three turns, *against the lay of the rope,* round both rope and inert end. Pull the turns taut, and hold them in place with the left thumb and index finger.

Fig. 3B: Lay the working end of the twine along the rope, pointing to the *left.* (The loop should be much larger than is shown in fig. 3B.) Take several turns, pulling each turn tight and making sure that the inert end and the loop do not become snarled.

Fig. 3C: When the whipping attains a length roughly equal to the diameter of the rope, pull the working end through to the left. As you do so, the turns will tend to work loose, and the loop will be-

come twisted. To prevent the former, hold the turns in place with the left thumb and *middle* finger. To prevent the latter, raise the left *index* finger, and place the loop over it. When the twine has been pulled almost all the way through, withdraw the finger.

Figs. 3D and 3E: Pull the ends of the twine taut and cut them off. Trim the end of the rope.

Second Method

Fig. 3F: This is called American whipping in British knot books. Bring the ends of the twine out between the same two turns, and knot them with a square knot. (Only the first half of the knot is illustrated.)

Third Method

Fig. 3G: To whip a spar or fishing rod in the middle, begin as in fig. 3A, but take the last five or six turns round a small wedge or round the left index finger. Remove the wedge (or finger) and stick the working end of the twine through to the left under the loose turns.

Fig. 3H: Pull each turn taut, and cut off the ends of the twine. The result is identical to fig. 3F.

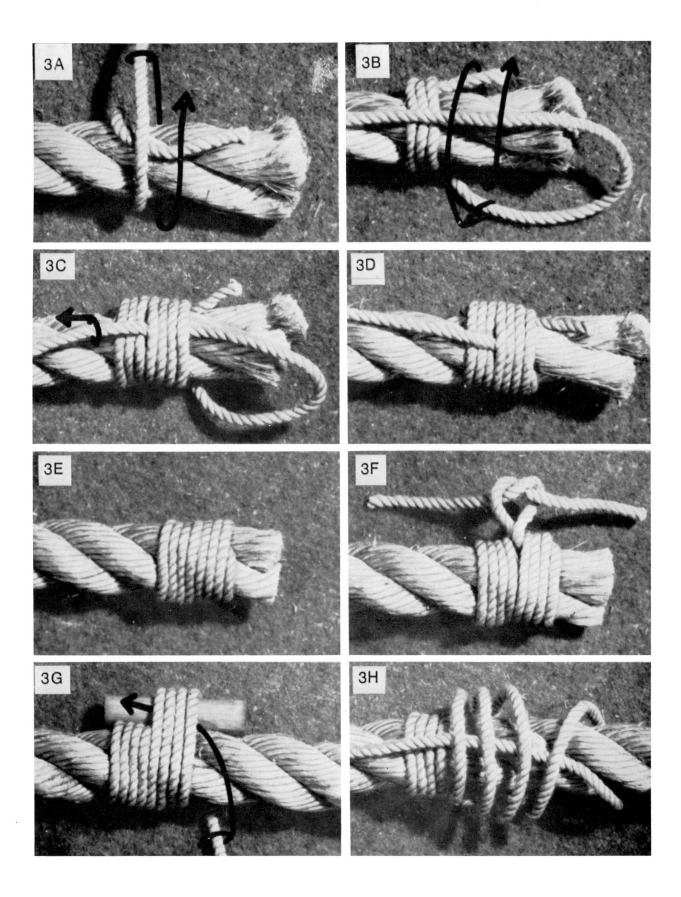

Fourth Method

Fig. 3I: Double back the end of the twine, and take a number of turns round both the rope and the doubled end, drawing each turn taut.

Fig. 3J: When the whipping is long enough, stick the free end of the twine through the loop in the doubled end.

Fig. 3K: Pull the doubled end to the left, carrying the free end with it, until the loop has reached a point under the turns about midway from left to right.

Fig. 3L: Cut off the ends of the twine, and trim the end of the rope.

This method is ingenious and easy. However, if the turns are as taut as they ought to be, it is sometimes hard to pull the free end under without breaking the twine. It is also difficult to judge when the middle point has been reached. The ordinary method seems to be preferable.

Fifth Method

A variation of the foregoing method is described in Martta Ropponen's *Solmukirja* (1931), a Finnish knot book. Instead of the doubled end of the whipping twine (fig. 3I), a separate piece of twine, doubled, is laid down in exactly the same position as the doubled end of fig. 3I. This separate piece is then covered by the turns of the whipping, the end of which is put through the loop (as in figs. 3J and 3K) and pulled to the left under the whipping. It is pulled completely through, however, and not halfway through. The separate piece of twine is then discarded, and the two ends of the whipping can be pulled very tightly to the left and right before being cut off.

4. Palm-and-Needle Whipping is the neatest and most permanent method.

Fig. 4A: Wax the twine with beeswax, and stitch it through the rope once or twice with a sail needle. Wind the twine round the rope several times, drawing each turn taut.

Fig. 4B: When enough turns have been taken, stitch the twine through the rope in such a way that it will come out between two strands, close to the whipping.

Fig. 4C: Bring the end back to the left along the spiral groove between the strands, and stitch it through again.

Fig. 4D: A more secure whipping results if the twine is stitched through diagonally, as shown here, instead of at right angles to the axis of the rope, as shown in fig. 4C. However, the rope is often too large or too stiff or both to permit diagonal stitching.

A sailor's palm (fig. 1B) is used in forcing the needle through the rope.

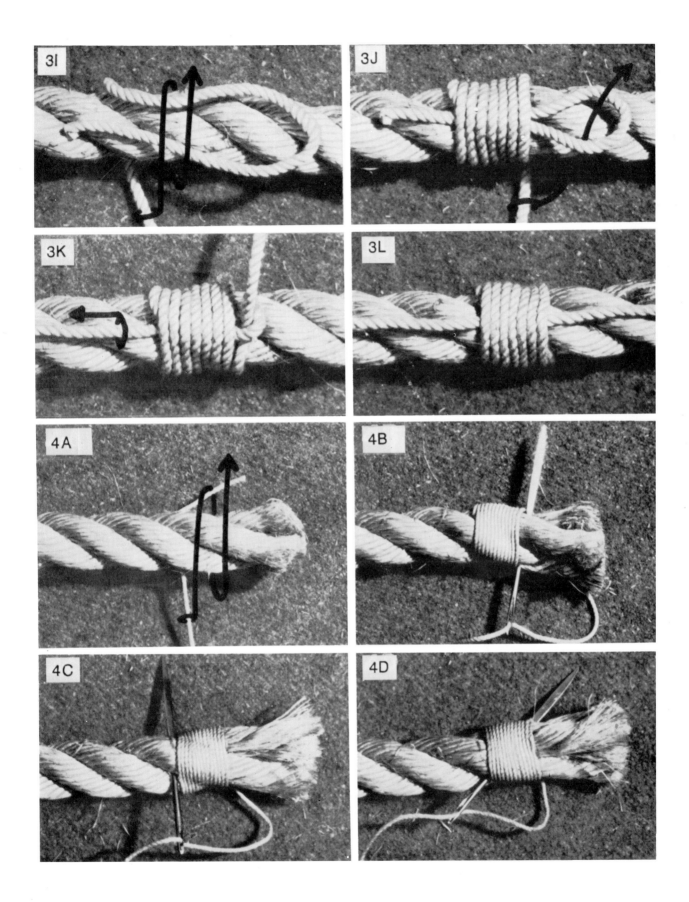

Fig. 4E: Continue stitching, as described above, until all the spiral cross-turns are doubled. (Diagonal stitching, as shown in fig. 4D, is preferable to the perpendicular stitching illustrated here, but, again, it is often impracticable.) When all the cross-turns are doubled, stitch the twine through two or three times in order to secure the end, and then cut it off.

Fig. 4F: The finished whipping.

5. Snaking. Instead of the spiral cross-turns of palm-and-needle whipping (no. 4), the stitching shown in figs. 5A and 5B may be used for the same purpose (i.e., to contain the turns of the whipping and make them more snug and secure). (Keep in mind that the twine used in the illustrations of whipping and snaking is heavier than would be desirable in practice.)

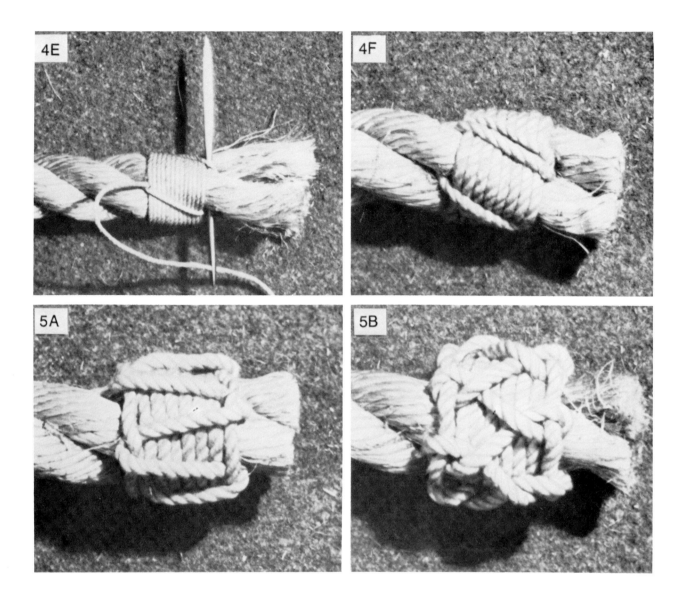

6. Tape and Heat Sealing. Plain whipping, palm-and-needle whipping, and snaking can be used for both natural and synthetic fiber ropes. But since synthetic ropes, whether they are braided, plaited, or twisted, fray quickly, their ends must be secured immediately, even if only in a temporary fashion. Tape and heat sealing is a good temporary method of securing the ends of most synthetic lines.

Fig. 6A: Wrap the line with two turns of electrical or masking tape near the end.

Fig. 6B: Using a hot knife, melt through the line inboard of the tape.

Figs. 6C and 6D: This method can also be used to wrap and cut a line into two lines, thus sealing both ends at once. In this instance, cut (melt) through the center of the tape.

Fig. 6E: Remove the tape and run the hot knife lightly around the outside of the line to prevent future cracking and fraying of the line. This procedure should be followed whenever a synthetic line is sealed with a hot knife.

The high melting point of Kevlar lines makes this method useless for them. Kevlar lines must be whipped by one of the previously discussed methods.

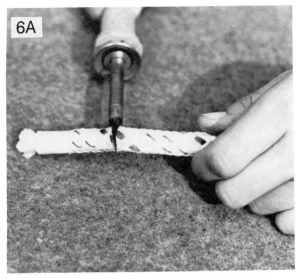

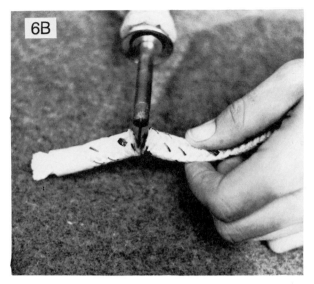

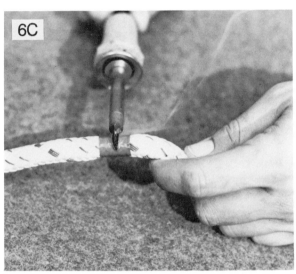

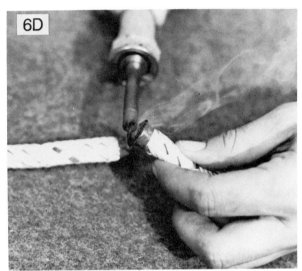

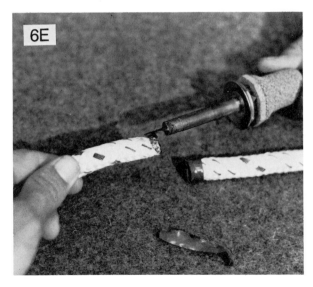

31

7. Liquid Vinyl Sealing. Another simple method of securing a line's end is to use liquid vinyl developed for this purpose.

Fig. 7A: First coat the section of the line to be cut, and allow approximately five minutes for the liquid vinyl to dry.

Fig. 7B: Cut the line through the center of the coated area.

Fig. 7C: Either dip both ends of the line into the liquid vinyl or apply the vinyl with a brush. The vinyl fully cures overnight. Manufacturers recommend two dips for ropes half an inch or less in diameter, and three dips for larger ropes.

Fig. 7D: Liquid vinyls are available in clear, white, and a variety of colors. Colored vinyl can be very useful for quickly marking docking or mooring lines.

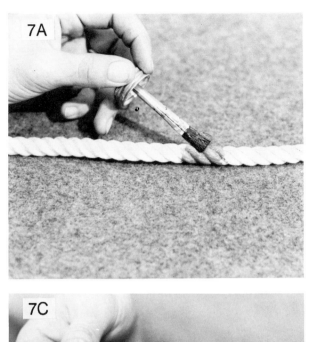

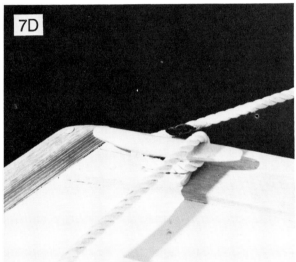

8. Wire-Rope Seizings. Temporary seizings of annealed iron wire are put on wire rope before it is cut and spliced. *The Splicing of Wire Rope* (1932), a booklet issued by the John A. Roebling Company, recommends the method shown here. If the ends of the rope are not firmly seized, this booklet warns, the balance of tension in the rope will be disturbed, and some strands will carry a greater portion of the load than others. "Before cutting steel wire rope," the booklet continues, "it is essential to place at least three sets of seizings each side of the intended cut to prevent disturbing the uniformity of the rope. On large diameter ropes more seizings are necessary." Seizing wire of the proper size should be used. The Roebling Company's recommendations are given in table 5.

Seizings such as the one pictured in figs. 8A to 8C are unsuitable for permanent purposes, for they would cut or tear the hands of the individuals who handled the rope. Before wire rope is put into service, all splices and ends should be wrapped (served) with serving wire to prevent injury. A serving mallet with a spool of wire on it is used in serving large wire rope. Small wire rope is often served with marline or sail twine.

Table 5. Size Guidelines, Seizing Wire to Wire Rope

Diameter of Wire Rope (in inches)	Diameter of Seizing Wire (in inches)
⅜ to ½	.047
⅝	.054
¾	.063
⅞ to 1⅛	.080
1¼ to 1⅞	.105
2+	.135

SOURCE: *Instructions for UniGrip Tools and Sleeves.*
Table courtesy of Universal Wire Products, Inc.

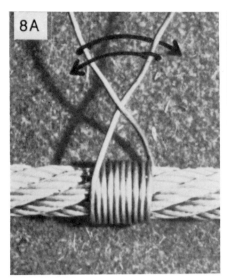

9. A Loop is a closed or nearly closed curve in a rope or line. The letter *A* indicates what is called, in knotting, the *end, free end,* or *working end.* The letter *B* indicates the *bight,* or the part of the curve on which the knot is formed. The letter *C* indicates the *standing part,* or the main part of the rope, as distinguished from the bight and the end. The word *bight* also means the middle of a rope or line, as opposed to the two ends, and the word *loop* is often used to mean a fixed loop, or loop knot, such as the honda (no. 72).

10. A Turn. A loop round an object is called a *turn.*

11. A Round Turn. Two turns are called a *round turn.* "There's a lot of virtue in a round turn," according to an old saying, which means that a round turn increases the security of a hitch (i.e., its resistance to slipping).

12. A Hitch. A turn with the end under the standing part is called a *hitch* or *single hitch.* Sometimes the end is actually nipped under the standing part, as in fig. 12, and sometimes it is merely under the standing part in relation to a second hitch or other formation, as with the clove hitch (no. 112). Thus, the first half of a clove hitch, considered by itself, would be a mere turn, but considered in relation to the rest of the knot, it is a hitch. In practice, a single hitch is often called a *half-hitch,* particularly when it is made round another rope.

13. A Half-Hitch. In distinguishing the single hitch (no. 12) from the half-hitch (no. 13), I am following Ashley (1944). Structurally the two are identical, but the half-hitch is made by securing the end to the standing part, whereas the single hitch is secured directly to another object. This distinction, though a real one, becomes rather tenuous under certain conditions. For instance, it is impossible to tell whether the hitch in fig. 13C is a single hitch or a half-hitch unless one knows whether *D* and *B* are separate ropes or parts of the same rope, with *D* and *B* joining just off the edge of the photograph. If *D* and *B* are separate ropes, the hitch, strictly speaking, is a single hitch, though it would generally be called a half-hitch in practice. If *D* and *B* are parts of the same rope, the hitch is a genuine half-hitch.

Figs. 13A and 13B show right-handed and left-handed half-hitches respectively.

Figs. 13C and 13D show how a hitch can be transferred from one rope to another. Pull *A* and *B* apart (fig. 13C) until *AB* is straight, and the hitch is transferred to *CD* (fig. 13D).

14. A Slippery Hitch is similar to no. 12, but the end is doubled back before being nipped under the standing part. The sheet of a small sailboat can be safely secured with a slippery hitch, since a quick pull on the end releases it instantaneously.

15. A Slipped Half-Hitch is a useful temporary tie. The end and the part adjacent to it must be well nipped.

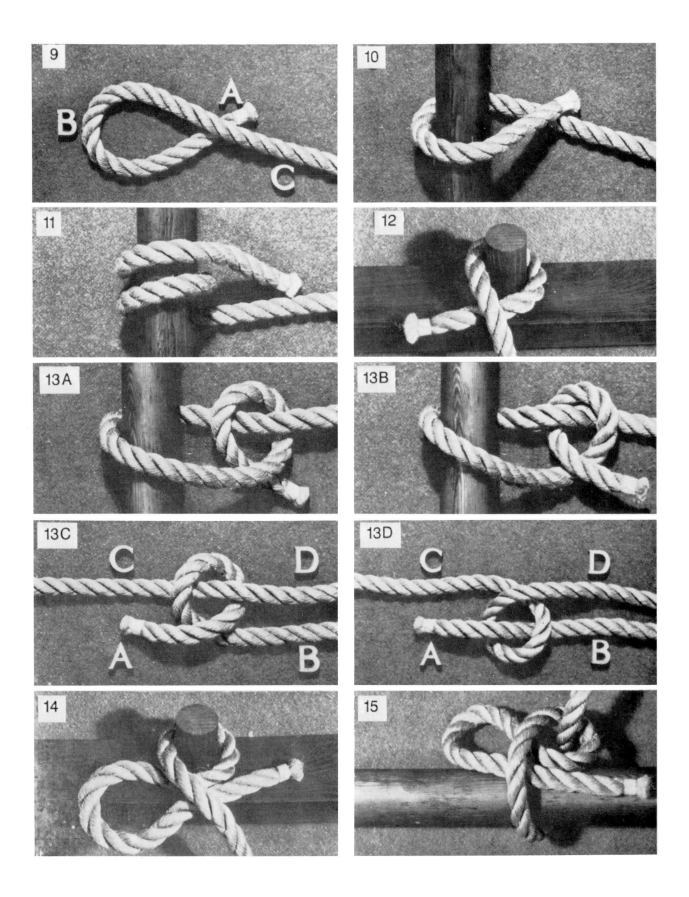

16. The Overhand Knot or Thumb Knot is a basic knot of great utility. It is the principal element in many knots, and it is often used alone—for example, as a temporary stopper knot to prevent a line from running through an opening. It is commonly tied in thread, twine, and other small material, to keep the ends from unravelling, but it is thought to be unseamanlike to tie it in rope for this purpose. It is the smallest of all knots, and the easiest to tie, but it jams hard under tension, and it weakens the rope in which it is tied.

Fig. 16A: A right-handed overhand knot, tied with the lay, in right-laid rope.

Fig. 16B: A left-handed overhand knot, tied against the lay.

When tied round an object, an overhand knot can be transformed into a half-hitch (no. 13) by pulling on the end.

17. The Half-Knot is similar in structure to the overhand knot, and in fact the two are not usually differentiated. However, the half-knot is made with the two ends rather than with one end, and it is a binding knot rather than a stopper knot. Ashley (1944) is the first writer to insist upon the distinction between the half-knot and the overhand knot, a more useful distinction than that between the single hitch and the half-hitch (nos. 12 and 13).

Fig. 17A: A right-hand half-knot.

Fig. 17B: A left-hand half-knot.

The half-knot is used in tying the square knot (no. 24).

18. The Slipped Overhand Knot is a stopper knot that can be quickly released by pulling on the end. It should not be confused with no. 88.

Fig. 18A: To tie the slipped overhand knot, pull a bight through a loop.

Fig. 18B: The completed knot.

19. The Blood Knot or Multiple Overhand Knot was used by the ancient Incas of Peru in their quipus, or knot records. It can be tied in either of two ways.
First Method

Fig. 19A: A small specimen, say a double or triple knot, can be tied by reeving the end through the loop one or two extra times, and then drawing the knot taut.

Fig. 19B: A right-hand double overhand knot (*A*) and a left-hand double overhand knot (*B*).
Second Method

Fig. 19C: Larger multiples are more easily tied by twisting the end back round the standing part, and sticking it through the loops, as shown by the arrow.

Fig. 19D: A six-fold overhand tied by this method.

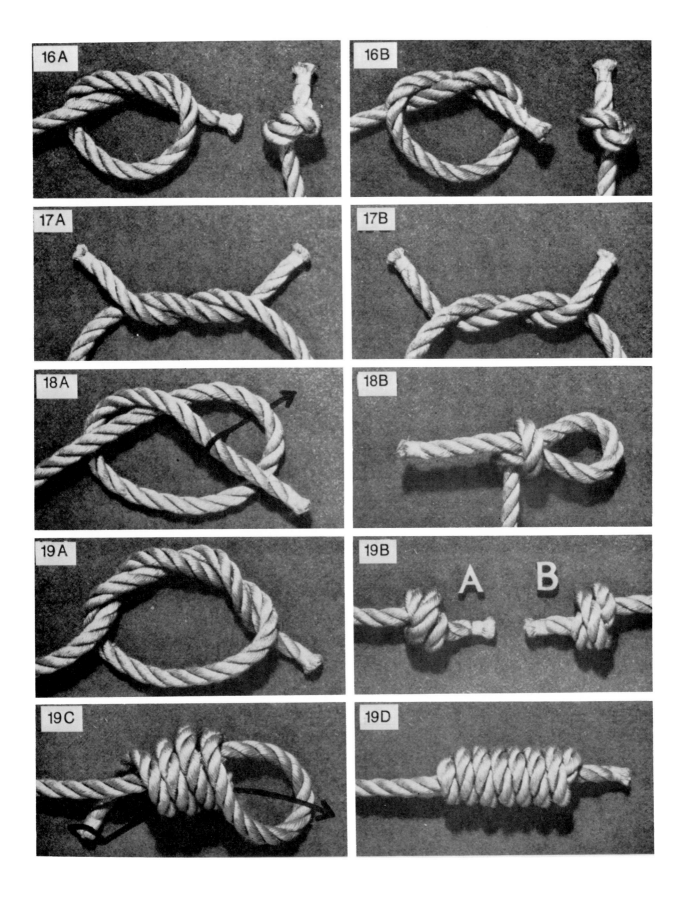

16 A 16 B
17 A 17 B
18 A 18 B
19 A 19 B A B
19 C 19 D

20. The Figure-Eight Knot, because of its symmetry rather than because of its utility, has been called the perfect knot. It serves the same general purposes as the overhand knot (no. 16). However, it is easier to untie than the overhand, because it does not jam quite so hard, and it is somewhat bulkier. For these reasons it is sometimes preferred as a temporary stopper knot. Many of the knots that begin with the overhand knot can be paralleled using the figure-eight knot as a base.

21. The Slipped Figure-Eight Knot is analogous to the slipped overhand knot (no. 18). To tie the slipped figure-eight knot, pull a bight instead of an end through the upper loop of the figure-eight. Do not confuse this knot with no. 92.

22. The Multiple Figure-Eight Knot is tied as illustrated. It has no particular utility.

23. The Stevedore Knot is a temporary stopper knot. It has no special connection with stevedores or the work of stevedores. The name originated in a pamphlet issued about 1890 by the C. W. Hunt Company, which sold rope under the trade name Stevedore. It was subsequently adopted by dictionaries (Funk and Wagnall, 1893, Webster, 1909), engineers' handbooks (Kent, Marks), and other works of reference, and it is now firmly established in books, if not in the vocabulary of seamen.

24. The Square Knot or Reef Knot is a familiar and important knot. It is indispensable when a bundle or anything in the nature of a bundle is to be bound up and secured, and it is the most convenient way to tie two cords together when there is tension on both of them. Traditionally, two of its chief uses have been to tie the reef points when reefing (hence one of its names) and to secure the robands to the yards (hence its Swedish name *råbandsknop* and its Norwegian and Danish name *raabandsknob*).

Fig. 24A: To tie the square knot, tie two half-knots (no. 17) one on top of the other. If the first half-knot is right-handed, the second must be left-handed, and vice versa. If both half-knots are alike, the result is a granny (no. 28).

Fig. 24B: In the completed knot, each end lies alongside its own standing part (*A* and *C; B* and *D*).

The square knot has three limitations: (1) it jams under great tension; (2) it spills if the ropes are of different sizes or materials; and (3) it upsets and falls into two half-hitches if the pull comes unevenly, on one part only, as for example on *BD* in fig. 24B.

Fig. 24C: Under these circumstances, *BD* becomes straight and slips out through the hitches in *AC*. This characteristic is in one way an advantage and can be utilized when untying the knot. Indeed, a sharp pull on one of the ends is the way to loosen the reef points when shaking out a reef. Nevertheless, the limitations mentioned make it inadvisable to unite two hawsers, or any two free lines, with the square knot.

Fig. 24D: To make the square knot more secure, tie an overhand knot in each end or hitch the ends to the standing parts.

25. The Draw Knot or Half-Bowknot is a form of the square knot. To tie the draw knot, double back one of the ends when forming the second half-knot, or, in other words, do not pull one of the ends all the way through. This knot is customarily used to tie the reef points on yachts.

26. The Bowknot is a square knot with both ends slipped. It is used in tying shoelaces, in doing up Christmas parcels, and whenever a decorative way to dispose of the ends is desired. In tying nos. 25 and 26, be careful to avoid the granny (no. 28).

27. The Surgeon's Knot is a variation of the square knot.

Fig. 27A: The usual form consists of a half-knot on top of a double half-knot. The increased friction of the double half-knot prevents it from slipping while the second half-knot is being tied.

Fig. 27B: This form of the surgeon's knot consists of two double half-knots. It is more symmetrical than fig. 27A and perhaps more secure.

Diderot's *Encyclopédie* (1778, vol. 23, p. 44) describes the surgeon's knot very clearly. According to an unverified story I have heard, a California surgeon who murdered a woman was caught and convicted because he used a surgeon's knot to tie up the body before throwing it into a river.

28. The Granny Knot or Lubber's Knot. Nos. 28, 29, and 30 resemble the square knot, but they are inferior to it and should be avoided.

Fig. 28A: Since the two half-knots that make up the granny are both tied the same way (i.e., both right-handed or both left-handed), the granny is easier for the beginner to tie than the square knot is. Therefore, anyone learning to tie the square knot must make a conscious effort not to blunder into the granny, which is apt to slip or jam or both.

Fig. 28B: When tension comes on one side only, say *BD* in fig. 28A, the granny upsets and falls into two half-hitches, as shown here. This characteristic gives rise to the one occasion when the granny can be legitimately used, as explained in fig. 98C.

29. The Thief Knot or Bread-Bag Knot slips under slight tension and would be even more treacherous than the granny except that it is not apt to be tied by mistake. Superficially it looks like the square knot.

Fig. 29A: Note that the ends are diagonally opposite each other, and not on the same side, as in the genuine square knot.

Fig. 29B: When upset, the thief knot takes the form of two half-hitches, each tied round the opposite standing part.

30. The What Knot (so named by Ashley) resembles the granny knot and is even less reliable.

Fig. 30A: The ends, unlike the ends in no. 28, are diagonally opposite each other.

Fig. 30B: When tension is applied, the knot tends to assume the form shown here, and slips apart with astonishing ease. Note that the end *A* is on top of the end *B*.

Fig. 30C: If the position of the two ends is reversed—that is, if *B* is placed on top of *A*—then the knot holds extremely well and is comparatively easy to loosen after a strain.

Seaman 2c. Edward Ross, in a letter dated September 1943, writes that he pulled a truck out of a ditch with a bulldozer, using this knot in 1-inch rope, with the ends crossed as in fig. 30C. Further experiments he has undertaken indicate that the knot does not jam as hard as the square knot or the sheet bend. However, it is a risky knot to use in view of what happens when it is in the position of fig. 30B.

Fig. 30D: The what knot is the same in structure as the strap knot (no. 46). The easiest way to tie it is to join the ends by means of a half-knot (no. 17), and then to stick both ends together through the center of the half-knot. The result is two half-hitches, one in each end round the opposite standing part. Note carefully the difference between fig. 30D and fig. 29B, and compare also nos. 43, 44, and 45.

31. The Sheet Bend or Weaver's Knot is also called the *single bend, simple bend, common bend, becket bend,* and *swab hitch.* It is strong, secure, and easy to tie, and it holds well with ropes of different sizes and materials. Its chief limitation is that it tends to jam under great tension. On the whole, however, it is the most useful bend for all kinds of miscellaneous purposes. In fact, it is one of the eight or ten most indispensable knots. There are several ways to tie it.

First Method

Fig. 31A: Hold *A* in the right hand and *B* in the left hand. Cross *A* over *B;* then bring *A* down, round *B,* and up. At the same time, and simultaneously with the foregoing operation, turn a hitch in *B,* using the thumb and forefinger of the right hand and also, to some extent, the left hand. If this operation, so easy to perform but so difficult to describe, has been completed successfully, the end *A* should now be sticking straight up through the hitch in *B.*

Fig. 31B: Pass *A* round behind the standing part and down through the hitch in *B.* Draw taut, and the hitch is complete.

Figs. 31C and 31D: Since knots sometimes look different from different angles, front and rear views of the sheet bend are shown here.

Figs. 31E and 31F: An inferior variety of sheet bend, sometimes called the *left-handed sheet bend,* results if the end is passed in the opposite direction round the standing part. Note that the ends come out on opposite sides of the knot, instead of on the same side, as in fig. 29C. This form of the sheet bend tends to slip, especially if the rope is at all smooth or slippery.

Figs. 31G and 31H: A third variety of sheet bend is shown here. The ends are on the same side of the knot, and it seems to be just as secure as fig. 31C. Except for the lay of the rope, it looks the way fig. 31C would look in a mirror, and it is the form that a left-handed person would naturally tie.

Figs. 31I and 31J: A fourth variety, with ends opposite each other, resembles fig. 31F, and it also has a tendency to slip.

The foregoing analysis is more complete than is usually provided in books on knots, but not so complete, let us hope, as to be confusing. To recapitulate: avoid the forms with ends on opposite sides (figs. 31F and 31J); use the forms with ends on the same side (31C and 31H).

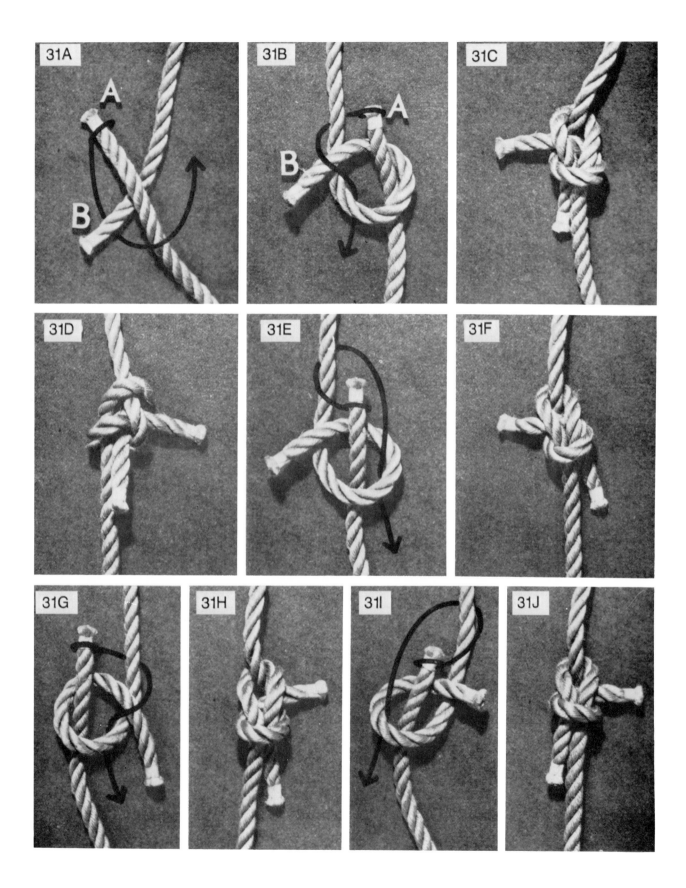

Second Method

Fig. 31K: Make a bight in the end of one of the lines (the larger of the two, if there is a difference in size), and pass the other end round and under, as shown by the arrow. This method is about as quick as the standard method, described on the preceding page, and is sometimes more convenient. All four varieties of the sheet bend (figs. 31C, 31F, 31H, and 31J) can be tied by this method, fig. 31C being the one that normally results.

Fig. 31L: Two lines can be bent to one by means of the sheet bend.

Third Method

This method, said to be used by weavers, is especially effective in very small material like thread or twine.

Fig. 31M: Cross *A* over *B*, and take a turn with the standing part of *B* over its own end.

Fig. 31N: Push *A* through *B*. The result by this method is identical to fig. 31C on the preceding page.

Fourth Method

Fig. 31O: Push a bight *A* through a loop near the end of the thread, or, in other words, tie an overhand noose (no. 88) in one of the threads.

Fig. 31P: Stick the other end up through the noose *A*, and pull *B* and *C* apart, until the noose and the end are drawn back through the center of the overhand knot. This method is useful when one end is very short, as when a shoelace breaks. It is illustrated in Douglas Cockerell's *Bookbinding* (1906, p. 106).

Other Methods

E. D. Fowle (*Textile World,* 21 May 1927, pp. 96–99) illustrates a quick way to tie the left-handed sheet bend or weaver's knot (i.e., the form with the ends on opposite sides). From the weaver's point of view, he argues, the left-handed knot is preferable to the knot with the ends on the same side, in that it "more evenly distributes the interference of the ends with the neighboring warp threads. It also makes it impossible for the two ends to become glued together in sizing and increases the likelihood of the knot being concealed in the woven or knitted fabric." Moreover, the ends are less likely to hang on "heddle eyes, reed dents, and the hoops of knitting needles." This last point is stressed again in an anonymous article in *Textile World* for June 1946 (pp. 101–5), which also illustrates two additional techniques of tying the left-handed knot.

Lingual Method

"With the flexure of her Tongue only she could readily tye that fast Knot, which we call the Weaver's Knot"—Nathaniel Wanley, *Wonders of the Little World,* 1678 (cited by the *New English Dictionary*).

32. The Slipped Sheet Bend is convenient when quick release is desired. It does not matter whether the slip hitch is arranged as in fig. 32A or as in fig. 32B.

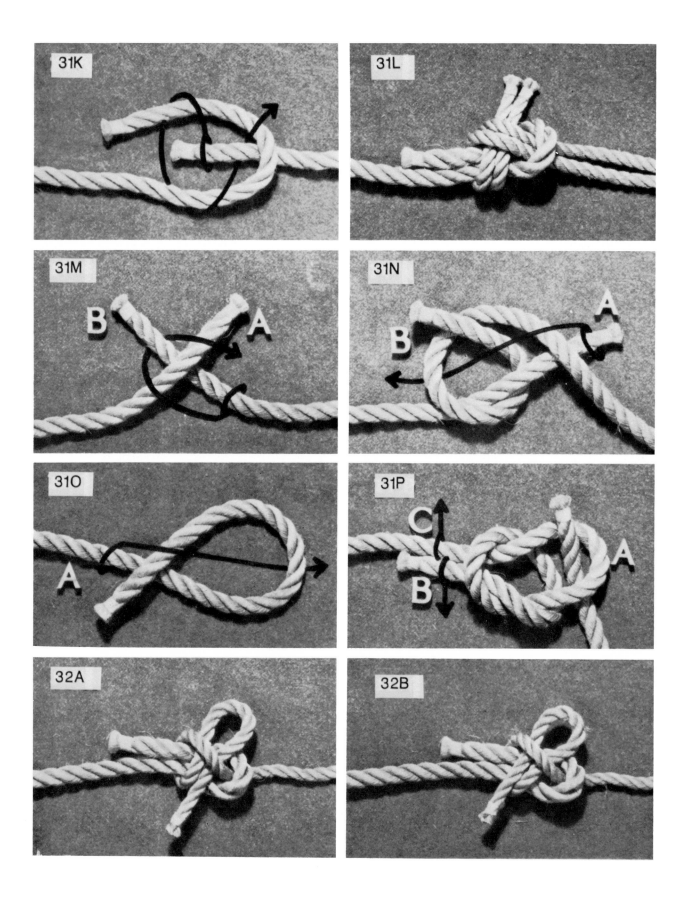

33. The Double Sheet Bend is more secure than the single sheet bend and should be used when one rope is considerably larger than the other. It has two forms.

First Method

Fig. 33A: This is the usual form. Note that the bight is made with the larger rope, the double hitch with the smaller.

Second Method

Fig. 33B: The advantage of this method is that the end has to be tucked only once.

Third Method

An anonymous author in *Textile World* (June 1946, pp. 101–5) says that the single weaver's knot slips in nylon yarns and recommends the double knot, like fig. 33B, but with ends on opposite sides. A technique of tying the double knot is illustrated. However, in the July issue (p. 186), C. S. Bicksler objects that the double knot is too bulky to pass smoothly through heddles and reeds. (Query: Would the single weaver's knot slip if the orthodox form, with ends on the same side, was used?)

34. The Tucked Sheet Bend. Since both ends lead the same way, this form of the sheet bend is supposed to be less likely than an ordinary sheet bend to catch in an opening.

35. The Becket Hitch or Becket Bend. This is the same knot as the sheet bend but is sometimes given a different name because one of the ropes has an eye or becket in the end.

36. The Halter Hitch. Horses are hitched with this knot the world over.

Fig. 36A: Sailors frequently use this knot to secure doused sails to their booms.

Fig. 36B: The end may also be loosely tucked through the loop created by the knot to keep the end out of the way. Note that the loop is not drawn tight. A pull on the end after taking it out of the loop releases the knot easily.

37. Lines with eye-splices in the ends can be joined in various ways.

Fig. 37A: Two interlocking eye-splices are extremely strong and cannot possibly jam. Barnes (1951) recommends this device for attaching a fishing line to a cast.

Fig. 37B: This device is similar to fig. 37A. It is released instantly when the toggle is withdrawn.

Fig. 37C: This type of toggle is described by Steel (1794) as follows: "Small toggles are little wooden pins, 3 to 9 inches long, and taper each way from the middle, round which is a notch, whereby they are seized to the topmast cross-trees, or elsewhere in the rigging."

Fig. 37D: A circular piece of wood with a hole in the center, such as an old sheave, serves a similar purpose. The end of one line is rove through the hole and knotted, preferably with a Matthew Walker knot (no. 212); the other end has an eye-splice in it.

38. The Thumb Knot, also called the *openhand knot* and the *creeler's knot,* consists of an overhand knot tied with the ends of two cords. It is an ungainly knot that tends to jam, but it is secure, and it is easy to tie in thread and twine, which are hard to manipulate because they are small. It is tied mechanically by grain binders and by machines that tie packages in stores.

39. The Ring Knot or Water Knot, also known as the *ordinary knot* and the *overhand tie,* is a time-honored way to join two leaders. Barnes (1951) thinks it is the same knot as the "water knotte or duchys knotte" mentioned by Dame Juliana Berners in 1496 (*A Treatyse of Fysshynge wyth an Angle*), and Ashley (1944) identifies it with the water knot mentioned in the seventeenth century by Izaak Walton. Although secure, it is weaker than the barrel knot (no. 45), which, says Barnes, has superseded it.

Fig. 39A: Tie a loose overhand knot in the end *A,* and follow back round this overhand with the end *D,* as shown by the arrow.

Fig. 39B: The completed knot is identical in structure to no. 38. The difference is that *D* is a standing part in fig. 38B, whereas it is an end in fig. 39B.

40. The Fisherman's Knot, also called the *Englishman's knot,* the *true-lover's knot,* the *waterman's knot,* and the *water knot,* is composed of two overhands, each tied round the opposite standing part. When drawn taut, the two overhands jam against each other, back to back, and prevent the knot from slipping. This knot is no longer used as a leader knot, since it is insecure in nylon. Books on mountain climbing have recommended it for more than half a century as a way to tie two climbing ropes together.

41. The Grapevine Knot resembles no. 40, but is made with double or triple overhands. With triple overhands, Barnes (1951) reports, it is secure in nylon monofil.

The point about knots and jamming is this: since rope is expensive, it is usually desirable to untie the knots that are tied in it, and use it again. On the other hand, it is uneconomical if not impossible to untie the knots in thread, artificial gut leaders, and other very small cords, so knots in these materials are simply cut off and discarded when they have served their purpose. Knots that jam are unsuitable in rope because they cannot be untied without injuring the fibers of the rope. Nearly all knots that are based on the overhand knot (e.g., nos. 38 to 41) tend to jam.

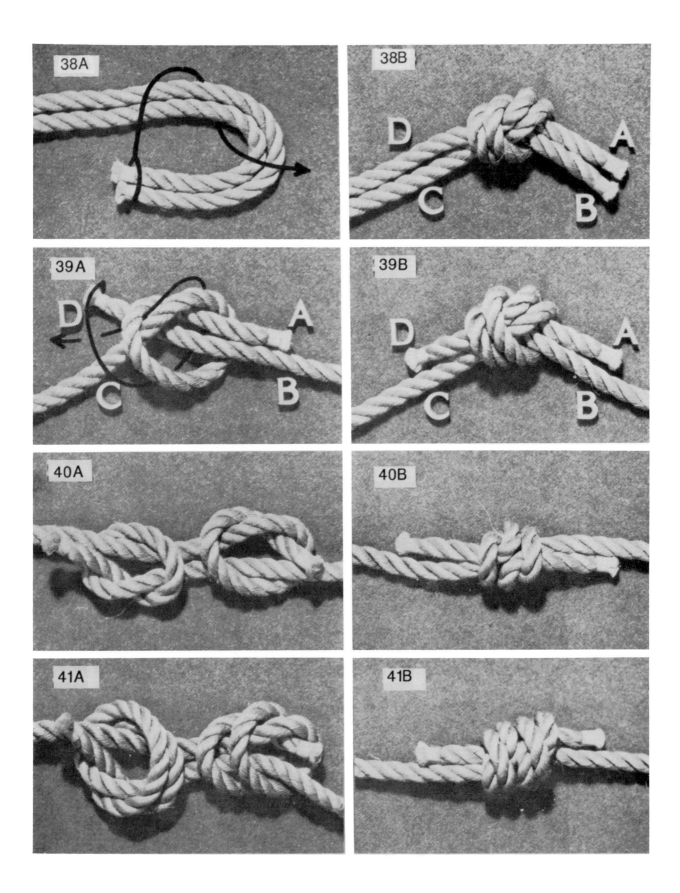

42. This knot, analogous to no. 40, is made with figure-eights instead of overhands. It has no name.

43. The Harness Knot is related to the thief knot and the what knot (figs. 29B and 30D), to the man-harness knot (nos. 82 and 83), and also, since it consists of two knots that jam against each other, to nos. 40, 41, and 42. It is tied with a half-hitch and a crossing knot (no. 131). It holds well when the ends are opposed, as in fig. 43B. Should the half-hitch be reversed, the ends would lie side by side and the knot would be insecure.

The harness knot, like the square knot, can be tied when there is a moderate pull on both cords.

44. The Double Harness Knot is made with two crossing knots (no. 131). It is safer to use than no. 43 because the ends may be either opposed (fig. 44B) or side by side (not illustrated). Both forms are equally secure. Another way to tie the double harness knot is to join the ends with a double half-knot (no. 17), and then to thrust the ends back through the center. When the knot is tied thus, the ends lie side by side.

45. The Barrel Knot, called the *blood knot* in England, is a development of the principles of nos. 43 and 44. It is an angler's knot, and its chief function is to join gut or nylon leaders. It has two forms, and it can be tied by two methods or techniques.

The two forms differ as follows. In one form (not illustrated), the turns in the two halves of the knot are continuous. This form is analogous to the what knot (fig. 30D). In the other form (figs. 45A and 138A), the turns are reversed. This form is analogous to the thief knot (fig. 29B). Both forms are equally strong and secure.

When the turns are continuous, the ends lie side by side (unless one half of the knot is made longer by half a turn than the other). When the turns are reversed, the ends are opposed (unless one half of the knot is made longer by half a turn than the other). Hence, the ends may be either opposed or side by side, and the two halves of the knot may be the same length, or one half may be longer by half a turn than the other.

The two methods or techniques of tying are illustrated in figs. 45A and 138A. In fig. 45A the turns are applied from the outside toward the center. In fig. 138A the turns are applied from the center toward the outside. Both techniques produce the same result provided the knot is tied in slippery enough material. Whatever technique is adopted, manual dexterity and much practice are the prerequisites for success in gut or nylon monofilament.

Fig. 45B shows two full turns in each half of the knot; fig. 138B shows two and a half turns. Three or three and a half turns are necessary (and sufficient) in nylon monofil.

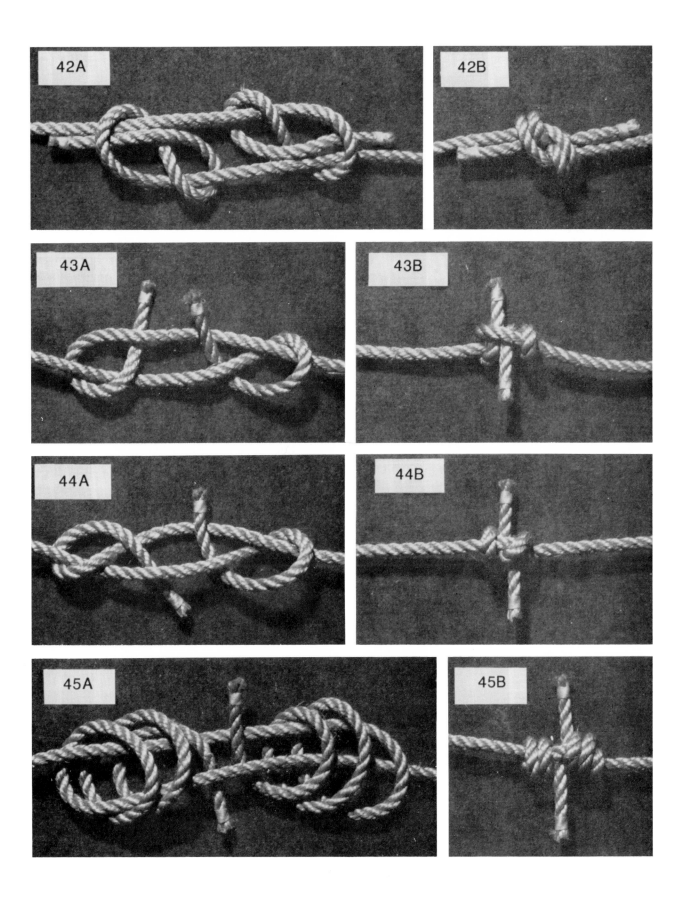

46. The Strap Knot or Grass Knot is identical in structure to the what knot (fig. 30D), but when tied in flat material like leather, it does not tend to slip, as the what knot does.

47. This strap knot requires a slit near the end of one of the straps. It is similar in structure to the sheet bend (no. 31).

48. The Rope-Yarn Knot can be tied either with single yarns or with small stuff of 2 to 4 yarns, like marline. In the former case, the single yarns are split for a short distance and crotched. In the latter case, the yarns are divided into two groups of 1 or 2 yarns each and crotched.

Fig. 48A: Pass the ends around as shown by the arrows.

Fig. 48B: Join the ends with a half-knot (no. 17).

Fig. 48C: For greater security, pass the ends as shown here, and join them with a half-knot.

When drawn taut, the rope-yarn knot is very small, especially after it has been rolled between finger and thumb. It is not a strong knot, but it is strong enough for its purpose—that is, joining the ends of the yarns when serving (no. 176).

49. The Heaving-Line Bend. We now pass from small to large cordage through the more or less appropriate medium of the heaving-line bend, intended for bending a small line, such as a heaving-line, to a large one, such as a hawser or cable. The several racking turns of this bend prevent jamming and make untying easy.

50. Ashley's Bend. This excellent bend is no. 1452 in *The Ashley Book of Knots* (1944). According to Ashley's tests, it ranks with the ring knot (no. 39) and the barrel knot (no. 45) in security, and it has the great advantage, not shared by those two knots, that it does not tend to jam. Indeed, it seems to jam less than any bend except the carrick bend (no. 51). It is therefore suitable both for small cords and for rope.

Fig. 50A: To tie Ashley's bend, form a loop with one end, and reeve the other end alternately under, over, under, and over, as shown by the arrow.

Fig. 50B: Stick both ends through the center.

Fig. 50C: The completed knot. This method of tying differs slightly from Ashley's method.

This bend is structurally similar to the lineman's loop knot (no. 81). Another good bend (structurally identical to the lineman's loop) can be tied as follows: hold the ends together, as if at the bottom of the loop in fig. 81A, and then follow the directions for figs. 81A and 81B.

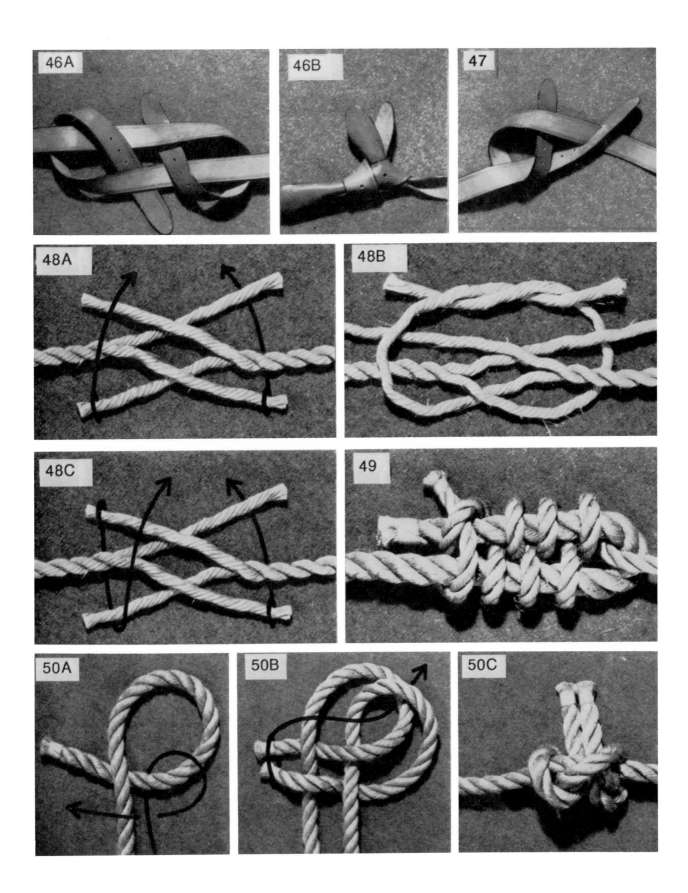

51. The Carrick Bend has less tendency to jam than any other bend, and it is therefore a good way to bend two hawsers together. It might well be used more often than it is for other purposes, also.

Fig. 51A: The basic form of the knot has a regular over-and-under weave, and the ends are oblique (i.e., diagonally opposite each other).

Figs. 51B and 51C: There are two ways to use the carrick bend. Let us consider fig. 51C first. When tension is exerted, the carrick bend upsets and falls into two loops, as illustrated in fig. 51C. In this position it has a fairly high breaking strength, and it neither slips nor jams—in fact, it satisfies all the requirements of a perfect bend. One warning: if the bend is allowed to adjust itself under tension, there is likely to be a good deal of initial slip, and the ends may even pull entirely out. Therefore, it should be upset and carefully adjusted by hand before being used. The initial slip occurs only while the process that I have called upsetting is being completed.

Fig. 51B: A second way to use the carrick bend is shown here. Very large hawsers are too heavy to be upset and adjusted by hand in the manner just described. Moreover, when the ends are seized to the standing parts, as illustrated in fig. 51B, the carrick bend is especially well adapted to hawsers without being upset. Hawsers thus bent together cannot jam, no matter how long they are in the water, and they can always be untied without injuring the fibers of the rope. This is the traditional way to use the carrick bend, but nowadays, apparently, more honored in the breach than in the observance. Lescallier pictures a seized carrick bend in 1791 and calls it a *noeud de vache*.

Fig. 51D: The ends in this form of the carrick are on the same side of the knot, instead of on diagonally opposite sides, as in fig. 51B. When upset (not illustrated), this form of the carrick looks very similar to fig. 51C. It is nearly as strong as the oblique form, but, according to Ashley's tests, it is much less secure.

52. This form of the carrick bend, pictured by Lever (1808), does not have the regular weave of no. 51. It does not have the two-fold function of no. 51, either, but holds only when the ends are seized to the standing parts. However, when the ends *are* seized, it is probably a good hawser bend. The same is true of nos. 53, 54, and 55.

53. This form of the carrick bend is called the *half-carrick* by Shaw (1933). The ends must be seized to the standing parts.

54. Shaw (1933) calls this the *single carrick bend*. The ends must be seized to the standing parts.

55. This is a sort of double single-carrick. The ends must be seized to the standing parts.

56. The Bowline Bend, made with two interlocking bowlines (no. 61), is one of the most common ways to join two hawsers, and also one of the strongest and most secure. It is advisable to stop the ends to the loops in order to keep them out of the way.

57. Twin Bowlines are somewhat troublesome to adjust, but in other respects they are as good as no. 56.

58. The Half-Hitch-and-Seizing Bend is recommended for hawsers by Lever (1808). Throat seizings (no. 157) are used at the two points marked *A,* and round seizings (no. 153) at the points marked *B.* Bends like nos. 58 to 60 can be untied without injuring the fibers of the rope. These bends are pictured in many old manuals of seamanship.

59. The Reeving-Line Bend is similar to no. 58 but more suitable for small hawsers, according to Luce (1863). Each end has two round seizings (no. 153).

60. This Hawser Bend is pictured and described by Lever (1808). Three throat seizings (no. 157) are used at the intermediate points marked *B,* and round seizings (no. 153) at the points marked *A.* Luce (1863) says that racking seizings (no. 156) should be used if unusual strain is expected.

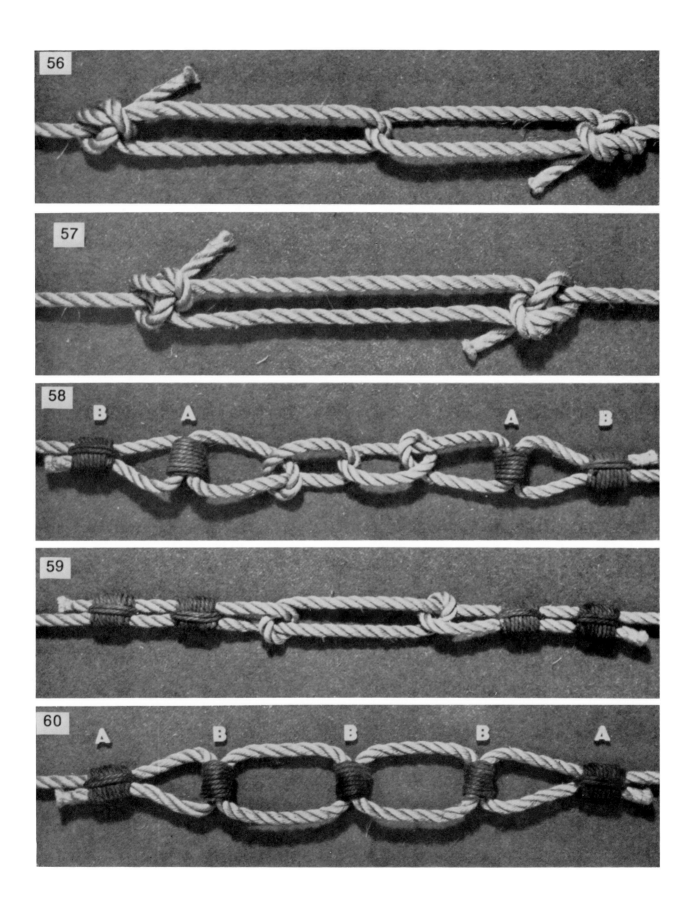

61. The Bowline Knot is the most useful way to form a fixed loop in the end of a rope. It is easy to tie, has a high breaking strength, and never slips or jams.

First Method

Fig. 61A: Hold the end *A* in the right hand and the standing part *C* in the left hand, and cross *A* over *C*. With the right hand, bring the end *A* round under *B* and up toward *C*. This would ordinarily result in a half-hitch round the standing part, but at the very moment when the half-hitch is being formed, it is transferred to the standing part (see no. 13), chiefly with the right hand, but with some help from the left hand. The end *A* should now come up straight through the hitch *D,* as shown in fig. 61B. The hitch *D* is called the *cuckold's neck*.

Fig. 61B: Pass the end *A* round behind the standing part *C* and down through the hitch *D*. This way of tying the bowline is identical to the standard way of tying the sheet bend, as explained in no. 31. The two knots are closely related in structure, though not in function; indeed, if the loop of a bowline is cut, the result is a sheet bend.

Fig. 61C: The knot is now complete and needs only to be properly drawn up and adjusted before being put into service.

Figs. 61D and 61E: The bowline is shown here from the front and back respectively. Under tension, the end sticks out a bit toward the back, as illustrated.

Fig. 61F: When the rope is new and springy, and the line slack a large part of the time, the end may have a tendency to work out. To prevent this, stop the end to the loop.

Fig. 61G: If the end, in fig. 61B, is passed round the standing part in the opposite direction, the resulting knot looks like fig. 61G. This form of the bowline is sometimes called a *left-handed bowline* and appears to be perfectly safe and secure.

Fig. 61H: This is the way a left-handed person would tie a bowline. Except for the lay of the rope, it is the way fig. 61D would look in a mirror. It is as good in every way as fig. 61D.

Fig. 61I: This is the way a left-handed person would tie a *left-handed bowline*. The terminology may be confusing, but I trust that the knots themselves are not. Except for the lay of the rope, fig. 61I looks the way fig. 61G would look in a mirror. This variation, too, is secure and safe.

An amusing and witty poem entitled "The Bowline," by A. P. Herbert, is printed in David McCord's anthology *What Cheer?* (1946, pp. 35–37). The *New English Dictionary* cites John Smith's *Seaman's Grammar* (1627) as follows: "The Boling knot . . . is fastened by the bridles into the creengles of the sailes."

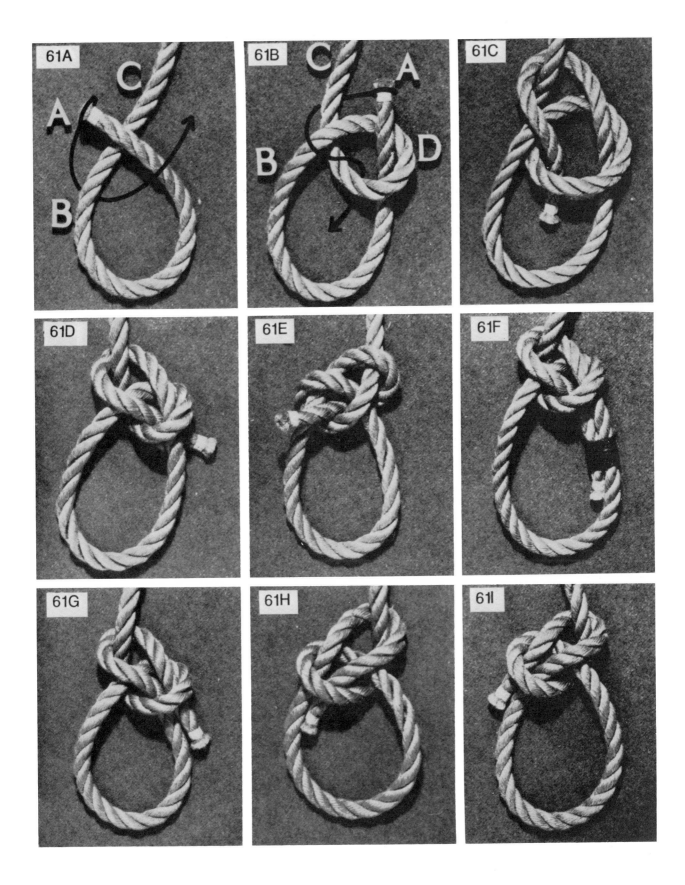

61A   61B   61C

61D   61E   61F

61G   61H   61I

Second Method

When the standing part is behind you, and the end has been passed round an object that is in front of you, another way of tying the bowline is in order.

Fig. 61J: Under these circumstances, make a hitch *C* with the end round the standing part, and then transfer this hitch to the standing part by pulling *A* and *B* apart.

Fig. 61K: Pass the end round behind the standing part and down through the cuckold's neck. The knot is now complete and looks like fig. 61D on the preceding page.

Fig. 61L: If the end happens to be passed in the other direction round the object in front of you, the knot is tied as illustrated in fig. 61L and looks, when complete, like fig. 61H on the preceding page.

A variation of this method is desirable if the rope is very large and heavy. Under these circumstances, omit the step shown in fig. 61J, and form the hitch in the standing part directly, as shown in fig. 61K. Then pass the end through this hitch, round behind the standing part, and down through the hitch.

Third Method

Fig. 61M: Pass the end *A* round the object to be secured, and pull a bight *B* up through *C* in the standing part. In other words, tie an overhand noose (no. 88) in the standing part.

Fig. 61N: Stick the end *A* through the noose *B*.

Fig. 61O: Pull *E* and *D* apart until *B* has been withdrawn through the center of the knot. The result is like 61D on the preceding page.

Fourth Method

A bowline can be tied to a ring without reeving the end of the line through the ring.

Fig. 61P: Push a bight through the ring, and hitch the standing part round this bight, as shown by the arrow.

Fig. 61Q: Reeve the end of the line through the bight.

Fig. 61R: The completed bowline.

This form of the knot, sometimes called the *ring bowline* or *snap bowline* (E. W. Williams, *Fire Fighting,* 1935), can be used to secure a police line to a series of rings in order to hold back a crowd. If toggles are available, the line need not be rove through the bights of the knots, and the knots can be quickly released from the rings.

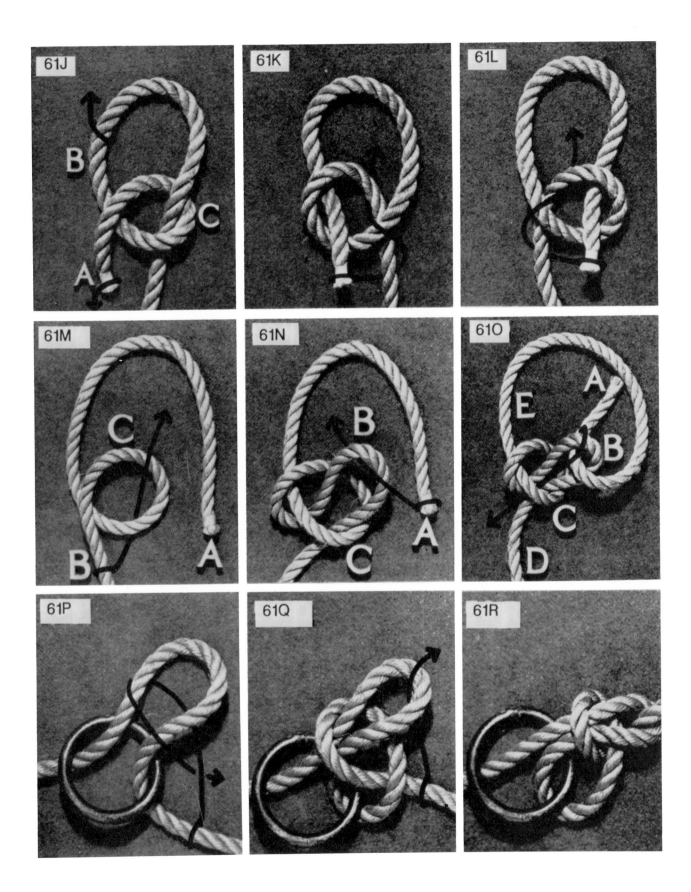

Fifth Method

Mountain climbers use the bowline as an end loop to secure the two people who are at the ends of the climbing rope. They tie the knot in a way that is nicely adapted to the purpose.

Fig. 61S: Tie a half-knot round the chest under the armpits. Then, holding the standing part in one hand and the end in the other, pull the end forward, away from the body, in such a way as to form a hitch in the standing part.

Fig. 61T: Transfer the end to the other hand and pass it round behind the standing part and down through the hitch or cuckold's neck. Adjust the loop snugly round the chest. This method of tying the bowline was developed by R. L. M. Underhill (*Appalachia,* 1928).

Sixth Method

Figs. 61U and 61V: Another use of the bowline is to secure the end of a vertical line to the bight or middle of a horizontal line of the same or greater diameter. This is a good way to tie the painter of a dinghy to a rope outhaul or traveler when the outhaul does not have any eyes spliced in it. Strictly speaking, the term *bowline* is inaccurate, since there is no loop; but it is called a *bowline* in Maine, where I learned it. When the horizontal or taut line is under considerable tension, it is difficult or impossible to turn the cuckold's neck and tie the knot.

Seventh Method

Two reverse half-hitches can be quickly changed into a bowline as follows:

Fig. 61W: Pull *A* and *B* apart, and transfer the hitch *C* to the standing part.

Fig. 61X: Push the end down through the hitch *C*. This way of tying the bowline is a mere trick, of small practical value.

62. The Bowline on the Bight is tied in the bight or middle of a line when both ends are inaccessible and when the strain is expected to come on both standing parts. It makes a good sling or boatswain's chair, because a doubled loop is more comfortable to sit in than a single loop. It holds well enough when the strain comes on only one of the standing parts, but generally when this condition obtains, the Portuguese bowline (no. 63) is to be preferred.

First Method

Fig. 62A: Pass the bight *A* up through the hitch *B*. Enlarge *A* and fold it down over *B* and *C*.

Fig. 62B: Bring *A* up behind the knot, and adjust the loop *C* to the desired size.

Fig. 62C: The completed knot.

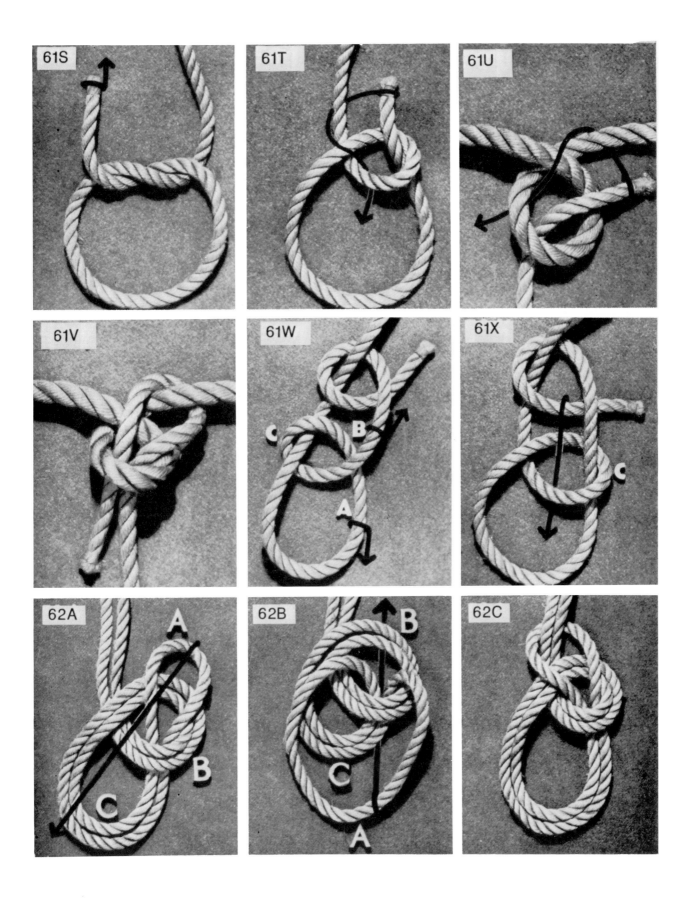

Second Method

Fig. 62D: Start with an overhand knot tied with the bight *A*.

Fig. 62E: Spread this bight out and bring it up behind the overhand knot. Then pull down *B*.

Third Method

Fig. 62F: Tie an overhand knot with the bight *A*, as before, but bring *A* up in front of the overhand instead of behind it. Pull *B* down (fig. 62F) while holding *A* firmly in place.

Fig. 62G: If a bowline on the bight is tied near one of the ends, it is well to secure the end to the standing part with a bowline knot. This combination is sometimes called a *bowline on the bight with a bowline on it.*

63. The Portuguese or French Bowline also has a double loop, but it is tied in the end of a line. The traditional name is *Portuguese bowline,* but the late Felix Riesenberg, who learned it from a French shipmate during the voyage described in *Under Sail,* gave some currency to the name *French bowline.* In his *Standard Seamanship* (1922), he explains how a person can sit in one loop and adjust the other loop round his chest under the armpits, so that he can use both hands while working, or even lose consciousness without falling out.

First Method

Fig. 63A: Start with two loops instead of with one, and bring the end round the standing part and up through the loops (see the arrow in fig. 63A), just as in tying an ordinary bowline.

Fig. 63B: Pass the end round behind the standing part and down through the cuckold's neck.

Fig. 63C: The completed knot.

Fig. 63D: A fairly large coil consisting of several loops can be handled by this method. However, with right-laid rope, it is advisable to coil the loops clockwise, or with the sun, in the manner natural for right-laid rope, and to tie the bowline the way a left-handed person would tie it, as shown in fig. 61H. The completed knot, with five loops, is shown in fig. 63D.

Second Method

Fig. 63E: Riesenberg's method of tying the knot is shown here. Start as if tying an ordinary bowline, but before passing the end round behind the standing part, make another loop and bring it up through the cuckold's neck, as shown by the arrow. Then pass the end round behind the standing part and down through the cuckold's neck. The result, after the parts have been adjusted, is identical to fig. 63C, though at first it may look a little different.

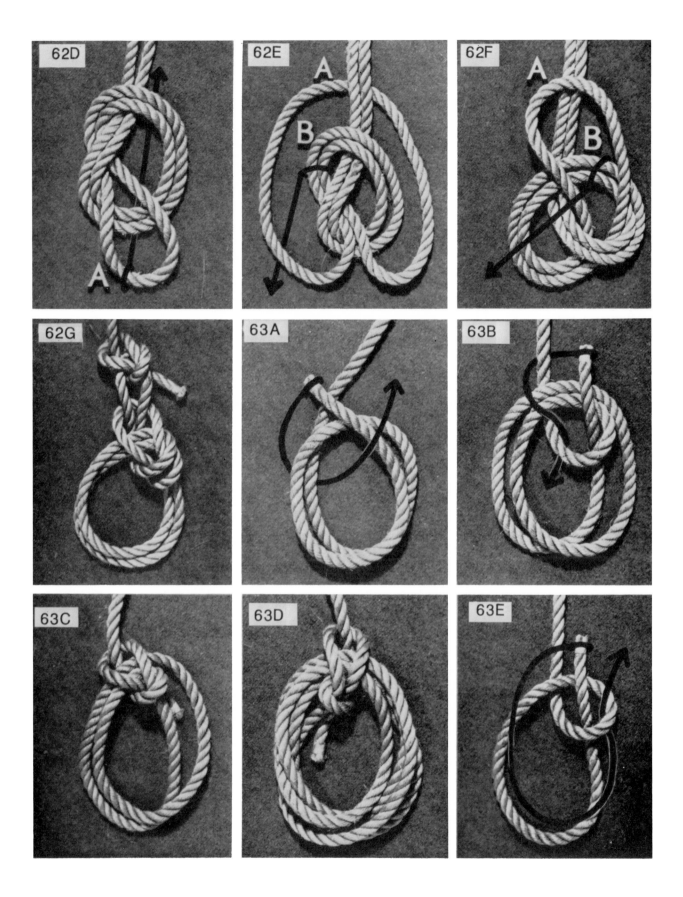

64. The Portuguese Bowline on the Bight is a combination of nos. 62 and 63. It can easily be tied by anyone who has mastered those two knots.

65. The Double Bowline or Round-Turn Bowline is probably stronger and more secure than the ordinary bowline. The cuckold's neck is the part that is doubled.

Underhill's method of tying this knot is as follows: join the end and standing part with a double half-knot, and then proceed as explained for figs. 61S and 61T.

66. The Water Bowline has two cuckold's necks, which are supposed to make untying the knot in a wet rope easier. Probably, however, the real virtue of this form of the bowline is that the size of the loop can be changed (after the knot is tied) by adjusting the lower cuckold's neck or hitch.

67. The Bowline with a Bight is a way of doubling or tripling the loop.

First Method

Fig. 67A: Tie a bowline with the doubled end.

Fig. 67B: Pull the bight of the doubled end down until it is the same size as the loop.

Fig. 67C: This form of the knot has a double loop.

Second Method

Fig. 67D: Double back the end farther than before, and tie a bowline with the doubled end.

Fig. 67E: Pull the bight of the doubled end down until it is the same size as the loop.

Fig. 67F: Join the end and the standing part with a bowline knot. This form of the bowline has a triple loop.

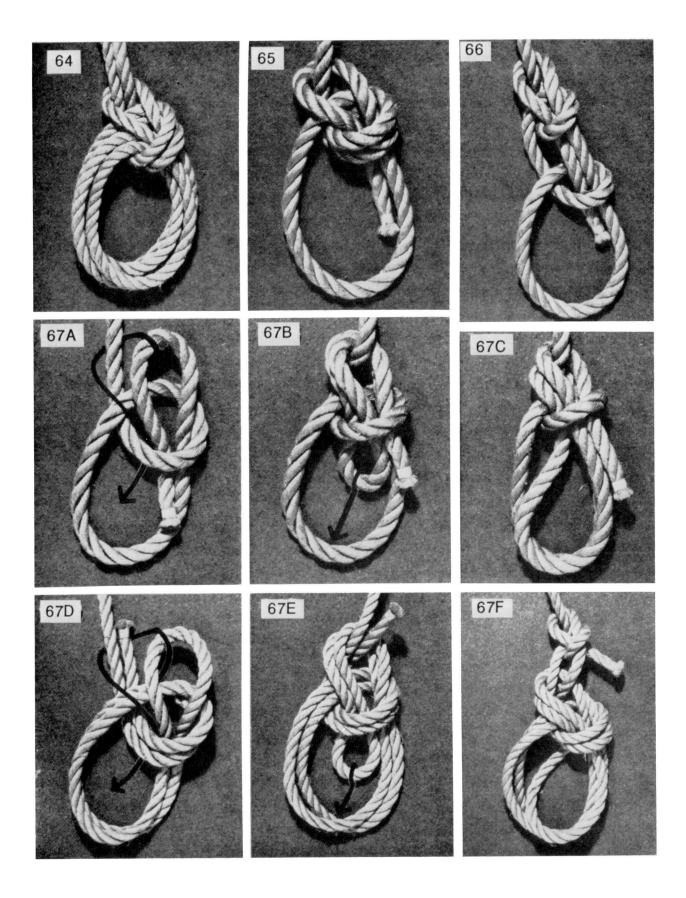

68. The Spanish Bowline has two adjustable loops, which can be fitted over two objects, such as a person's legs when the knot is used as a boatswain's chair, or the two legs of a ladder, when a ladder is slung horizontally as a scaffold. When the Spanish bowline is used as a boatswain's chair, a half-hitch can be tied in the standing part round the chest under the armpits. It is possible to sling an unconscious person in this way.

First Method

Fig. 68A: Form three loops *A, B,* and *C,* and fold *B* up as shown by the arrow.

Fig. 68B: Enlarge *B* until it covers both *A* and *C.*

Fig. 68C: Pull bights from *B* up through *A* and *C.*

Fig. 68D: This illustration shows one side of the finished knot.

Second Method

Fig. 68E: Form two loops *A* and *B,* and fold them up as shown by the arrows.

Fig. 68F: Pull *C* and *D* down through *B* and *A* respectively.

Fig. 68G: This illustration shows the other side of the finished knot.

Frank and John Craighead used the Spanish bowline some years ago when climbing down perpendicular cliffs in order to photograph birds of prey in their nests. (See their book *Hawks in Hand,* 1939, p. 286 and plates 4, 23, and 49.) They used two ropes, a large one (⅞ to 1 inch in diameter) and a small one (½ inch in diameter). They climbed down the large one and sat in a Spanish bowline at the end of the small one. They stepped into the loops of the bowline in the usual fashion, but they tied the end of the knot round the waist instead of hitching the standing part round the chest. The large rope was tied to a tree at the top of the cliff. The small one was paid out by reliable helpers as required.

See also "Plainsman's" methods of tying the Spanish bowline in the *Christian Science Monitor,* 11 November 1945.

69. Two loops in the bight can also be made by bringing the two hitches of a sheepshank (no. 147) together in the middle of the knot, and using the end loops in the same way that the loops of the Spanish bowline are used. The knotted sheepshank (fig. 147H) is a good form of the sheepshank to use for this purpose, since the material of one loop cannot pass over into the other loop, as is the case with the Spanish bowline.

Fig. 69A: Follow the directions indicated by the arrows to tie two loops in the bight.

Fig. 69B: The completed knot.

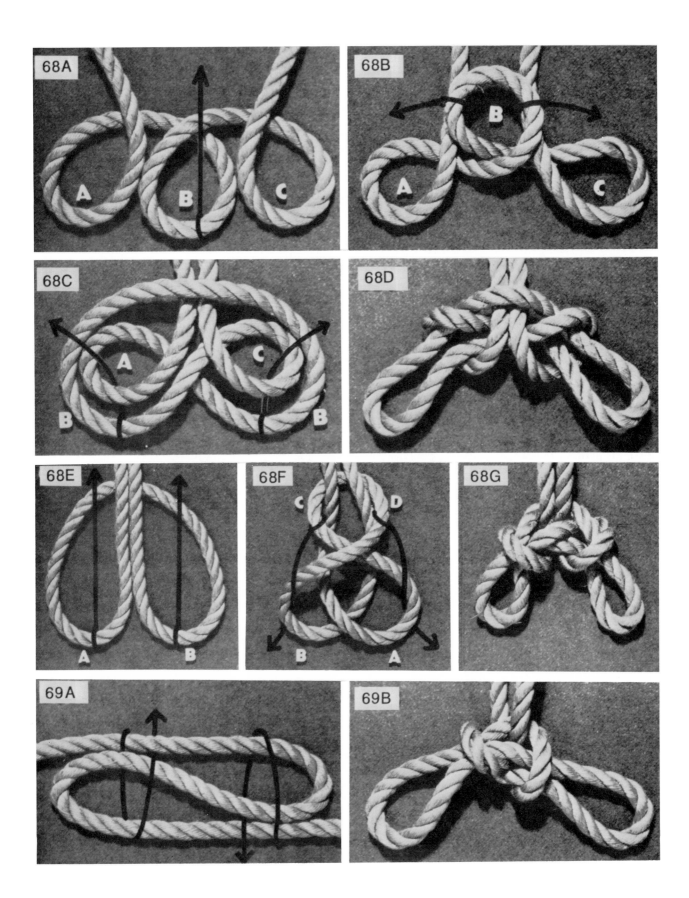

70. The Overhand Loop Knot. Other than the bowline, few loop knots are suitable for rope. However, several are well adapted to thread, twine, artificial silk gut, and other small cords. The overhand loop knot is an example. It is easy and natural to tie, for it consists merely of an overhand knot tied with the doubled end. It is strong and perfectly secure. It jams under tension, however, and therefore is unsuitable for rope. The speed with which it can be tied in thread, when fingers are usually all thumbs, partly accounts for its popularity.

71. The Figure-Eight Loop Knot or Flemish Loop Knot is similar to no. 70 but bulkier and perhaps a trifle stronger. It is made by tying a figure-eight knot with the doubled end.

72. The Honda Knot is used to make lassos (no. 86).

Fig. 72A: To tie the honda knot, stick the *knotted end* through an overhand knot in the standing part. Stick it through exactly as illustrated, or an inferior construction will result.

Fig. 72B: The honda is the most nearly circular of fixed loops.

Fig. 72C: A honda knot from Mason's *How to Spin a Rope* (1928). It is made by sticking the end of a four-strand lariat rope between the strands, and tying a stopper knot (no. 206) in the end.

73. The Department-Store Loop Knot consists of a slipped overhand knot (no. 18) with an overhand knot in the end. It is not a strong loop, but it is quickly tied and is convenient in doing up parcels. An analogous knot can be made from a slipped figure-eight knot (no. 21).

74. Several other fixed loops or loop knots, all of them better adapted to small material than to rope, can be made from the slipped overhand knot (no. 18). Three such loop knots are shown as nos. 76, 77, and 80.

Fig. 74A: Three others are indicated by the arrows in this illustration. Of these, the one indicated by the upper arrow, in which the end is hitched round the standing part, is undoubtedly the best.

Fig. 74B: The knot drawn taut. The hitch may be passed round the standing part in either direction.

75. The knot shown in fig. 74B is pictured here with the end slipped for quick release.

76. This variation of fig. 74B is recommended by Hunter (1927) as a leader loop knot. It differs from fig. 74B in that a round turn is taken on the standing part before the end is hitched.

77. The Perfection Knot was first published in Genio C. Scott's *Fishing in American Waters* (ca. 1870). I do not know who gave it its name. It has long been a favorite loop knot among anglers, both in America and in England, and it has survived the advent of nylon monofil, a leader material that, because it is very slippery, has rendered many once-popular angler's knots obsolete.

The perfection knot is secure in both gut and nylon, and it is easy to tie and to remember. But it is 20 percent weaker than no. 137, according to Barnes's tests, and, moreover, the end sticks out at an angle. No. 137 is probably a better leader knot.

First Method

Fig. 77A: This method reveals the similarity in structure to the loop knot shown in fig. 74B.

Fig. 77B: The completed knot.

Second Method

Fig. 77C: Start as if tying a figure-eight knot, but instead of sticking the end back through the lower loop, pass it round the crossing, as shown by the arrow.

Fig. 77D: Push the upper loop down through the lower loop.

78. Several fixed loops can be made from the slipped figure-eight knot (no. 21). Three of them are indicated by the arrows in fig. 78. The one indicated by the upper arrow is analogous to fig. 74B. These knots jam and are unsuitable for rope.

79. This knot can either be made from a slipped figure-eight knot (as in fig. 79A) or tied in the bight. Wright and Magowan (1928) call it the *rover noose* and recommend it as a *middleman's knot* for the climbing rope of the mountaineer. No. 81, however, is probably a better knot for the purpose. Writers on mountain climbing often use the word *noose* to denote a fixed loop, despite Oscar Eckenstein's sly protest (the *Climbers' Club Journal,* 1909): "Any technical reader who understands knots will fully appreciate the humour of calling [the fisherman's loop knot] the 'middleman noose.'"

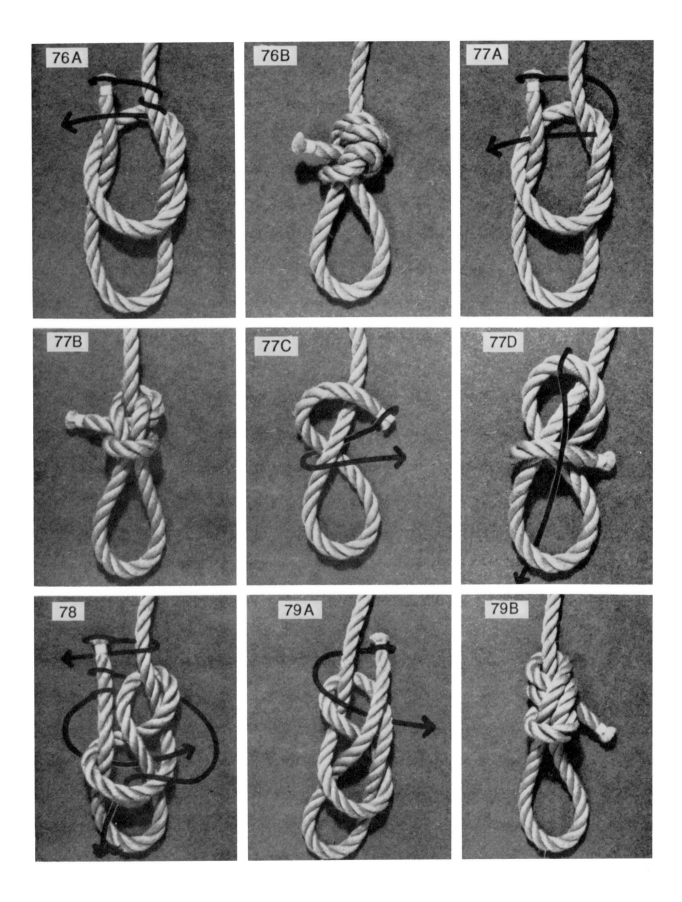

76A 76B 77A

77B 77C 77D

78 79A 79B

80. The Fisherman's Loop Knot, Englishman's Loop Knot, Dalliance Knot, or True-Lover's Knot.
First Method

Figs. 80A and 80D: This knot is similar to no. 74 (fig. 74B), except that the end, instead of being hitched, is knotted round the standing part.

Figs. 80B and 80E: When the knot is pulled taut, the two overhand knots fit snugly together (hence one of the names of the knot). The construction is the same as no. 40.

The second overhand knot can be tied in the opposite direction from the first (figs. 80A and 80B), or in the same direction (figs. 80D and 80E), with slightly different results.

Second Method

Fig. 80C: Form two loops, and pull *A* down through the center. This method produces fig. 80B, and permits the knot to be tied in the bight.

Third Method

Fig. 80F: This illustration shows how to tie fig. 80E in the bight, when the ends are inaccessible.

Fourth Method

Fig. 80G: Form three hitches, and place the left-hand hitch over the right-hand hitch.

Fig. 80H: Bring the left-hand hitch under the middle hitch, and then up. This method produces fig. 80E. If either the first or the last hitch in fig. 80G is made in the opposite direction from that shown, the result is fig. 80B.

The fisherman's loop knot has a low breaking strength and tends to jam if the tension is severe. It is inappropriate in rope, though it is often recommended in mountaineering books as an end loop for the climbing rope, and even, sometimes, as a middle loop.

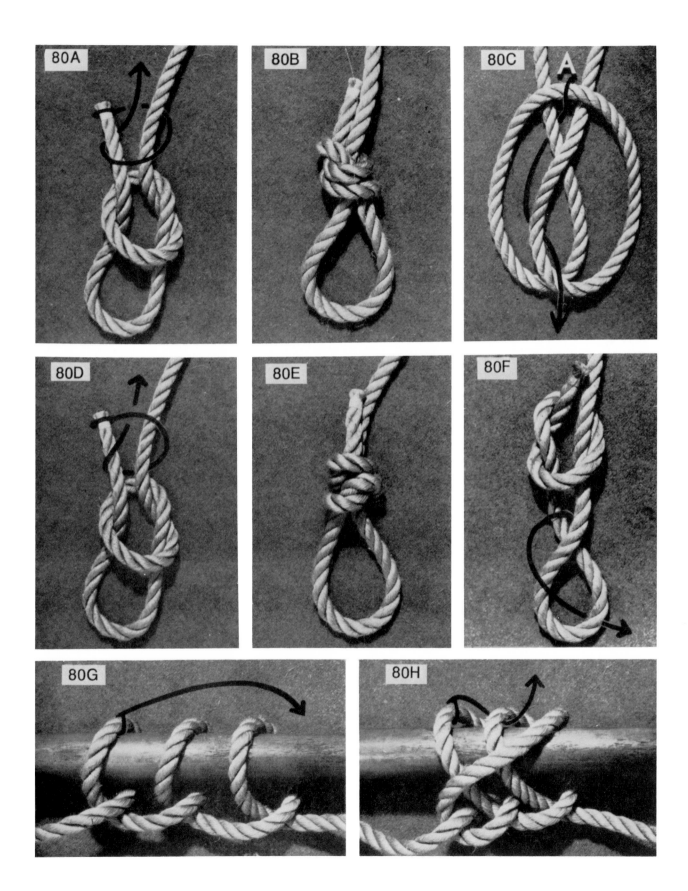

80A

80B

80C A

80D

80E

80F

80G

80H

81. The Lineman's Rider or Lineman's Loop Knot is the best of several loop knots that are tied in the bight and that are suitable for hauling in a direction parallel to the axis of the rope.

First Method

Fig. 81A: Twist a loop in the bight one full twist. Fold this loop up.

Fig. 81B: Pull *A* down through the center.

Fig. 81C: The completed knot.

Second Method

Fig. 81D: Form a loop in the bight.

Fig. 81E: Form another loop at point *A* in the first loop.

Fig. 81F: Pass *A* over the top and down through *B* on the other side.

Burger (1914–15), who first published this excellent knot, writes as follows: "Linemen and especially telephone men often use a knot which they term the lineman's rider. It is absolutely secure and will hold from any point upon which it may be drawn." Drew (1931) likens it to the bowline "in that it will not jam." "It is often used," he says, "when a crew of men are to pull on a rope and it is convenient for each man to have a loop rather than pull on the straight rope." Wright and Magowan (1928) call it the *butterfly noose* and recommend it as a middle loop for mountain climbers, a purpose to which it is perfectly adapted.

82. The Artillery Loop Knot or Man-Harness Knot is useful under the same conditions as no. 81. However, it is an inferior knot—in fact, a dangerous knot—because if yanked out of shape it is likely to turn into a running knot or noose. It is tied as follows.

Fig. 82A: Make a loop *AB*. Bring *B* down over the standing part, as shown by the arrow.

Fig. 82B: Pull *A* down behind the standing part and through *B*, as shown by the arrow.

Fig. 82C: The completed knot.

Note that fig. 82B is the same as the marlinespike hitch (no. 132).

Moreover, the completed knot is identical in construction to the inferior variety of the harness knot (no. 43), in which the end is hitched round the standing part in a direction opposite to that shown in fig. 43A.

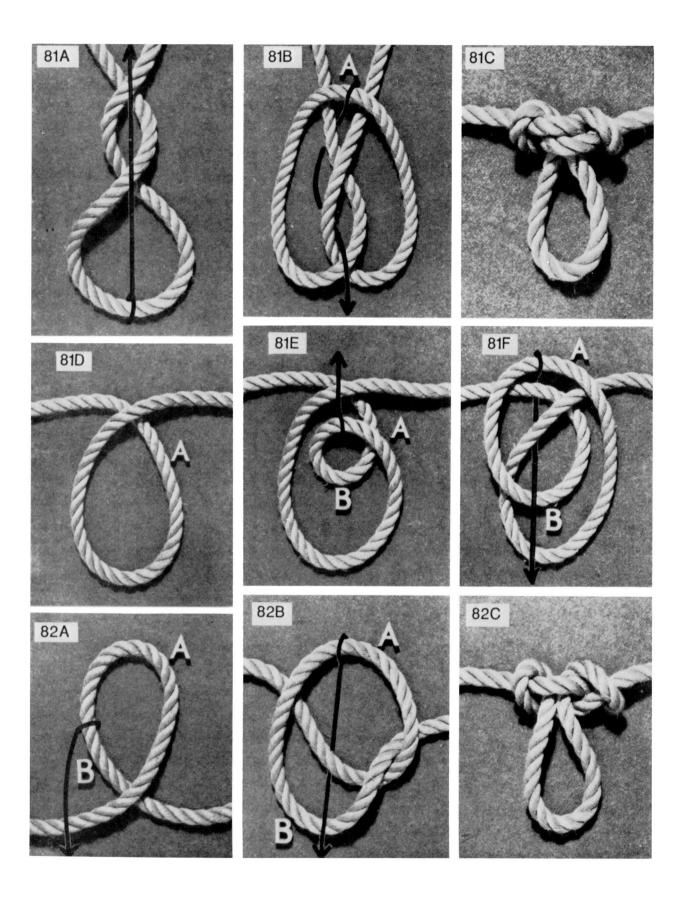

81A

81B

81C

81D

81E

81F

82A

82B

82C

83. The Double Artillery Loop Knot or Double Man-Harness Knot is a safer knot than no. 82, but it cannot be tied in the bight. It was first described by Öhrvall (1916).

Fig. 83A: Tie a double overhand knot at the desired point, and bring a bight down through the center.

Fig. 83B: The completed knot is identical in structure to the double harness knot (no. 44).

A similar knot can be tied by bringing the bight down through the center of a single overhand knot. The result, identical in structure to the what knot (no. 30), is a loop that is secure if the parts are properly crossed, but insecure if they are not.

When made with a six-fold overhand instead of with a double overhand, the double artillery loop knot is used by anglers as a dropper knot. (A dropper is a supplementary fly attached to a leader above the end-fly or tail-fly.) Barnes (1951) considers it one of the best of the several dropper knots he has tested. However, all dropper knots thus far devised, including this one, have a low breaking strength—as low, sometimes, as 30 percent.

The six-fold knot has three turns in each half of the knot. It is equivalent in structure to a six-fold barrel knot made with continuous rather than with reversed turns (see nos. 45 and 138). It is a difficult knot to tie in gut or nylon monofil, for the loop, after it has been pushed through the center, is apt to be lost when the knot is being pulled tight. To prevent this, Barnes suggests putting a pencil through the loop.

84. The Farmer's Loop Knot is a secure knot in the bight, the chief defect of which is that it requires a bit of adjusting when it is being drawn taut.
First Method
Figs. 84A to 84D: A method of tying this knot that was first illustrated by Riley (1912).

Fig. 84E: The completed knot.
Second Method
Fig. 84F: This method begins with a slipped figure-eight knot (no. 21). Arrange the parts as shown, and pull the upper loop down through the lower loop, as indicated by the arrow.

85. The Running Bowline consists of a bowline (no. 61) tied round the standing part. It is the most useful temporary running knot or noose. An early reference to it is found in *The Four Years Voyages of Capt. George Roberts* (1726): "And making a running bowling Knot on the End of another Rope, I cast it over" (quoted by the *New English Dictionary)*.

86. The Lasso is a noose made by reeving one end of the lariat through a small eye in the other end.

Fig. 86A: A lasso made with a honda (no. 72).

Fig. 86B: A lasso made with an eye-splice (no. 180). Oblong thimbles of aluminum or brass are often used when lassos are made with eye-splices.

87. The Clinch is made with two or three round seizings (no. 153). It was formerly used to secure the bowline bridles to the cringles in the leech of the sail, and to bend the cable to the bower anchor.

Fig. 87A: An outside clinch.

Fig. 87B: An inside clinch, which is a little more secure than an outside clinch because the end is nipped when the knot is drawn up. A clinch cannot jam; cutting the seizings will release it at once, without injuring the rope. The clinch as a method of bending the cable to the anchor is mentioned by John Smith in his *Seaman's Grammar* (1627).

88. The Overhand Noose, Running Knot, or Slip Knot is the most familiar and elementary of the nooses.

Fig. 88A: Pull a bight from the standing part through a loop in the end.

Fig. 88B: For added security, knot the end, or take a hitch round the standing part.

This knot has the same form as no. 18, but the standing part and the end have exchanged roles.

89. The Slipped Running Knot or Noose.

Fig. 89A: Double back the end, and pull a bight from the standing part through the loop made by the doubled end.

Fig. 89B: A pull on the end releases the knot.

90. The Crabber's Knot or Crossed Running Knot.

Fig. 90A: This knot has a dual function. It is a noose in the form shown here, but if *A* and *B* are pulled sharply apart, it becomes a fixed loop. In other words, the noose can be *locked* at any desired point.

Fig. 90B: As a fixed loop it looks like a bowline lying on its side—not, one would suppose, an especially effective construction.

The name of the knot has an interesting history, which was called to my attention by L. G. Miller. In 1891 and 1892, a series of articles titled "Knotting, Splicing, and Working Cordage," by Lancelot L. Haslope (pseudonym?), was published in the British magazine *Work*. No. 90 was first pictured in these articles, and Haslope, who said that he had learned it from an ardent crabber, called it the *crabber's knot*. Later Haslope's articles were incorporated in Paul N. Hasluck's book *Knotting and Splicing* (1905), and subsequent writers have copied the knot and the name. The knot has no special connection with crabbing.

91. The Capstan Knot is similar to no. 90 in function.

Figs. 91A and 91B: One way to tie the capstan knot.

Fig. 91C: Like no. 90, the capstan knot is a noose until *A* and *B* are pulled apart.

Fig. 91D: It then becomes a fixed loop.

"Tom Bowling" shows the capstan knot in 1866 but does not explain its use. Öhrvall (1916), who shows how to tie it, calls it the *Gångspelsknut,* which means *capstan knot* in Swedish.

92. The Figure-Eight Noose or Running Knot (1) is the converse of the slipped figure-eight knot (no. 21).

93. The Figure-Eight Noose or Running Knot (2) slides less easily than no. 92 and is probably more secure.

94. The Figure-Eight Noose or Running Knot (3).

First Method

Figs. 94A and 94B: Pass the end round the standing part and tie a figure-eight knot. It does not matter whether the figure-eight is tied in the way shown in fig. 94A or in the way shown in fig. 94B.

Second Method

Fig. 94C: Start with a slipped overhand knot (no. 18), and pull a bight down through the loop, as shown by the arrow. By this method, which produces fig. 94B, the knot can be tied in the bight.

95. The Double Running Knot or Double Lark's Head is useful when tension comes on both standing parts.

Fig. 95A: Start with a lark's head (no. 108) arranged in the form of a loop, and pull both ends all the way through the loop.

Fig. 95B: The finished knot is a strong, secure noose. It consists of a lark's head tied on the two standing parts.

96. The Double Overhand Noose.

Fig. 96A: Tie a double or multiple overhand knot (no. 19) round the standing part.

Fig. 96B: When drawn taut, this knot slides with difficulty, a useful characteristic under certain circumstances.

97. The Hangman's Noose, Knot, or Halter.

Fig. 97A: Eight or nine turns (not thirteen), passed as shown by the arrow, are customary.

Fig. 97B: This specimen has eight turns. The turns are supposed to strike the victim on the side of the head and break his neck.

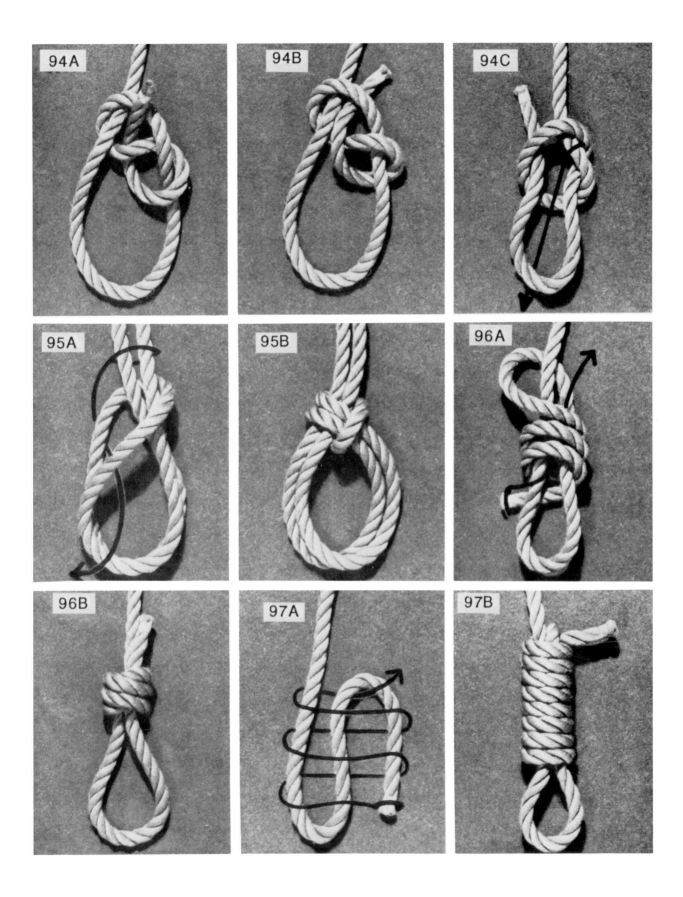

98. Two Half-Hitches are a quick and widely used way to hitch a line temporarily to a ring, spar, post, or other object.

Figs. 98A and 98B: The two hitches should always be alike—that is, both should be right-handed or both left-handed.

Fig. 98C: Two half-hitches can be tied either directly, or by first tying a granny knot (no. 28) round an object, and then pulling on the standing part, as shown by the arrow.

Figs. 98D and 98E: Here the hitches are unalike—that is, one is right-handed and one left-handed. Reverse half-hitches tend to slip and therefore should be avoided.

Fig. 98F: Reverse half-hitches can be tied by first tying a square knot (no. 24) round an object, and then pulling on the end, as shown by the arrow. This is one situation where the granny knot is preferable to the square knot.

Note that fig. 98B is equivalent to a clove hitch (no. 112) tied round the standing part, and that fig. 98E is equivalent to a lark's head (no. 108) tied round the standing part.

99. The Half-Hitch and Seizing is more permanent than no. 98.

100. The Round Turn and Half-Hitch is more secure than no. 99. Various combinations are possible, such as a round turn with two half-hitches and two seizings.

101. The Backhand Hitch requires only one turn round the spar or other object, yet it has two parts bearing on it. It is convenient when the object that is to be secured is more or less inaccessible, as, for example, the axle of an automobile.

102. Two Round Turns and Two Half-Hitches are called a *rolling hitch* by Lever (1808), but it is less confusing to reserve the name *rolling hitch* for no. 113.

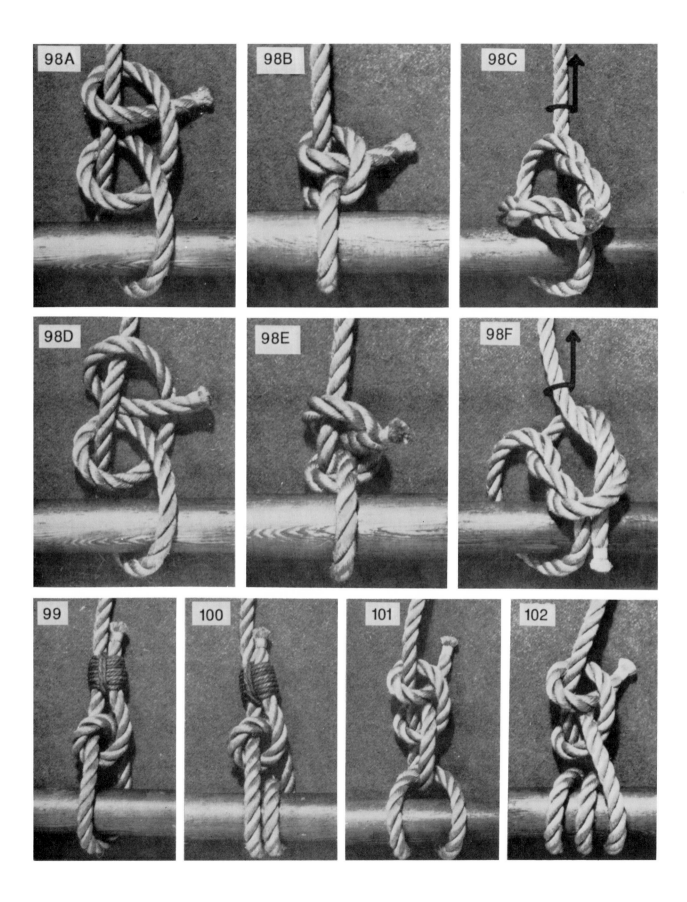

103. The Buntline Hitch or Studdingsail Tack Bend was formerly used to secure the buntlines to the foot of the sail. Since the second half-hitch is nipped or jammed inside the first when the knot is drawn taut, it is a very safe knot and could often be used to advantage instead of two half-hitches (no. 98). Four-in-hand neckties are usually tied with the buntline hitch.

L. G. Miller, in a letter dated 18 December 1947, makes this remark about the buntline hitch: "An interesting thing . . . which is not usually if at all mentioned, is that if you put the end through as a bight, the knot will dissolve perfectly clear without any half-hitches to catch when released by pulling the end."

104. The Lobster-Buoy Hitch, illustrated by Shaw (1924) and named by Ashley (1944), is similar to no. 103. It is very secure and, like no. 103, would be useful, if it were better known, on a variety of occasions.

105. The Fisherman's Bend or Anchor Bend is a beautiful example of simplicity, security, and strength.

Fig. 105A: Take a round turn on a spar or ring (it is equally secure on both), and then pass the end back of the standing part and under both turns.

Fig. 105B: Bring the end and standing part up together, as shown by the arrows.

Fig. 105C: The essential part of the knot is now complete, and all that remains is to dispose of the end.

Fig. 105D: One way to dispose of the end is by means of a half-hitch, or two half-hitches (not illustrated).

Fig. 105E: A seizing, two seizings (not illustrated), or a half-hitch and seizing (not illustrated) are more permanent than a single half-hitch.

Fig. 105F: Another good way to dispose of the end is to join the end and the standing part with a bowline knot.

106. The Studdingsail Halyard Bend is like the fisherman's bend, except that the end is tucked back under the first turn. It is an excellent knot, with an extremely high breaking strength and little tendency to slip.

107. The Timber Hitch is suitable for large convex objects, such as logs and spars. It is extremely strong and secure, and it cannot possibly jam.

Fig. 107A: Pass the end round the spar and then round the standing part. Then twist or dog the end with the lay three or four times.

Fig. 107B: When the timber hitch is used for towing a log or spar, a half-hitch or two can be added to keep the log or spar in line.

108. The Lark's Head, Cow Hitch, or Ring Hitch. This is a useful and familiar hitch, suitable for large objects, like casks and bales (see nos. 169 and 170), or for small objects, like keys, baggage tags, and rings. It should ordinarily be used only when the strain comes on both standing parts.

Fig. 108A: Sometimes, as with a key or ring, the lark's head can be made in the bight, without access to the ends; but when the object is large, or when it is attached to another object, the bight must first be passed through the ring, and the two ends then passed through the bight.

Fig. 108B: Front and back views of the lark's head.

Fig. 108C: A lark's head with a toggle. This form of the hitch can be released instantly.

Ashley (1944) argues convincingly that the term *lark's head* was coined by "Tom Bowling" in 1866 as a result of a misapplication of the French *tête d'alouette*. The term is pretty well established by this time, however. It is in all the dictionaries, and Öhrvall (1916) gives *Laerkehoved* as the Norwegian and Danish name. Lever (1808) pictures it without giving it any name at all.

109. The Latigo Knot, Girth Knot, or Cinch Knot is structurally the same as the lark's head.

Figs. 109A and 109B: It can be used to hitch the end of a leather strap to a ring.

Figs. 109C and 109D: It can also be used to join two rings, as for example on saddle girths, one end of the strap being secured permanently to the lower ring.

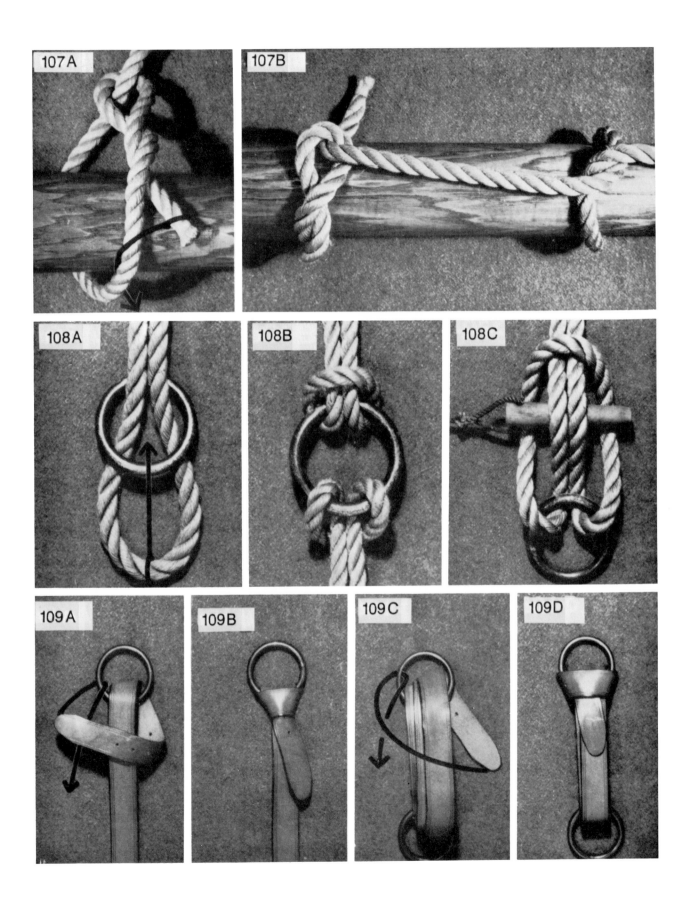

110. The Midshipman's Hitch consists of a rolling hitch (no. 113) tied on the standing part. Like the rolling hitch, it has several forms.

Figs. 110A and 110B: The most characteristic form starts with two turns round the standing part, the second turn being jammed inside the first.

Fig. 110C: The end is then seized or stopped to the standing part, or, for very temporary purposes, held against the standing part by the hand. Since the strength of this form of the hitch lies in the two turns, and particularly in the way the second turn is jammed inside the first, the seizing need not be strong. It is enough that the end remain in place while the hitch is in use.

This form of the hitch can be tied when the line is under tension, as when a man has fallen overboard and is being dragged through the water by a line to which he is clinging. A loop in the end of the line will make his situation more tenable, and the midshipman's hitch is the most convenient loop for him to use.

Fig. 110D: Another form of the midshipman's hitch. Here the second turn is *not* jammed inside the first, and the end is secured with a half-hitch.

Fig. 110E: When drawn taut, this form of the hitch closes round the object secured.

Fig. 110F: The final half-hitch can also be made in the opposite direction.

111. Three variations of the midshipman's hitch are shown here, some or all of which have at times been called by the same name. They function like the form shown in fig. 110F and are presumably just about as secure. However, they lack the characteristic virtues of the form shown in fig. 110C. Other variations can be devised.

112. The Clove Hitch or Ratline Hitch is an important basic knot. It is used to secure the ratlines to the shrouds (the process is called *rattling down*), to hitch the mesh lines to the head rope of a net, to secure the guy ropes to the head of a pair of shears, to make a painter temporarily fast to a post, and for many other purposes.

First Method

Fig. 112A: If the end of the post or other object is accessible, grasp the standing part of the line with one hand and the end with the other, and place a single hitch over the top of the post. (Leave the end longer than the illustration indicates.)

Fig. 112B: Let go of the standing part, grasp the end with both hands, one hand separated from the other, and place another hitch, exactly like the first, over the top of the post.

Fig. 112C: The completed hitch is shown here. This method of tying the clove hitch has the advantage that it can be used when there is considerable tension on the standing part.

The clove hitch is very useful as a temporary fastening when excessive strain is not expected. For greater permanence and security, the end should be secured to the standing part.

Figs. 112D and 112E: Two half-hitches or a seizing are common and excellent ways to accomplish this. Another way is illustrated in fig. 164.

Second Method

Fig. 112F: When the top of the object is out of reach, as when rattling down, the end of the line must be passed round twice, as shown by the arrow, in such a way as to form the hitch.

Third Method

Fig. 112G: Rotate both hands to the right, until the palms are up, and grasp the rope. Then rotate the hands to the left, as shown by the arrows.

Fig. 112H: Place *A* and *B* (the two hitches that are formed) on top of each other, as shown by the arrow.

Falconer (1769) refers to the clove hitch, and Lescallier (1791) pictures it under the name *demi-clef*. The similarity of sound between the English *clove* and the French *clef* suggests a linguistic relationship that has not been noted in the dictionaries.

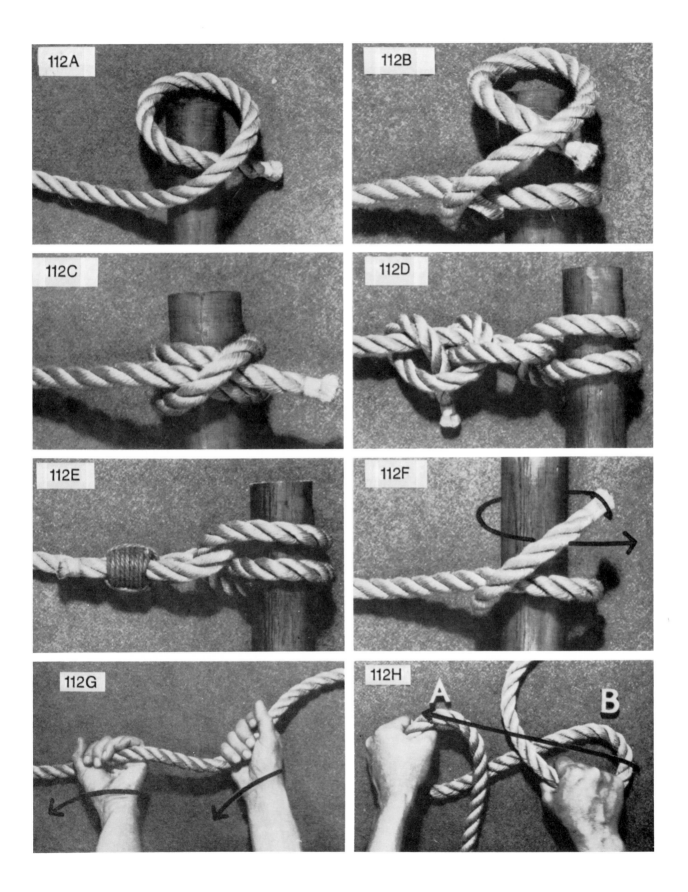

113. The Rolling Hitch or Magnus Hitch has several forms.

Figs. 113A and 113B: One form begins with a round turn but ends (as the clove hitch does) with a single hitch. This form is a sort of double clove hitch (compare figs. 113A and 112F). For greater permanence the end may be secured to the standing part by one of the methods described on the preceding page.

The rolling hitch may be used to take a strain at right angles to the spar, and when used in this way it is more secure than the clove hitch. However, it is especially adapted to bear strains that are parallel, or nearly parallel, to the spar, as for example a downward pull in figs. 113B, 113E, 113F, 113G, and 113H.

Figs. 113C and 113D: When used to secure a small rope to a large one, the rolling hitch is usually tied in a different and distinctive way. That is, the second turn is jammed inside the first. This is the construction that was explained in figs. 110A to 110C, in the description of the midshipman's hitch. When the stage shown in fig. 113D is reached, the end must be disposed of.

Fig. 113E: The simplest way to do this is to take a single hitch round the other rope.

Fig. 113F: A more effective way is to seize or stop the end to the other rope.

Fig. 113G: Several turns round the other rope, *with the lay,* provide additional security.

Fig. 113H: This method is illustrated in the British Admiralty's *Manual of Seamanship.*

For very temporary purposes, the end can simply be held against the other rope by the hand.

The rolling hitch has little inclination to slide as long as the second turn remains jammed inside the first, and the second turn remains so jammed as long as tension is continuous.

When the rolling hitch is used to secure a small rope to a large one, the hitch shown by the arrow in fig. 113A is sometimes tied in the reverse direction, especially by farmers and tree surgeons, who are apt to use the name *taut-line hitch* instead of *rolling hitch.* Another name that is sometimes used is *stopper hitch.* Lescallier (1791) pictures it under the name *tour mort avec deux demi-clefs.*

114. The Shiver Hitch was formerly used in the British merchant service, according to Lever (1808), when a jigger, or small tackle, was hitched to the anchor cable to assist in raising or lowering the anchor.

Figs. 114A and 114B: Lever shows the single variety; Ashley shows the double variety and supplies the name. The end of the jigger is rove through the hole in an old sheave and knotted with a multistrand stopper knot such as the Matthew Walker (no. 212).

115. A Stopper, either single (fig. 115A) or double (fig. 115B), also serves to take the strain temporarily from a larger rope when hauling, hoisting, belaying, etc. The lower end of the stopper has an eye-splice or a hook in it, or is fastened to a block. The upper end is held in place by hand, or temporarily stopped to the larger rope, while the operation is in progress.

116. A Selvagee Strap or Strop is made by winding a long piece of rope or small stuff several times round two pegs set the desired distance apart. The two ends are spliced or knotted together, and the whole is firmly marled (no. 133).

Fig. 116A shows how a tackle, such as a handy billy, can be secured to a rope with a selvagee strap.

Fig. 116B shows one way of hooking a tackle to a spar. Straps are used when setting up the shrouds to fasten the tackle to the shrouds.

117. A Grommet Strap is an endless piece of rope (i.e., the ends are spliced together). Fig. 117 shows one way in which a grommet can be used to secure a tackle to a spar. A grommet strap is less supple and strong than a selvagee strap of the same weight.

118. The Well-Pipe Hitch or Lifting Hitch will bear a strain parallel to the pipe or spar. It is sometimes used to secure the guy ropes of circus tents to stakes driven into the ground. Instead of the two half-hitches, a bowline can be used to join the end and the standing part.

119. The Telegraph Hitch is similar in purpose to no. 118.

120. The Fire-Hose Hitch, from Graumont and Hensel (1939), is supposed to be used in lifting fire hoses vertically up the sides of burning buildings. The end *A* is left long so that the hose can be secured to the building at the desired point.

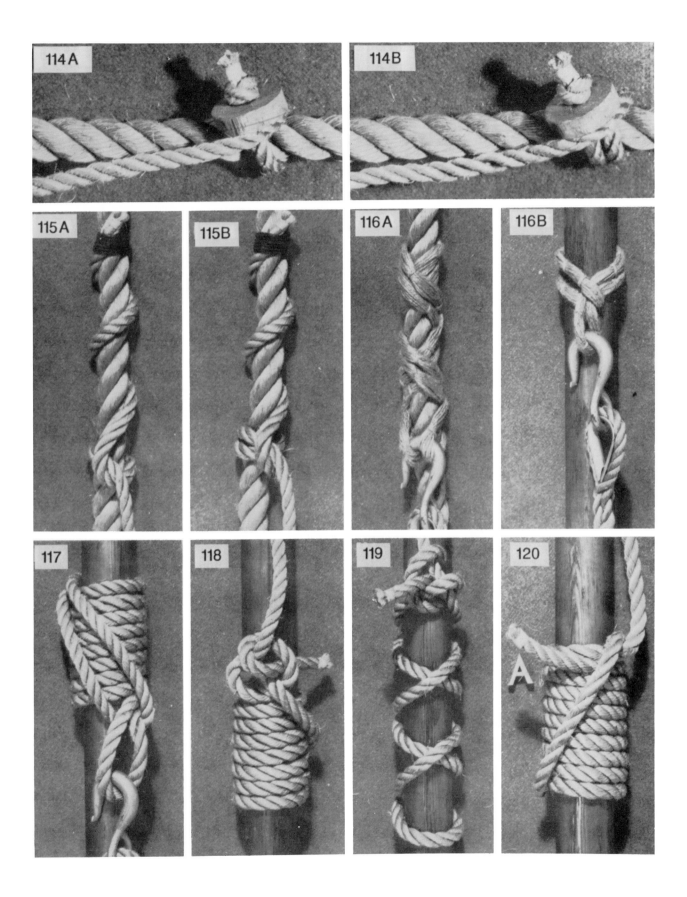

121. The Catspaw (1), sometimes called the *single catspaw,* is a way of hitching a line to a hook. It is less secure than no. 122.

Figs. 121A and 121B: Form two loops, and wind the standing part several times round them.

Fig. 121C: Place the two loops over the hook.

122. The Catspaw (2) is used when the bight of a rope—a sling, for example—is to be hitched to a hook. It is a strong, secure hitch that cannot slip or jam.

Figs. 122A and 122B: To tie the catspaw (2), twist the two loops *A* and *B* several times in opposite directions, and place them on the hook.

123. The Blackwall Hitch is a quick and convenient way to hitch a line temporarily to a hook. It does not hold unless the tension is continuous, and it should never be used when lifting heavy loads or when damage would result if it slipped. It was formerly much used to hook the lanyard to the tackle when setting up the shrouds. To tie it, bring a hitch up under the hook, and drop the end, and then the standing part, in place.

124. The Double Blackwall Hitch is similar to no. 123.

125. The Stunner Hitch is tied as illustrated, according to F. L. R. Murray, with one more turn than is usually pictured.

126. The Bill Hitch is similar in structure and function to no. 123.

127. A Clove Hitch (no. 112) is sometimes a convenient way to hitch a line to a hook.

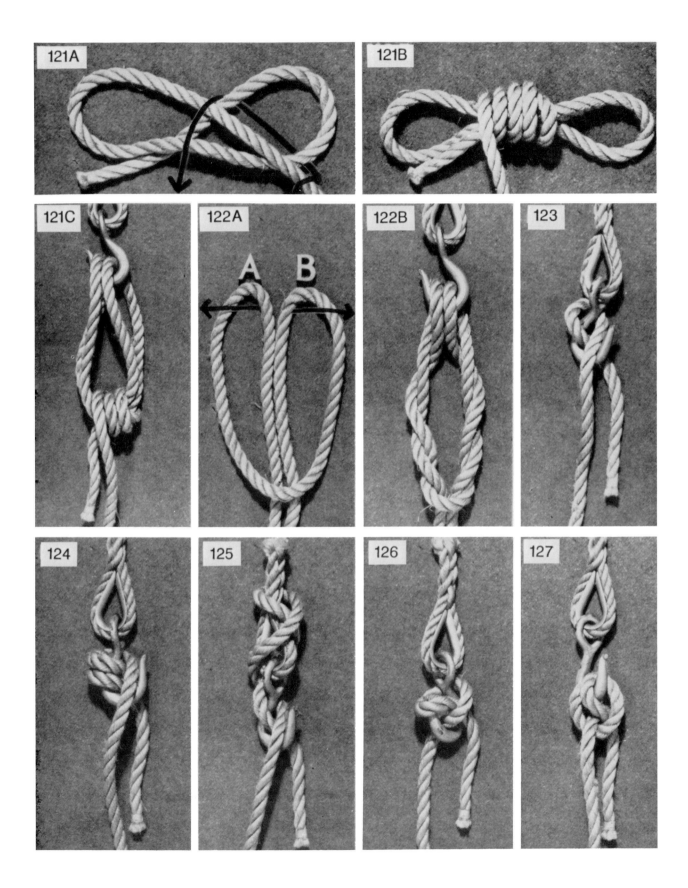

128. The Highwayman's Cutaway.

Fig. 128A: Pass a bight through a ring, or round a spar, rail, or post. Push a second bight (from the standing part) through the first bight.

Fig. 128B: Push a third bight (from the end) through the second bight.

Fig. 128C: The distinguishing characteristic of this ingenious hitch is that a tug on the end releases it instantaneously, without pulling any part of the line back through the ring or round the spar. Hal McKail says that Dick Turpin is supposed to have invented this hitch, and that it is useful in tying to a mooring or pier when sailing alone. The end of the line can be led to the stern of the boat, and the hitch released from there when it is time to cast off.

129. The Scaffold Hitch is a clove hitch (no. 112) arranged in a way convenient for slinging a plank on edge and similar purposes. Oribasius described it in the fourth century A.D. and recommended it as a sling for broken arms.

130. This is another application of the clove hitch (no. 112). It is a crossing knot, suitable for fence posts or the guy ropes of a derrick. The G.I. who showed it to me called it the *Oklahoma hitch.* Known in bandaging as the *Collins cinch,* it is used to apply traction quickly in fracture cases.

131. The Crossing Knot is used in wrapping parcels, where one part of the twine crosses another part at right angles.

132. The Marlinespike Hitch is used when increased power is needed to heave a length of small stuff taut, as, for example, the turns of a seizing.

Fig. 132A: Hold the end (at the bottom of the photograph) in the left hand, and take up all the slack. Hold the marlinespike in the right hand, and rotate the point so as to make a hitch in the rope.

Fig. 132B: Rotate the spike again in such a way as to fold the hitch up over the standing part.

Fig. 132C: Stick the spike through to the left.

Fig. 132D: The spike can now be grasped in the hand, and a pull exerted directly; or the spike can be used as a lever, with the point resting on a fixed object.

133. The Marling Hitch consists of a series of hitches round an object, such as a selvagee strop (no. 116), to contain the object, and it holds the parts in place. The verb *to marl* means to *secure with marling hitches.* The bolt rope is sometimes marled to the foot of the sail.

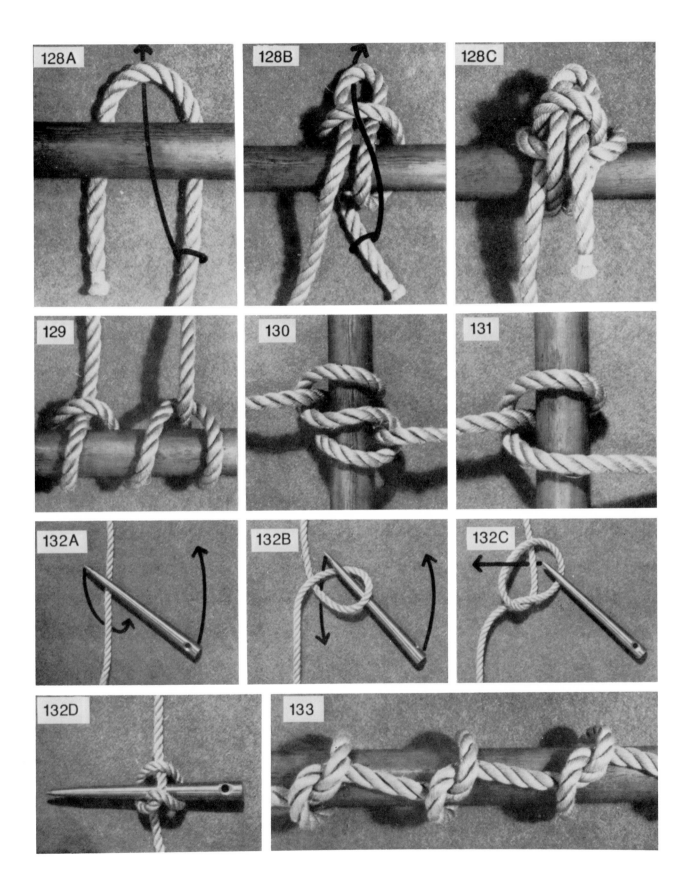

134. The Roband Hitch is, or was, used to secure the robands to the jackstays or to the yards. Robands were of two kinds: one kind consisted of a single length of braided cordage, seven to nine feet long, permanently secured at one end either to the head-rope or to an eyelet hole in the head of the sail. The other kind had two braided legs, one longer than the other, which, after being passed round the yard in any of several ways, were tied together at the top with a square knot. (Hence the Swedish word *råbandsknop* for *square knot*.) It is the first kind of roband, consisting of a single long leg, with which we are concerned here.

Fig. 134A: The small rope is supposed to represent a braided roband secured at one end to an eyelet hole in the sail. To tie the roband hitch, pass the free end round the yard, through the eyelet hole, and round the yard again.

Fig. 134B: Pass the end to the left, and hitch it round the yard.

Fig. 134C: The finished hitch looks something like the magnus hitch (fig. 113B). I am indebted to L. G. Miller for this reconstruction of this obsolete knot.

The word *roband* (pronounced "roe'bin" or "roe'bnd") is not related to the fanciful compound *rope-band*, as is sometimes incorrectly stated. Webster correctly relates it to the Danish word *ra*, meaning *spar*, a word that is common in the Scandinavian languages.

135. The Ossel Hitch or Net-Line Hitch (1) is from the 1939 edition of Spencer's *Knots*. When a net is made with backing, short lines, which Spencer calls *ossels*, are used to connect the backing and the head-rope. The ossel hitch is used to secure the ossels to the backing. Duhamel du Monceau (1769) pictures a hitch almost exactly like it (*Traité Général des Pesches*, vol. 1, plate 1).

136. The Ossel Hitch or Net-Line Hitch (2) is also from Spencer (1939). It is used to secure the ossels to the headrope of the net.

The word *ossel* does not appear in Webster or in the *Oxford English Dictionary*. Spelled *ossil* or *osil*, it is defined in Wright's *English Dialect Dictionary* as "a short line to which a fish hook is attached," and is said to be current in the Orkney and Shetland Islands.

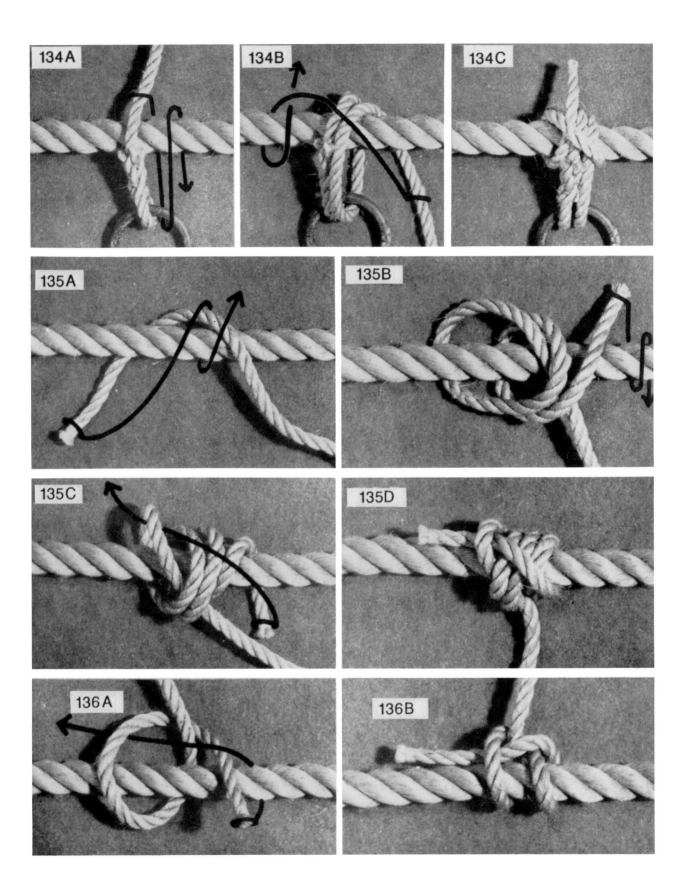

134A 134B 134C

135A 135B

135C 135D

136A 136B

137. A good angler's knot must be secure, strong, streamlined, and easy to tie. The loop knot for leaders and spinning lines illustrated in figs. 137A and 137B is superior to the perfection knot (no. 77) in two respects: it is stronger (80 percent, as compared to 60 percent, according to Barnes's tests), and it is more satisfactorily streamlined (since the end does not stick out at an angle). Because it is intermediate in structure between a figure-eight loop knot (no. 71) and a loop knot made with a stevedore knot (no. 23), the name Barnes has given it—*blood bight*—is somewhat inappropriate.

138. The Barrel Knot (called the *blood knot* in England) is the best way to tie the ends of two leaders together. It is strong (80 percent), secure in gut or nylon, and admirably streamlined. One method of tying it, called by Barnes the *incoil* method, is illustrated in fig. 45A. The *outcoil* method is shown in fig. 138A. Barnes prefers the former; the Du Pont Company, in its pamphlet *Spinning with Du Pont Tynex*, recommends the latter.

The turns in the two halves of the knot, as shown in fig. 138A, are reversed. Continuous turns (not illustrated) are easier to manipulate, requiring only that one tie a six-fold half-knot (no. 17) and stick the ends back through the center. The ends will then lie side by side.

139. The Turle Knot, for tying a leader to a fly or hook, is usually made with an overhand running knot (no. 88). Barnes prefers the form shown in fig. 139A because the end lies closer to the shank of the hook, or at least it does, he says, when the eye of the hook is bent up or down. The Turle knot was first illustrated by R. B. Marston in the *Fishing Gazette* (30 May 1884), and was named for a Major Turle, who is credited with having first used it for eyed hooks.

For large hooks, Barnes recommends a *two-circle Turle*. It is like fig. 139A except that two loops are formed instead of one before the overhand knot is tied.

140. The Clinch Knot is equivalent to half a barrel knot (no. 138). It is secure, strong (80 percent), and easy to tie. Both Barnes and Du Pont recommend it.

141. The Prefect Knot, recommended by Barnes for swivels, is both stronger and more satisfactorily streamlined than no. 140. To tie it, pass the turns successively, one after the other, to the right, over the metal eye, beginning with the outside turn. Then draw the knot taut. L. W. Darke showed this knot to Barnes, and they agreed to call it the *prefect knot* "because it is so nearly perfect."

For additional angler's knots, see nos. 34, 37, 39–42, 45, 77, 80, and 83, and consult the second edition of Barnes's book (1951).

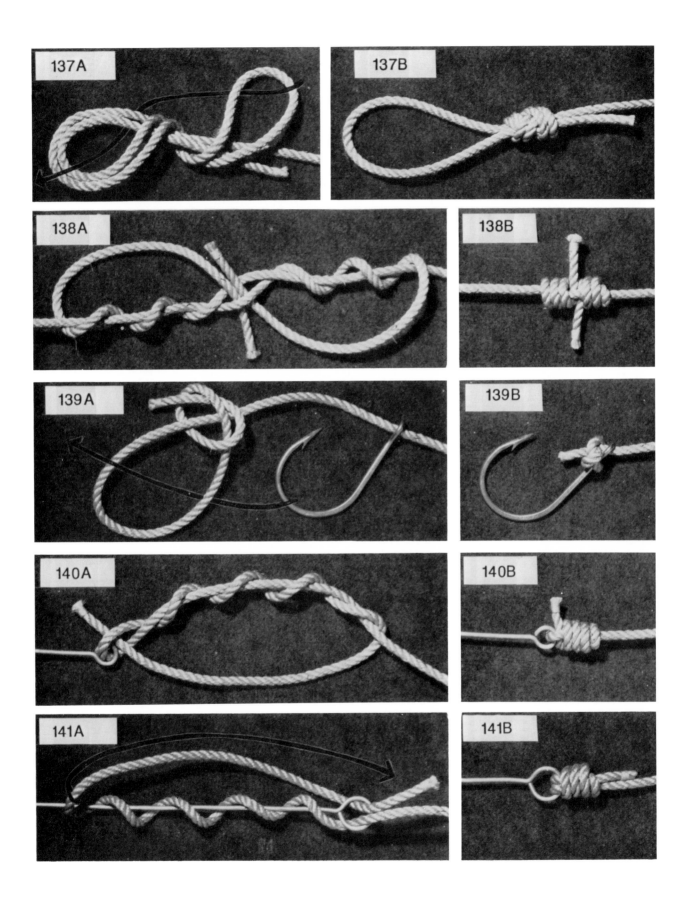

142. The Constrictor Knot consists of a half-knot under an exterior turn. Its function is to bind an object and keep it from expanding. It does not hold on flat surfaces or on corners, but it grips and closes down on *round* objects (such as spars, ropes, rubber tubes, the mouths of sacks, and the handles of tools) with the tenacity of a boa constrictor. It makes a good temporary whipping, and it can be used to repair or strengthen all kinds of household articles.

First Method

Fig. 142A: Begin as if tying a three-lead Turk's-head (fig. 222A). Bring the end down to the *left* of the standing part, and up under the central crossing.

Fig. 142B: Pull the knot taut, and cut off the ends.

Fig. 142C: This variation of the constrictor can be used as a transom knot to hold two rods or spars at right angles to each other.

Second Method

Figs. 142D and 142E: To tie the constrictor knot in the bight, make a loop *ABCD,* turn *AB* down (see the arrow), and bring *A* and *C* together under the knot.

Third Method

Figs. 142F and 142G: The double knot is stronger than the single knot, but the exterior turns are more difficult to draw taut.

Fourth Method

Fig. 142H: When the end is slipped, the constrictor knot can be used as a tourniquet. Take care, however, not to pull it too tight.

The constrictor knot was almost unknown in this country until Ashley published it in 1944. Ashley first tied it about 1919, and seems to have thought that he originated it; but Öhrvall (1916) had already described it (without benefit of diagram) as a variant of the strangle knot (Swedish *ålstek* or eel knot). Martta Ropponen-Homi, in her *Solmukirja* (1931, preface dated 1930), was the first to illustrate it. She called it the *whip knot* (Finnish *ruaskasolmu*) and showed how to tie it in the bight. In a letter to me dated 5 December 1954, she says she never saw it in Finland, but got it from Raphael Gaston of Zaragoza, Spain. She translated the name *whip knot* into Finnish from Esperanto, the language in which she and Gaston corresponded. Drew (1931), the first writer in the English-speaking world to describe the constrictor knot, also showed how to tie it in the bight, and (like Öhrvall) treated it as a variant of the strangle knot. Drew probably learned it from Ashley, whom he met in 1926 (letter from Drew to L. G. Miller). By 1944 Ashley had given it the name *constrictor knot* and fully appreciated its distinctive merits.

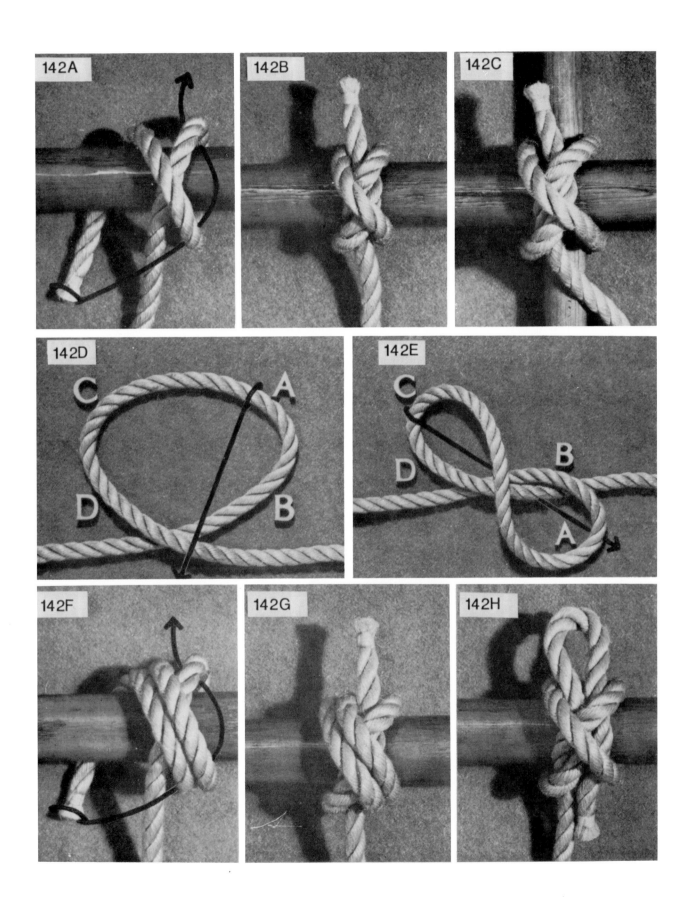

142A 142B 142C 142D 142E 142F 142G 142H

143. The Strangle Knot is similar in structure and purpose to the constrictor knot (no. 142), but it does not bind with the same relentless force, and it cannot be tied in the bight. On the other hand, it is somewhat more trim in appearance, since the turns lie close together all round the knot.

First Method

Fig. 143A: The best way to tie the strangle knot.

Fig. 143B: The completed knot.

Second Method

Fig. 143C: Take two turns round the object to be contained, and stick the end under both turns.

Fig. 143D: Place the right-hand turn over the left-hand turn. The result is like fig. 143B.

Third Method

Fig. 143E: Tie a double overhand knot (as illustrated in fig. 19A) and start to draw it taut. Before the two loops have come together, place them over the object to be contained, as shown by the arrow.

The strangle knot is nothing more nor less than a double overhand knot tied round an object. It is also closely related to the fisherman's bend (no. 105), as a comparison of fig. 105A and fig. 143C will show.

Drew pictured this knot in 1912 under the name *first-aid knot,* and showed how to use it to keep a bandage on an injured finger. In a later work (his chapter on knots in Griswold's *Handicraft,* 1931), written after he had met Ashley, he called it the *strangle knot,* a name he may have gotten from Ashley. Öhrvall (1916) called it the *ålstek,* or eel knot.

144. The Miller's Knot, Sack Knot, or Bag Knot (1) is used to close the mouth of a sack or bag. Normally it is tied in a horizontal position, but for the sake of comparison with nos. 142 and 143, it is here shown vertical. There are several miller's knots. This one is identical to a three-lead two-bight Turk's-head (no. 222).

145. The Miller's Knot, Sack Knot, or Bag Knot (2). This is similar to no. 144.

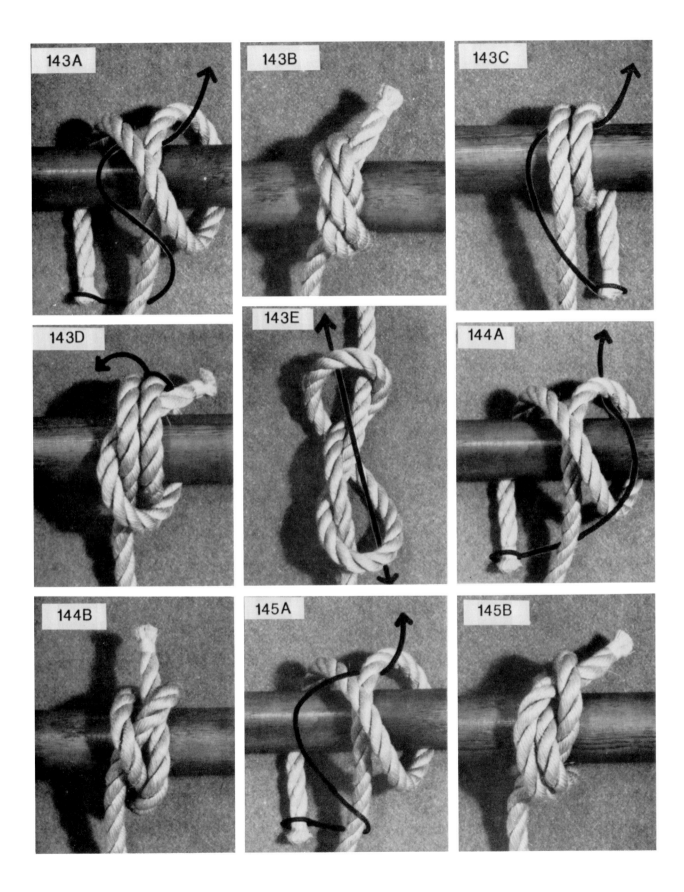

146. A Shortening for Slings.

Fig. 146A: Make a loop *AB* in the sling, and bring *B* down behind the standing part.

Fig. 146B: Bring *B* up to join *A*.

Fig. 146C: Place *B* and *A* over the hook.

147. The Sheepshank is a device for shortening a rope. Captain Felix Riesenberg (1922) remarks that it is used now about as often as the cross-bow, but our ancestors thought well of it. Captain John Smith (1627) speaks of it in the same breath with the wall knot and the bowline.

First Method

Fig. 147A: Double the rope and place half-hitches over the two bights *A* and *B*. Or form hitches in the standing part and push the two bights *A* and *B* through them.

Figs. 147B and 147C: The sheepshank holds only as long as tension is maintained, and even then it sometimes collapses. To make it more secure, toggles may be inserted, or the ends, if they are accessible, may be rove through the terminal bights. Another way (not illustrated) is to seize the terminal bights to the standing part.

Fig. 147D: This illustrates how the sheepshank can be used as an impromptu tackle or purchase. According to Hal McKail, this device is much used in Australia "by teamsters in bowsing down lashings on bales of wool." The upper end *A* goes over the top of the wagon, and the lower end *B* is hauled on. Hadfield (1912) calls the device a *hay knot,* and shows it with only half a sheepshank, the hitch at the lower end of the knot being omitted. Osborn (1915) calls it a *sheepshank cinch.*

The sheepshank is sometimes called the *dogshank* in books, presumably because the French name is *noeud de jambe de chien* (Lescallier, 1791). "Tom Bowling" (1866) probably inaugurated this innovation in nomenclature.

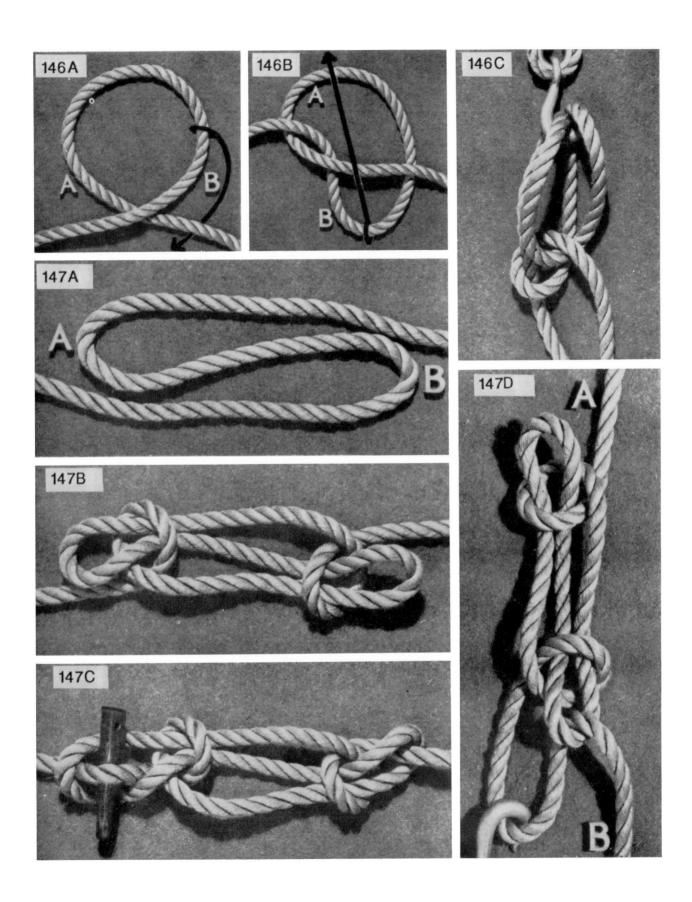

146A

146B

146C

147A

147B

147C

147D

A

B

A

B

A

B

A

B

117

Second Method

Figs. 147E and 147F: Lay down three loops and pull the middle loop apart. The result is a sheepshank with two of the parts crossed but otherwise identical to fig. 147B.

Third Method

Figs. 147G and 147H: Lay down four loops and pull the two middle loops apart, as shown by the arrows. The result is a so-called *knotted sheepshank* or *man-of-war sheepshank*. Remove the two half-hitches from this sheepshank and the result is the same as fig. 149B.

148. The Jug Sling, Jar Sling, Bottle Sling, or Hackamore. There are at least seven ways to tie this ingenious and useful knot.

First Method

Fig. 148A: Start with an overhand noose (no. 88), and make a loop X in the noose. Enlarge X until it covers the overhand knot.

Fig. 148B: Bring Y over X, under Z, and up. This method is described by Oribasius.

Fig. 148C: The completed knot is used as follows. Put the neck of the bottle through the center of the knot O, tie A and B together, and use Y and AB as handles. Fig. 148D shows the sling in use.

Fig. 148D: The jug sling in use. A bottle with the merest suspicion of a flange can be safely carried with this sling.

Second Method

Fig. 148E: Arrange the cord as illustrated, and then follow the arrow with the end. This method, which may be called the analytical method because it reveals the construction of the sling, has no practical value, for it is too difficult to remember.

Third Method

Fig. 148F: Start with a fisherman's loop knot (no. 80), and bring the upper overhand knot partly over the lower one.

Fig. 148G: Follow the arrow with the main bight. This is one of Oribasius's methods.

Fourth Method

Fig. 148H: Lay down two loops, and bring up a bight from the bottom, under, over, under, and over, as shown by the arrow.

Fig. 148I: Fold down the back loop.

Fig. 148J: Fold down the front loop.

Fifth Method

Fig. 148K: Arrange two loops as illustrated, and bring a bight up from the bottom, over, under, over, and under.

Sixth Method

Fig. 148L: Lay down two loops; push *B* to the right under *A*, and *A* to the left over *B*.

Fig. 148M: Bring a bight up from the bottom through the center. This method is a variant of the fourth method (figs. 148H to 148J). Another variant is pictured in *A Boy's Workshop* by Harry Craigin (Boston, 1884, chap. 23). This seems to be the first description of the jug sling since Oribasius's redaction of Heraklas in the fourth century A.D.

Seventh Method

For this method, contributed by L. G. Miller, see fig. F, p. 8.

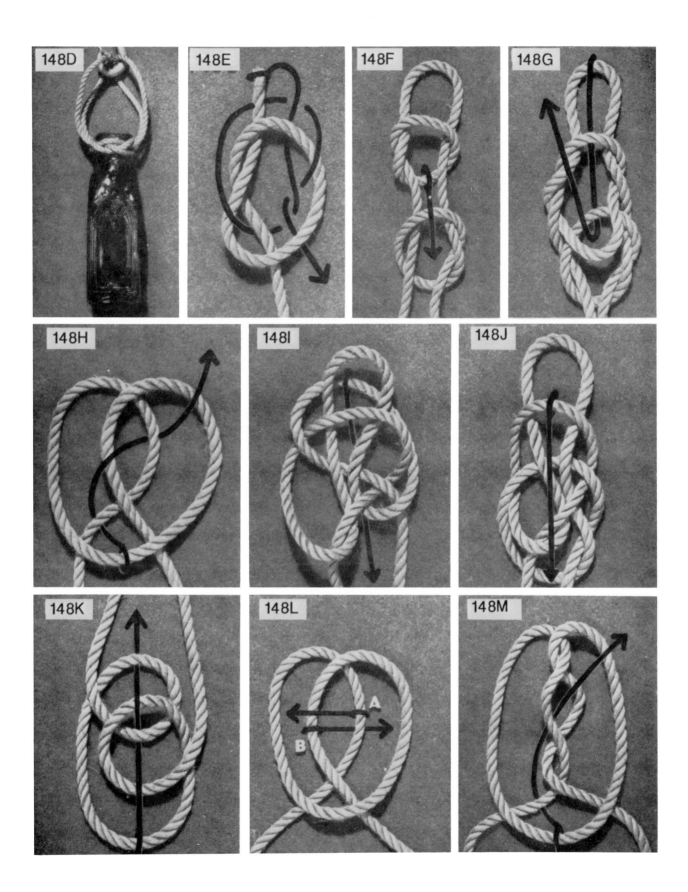

148D 148E 148F 148G

148H 148I 148J

148K 148L 148M

121

149. Rope Handcuffs or Single Jug Sling.

Fig. 149A: Lay down two loops, the second *on top of* the first, and pull them through each other, as shown by the arrows.

Fig. 149B: Place the prisoner's wrists in the two nooses, and knot the ends. Fig. 149B resembles fig. 150B; the difference is that the ends in fig. 149B are crossed as they leave the knot. According to Hal McKail, this crossing is called *the kiss,* and fig. 149B is sometimes called the *true-lover's knot,* a name that has been applied to a good many other knots, as well.

150. The Tom Fool Knot can be tied in several ways.

First Method

Fig. 150A: Lay down two loops, the second *under* the first, and pull them apart, as shown by the arrows.

Fig. 150B: The result is a double noose very similar to fig. 149B.

Second Method

Fig. 150C: Hold the cord with both hands, as illustrated. Grasp *B* with the index and middle fingers of the left hand, and grasp *A* with the index and middle fingers of the right hand.

Fig. 150D: Pull *A* and *B* apart. The result is the same as fig. 150B.

Third Method

Fig. 150E: Oribasius clearly describes this method. Wrap the cord twice round the left hand, the first time under the thumb, the second time over the thumb. Let the cord pass over the palm and between the little finger and the ring finger. Raise the thumb, reach under, and, with the right hand, pull the first turn to the right; with the little finger and ring finger of the left hand, pull the second turn to the left, as shown by the arrows. The result is like fig. 150B.

The Tom Fool knot is a conjuror's knot. When the knot is tied by the third method, the right hand can conceal the operation from the spectators.

Fourth Method

Fig. 150F: Make two bights in the cord and tie these two bights together by means of a half-knot. The result is like fig. 150B.

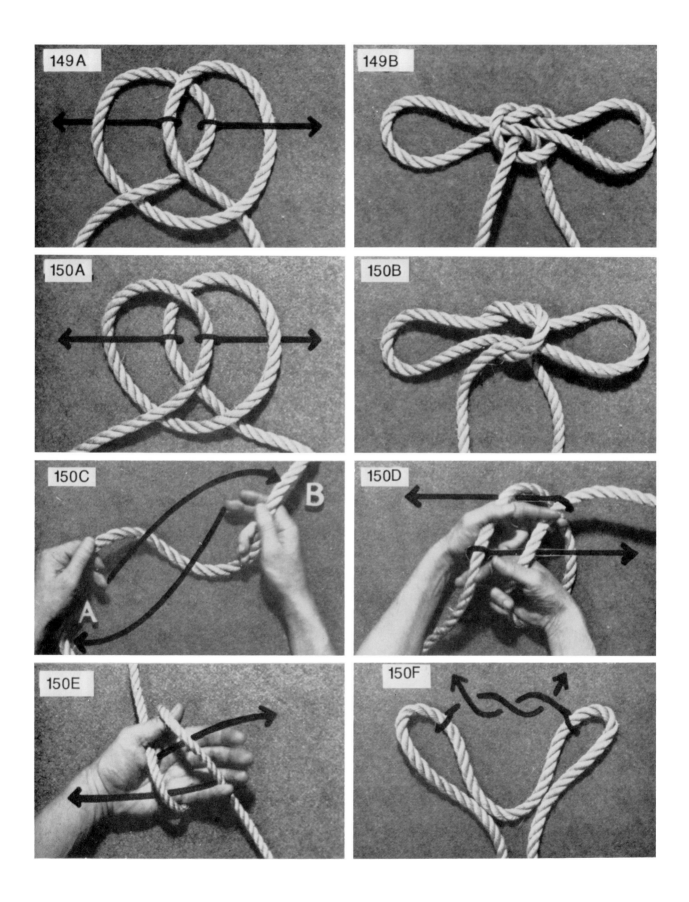

149A

149B

150A

150B

150C

150D

150E

150F

123

151. The Masthead Knot or Jury Knot can be tied in at least three ways, with a slightly different result in each case.

First Method

Figs. 151A and 151B: Lay down three loops, one *on top of* the other, and pull them apart, as indicated by the three arrows.

Second Method

Figs. 151C and 151D: Lay down three loops, one *under* the other, and pull them apart, as indicated by the three arrows.

Third Method

Figs. 151E and 151F: Lay down three loops one *on top of* the other, the second loop being formed in the opposite way from the other two. Pull the loops apart, as indicated by the three arrows.

This knot can be used as a jug sling with four handles, but it is not as good a knot for the purpose as no. 148. When used as a masthead knot, it is placed over the masthead of the jury mast, and guy lines or stays are hitched to the three bights. The two ends are then joined with a bowline knot, and the long end is used as a fourth stay or is bent to a fourth stay.

152. The Shamrock Knot or Japanese Masthead Knot.

Fig. 152A: Arrange two interlocking overhand knots, and pull them apart, as indicated by the arrows.

Fig. 152B: The resulting knot is inferior to no. 151 as a masthead knot. It is primarily a decorative knot.

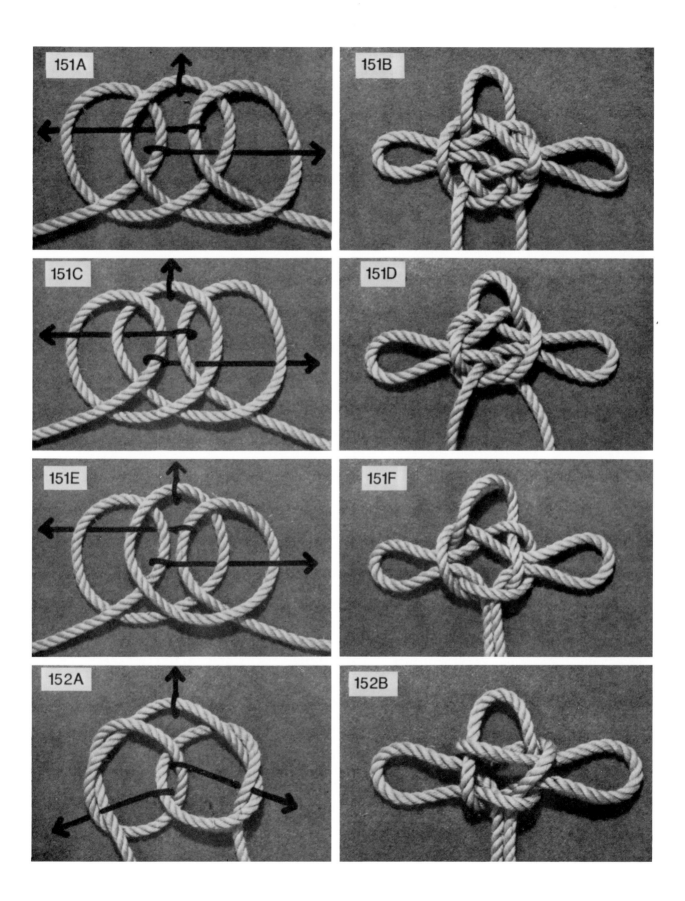

153. The Round Seizing. Seizings are lashings used to hold two ropes, or two parts of the same rope, together. They are made of various materials, from marline or spun yarn to three-strand tarred seizing stuff of 6, 9, or 12 threads. They are named according to their use and their construction. If the end of a rope is turned round a thimble, and five seizings are put on to hold the end and the standing part together, the seizings are called (1) *end seizing,* (2) *upper seizing,* (3) *middle seizing,* (4) *quarter seizing,* and (5) *eye seizing.* With respect to construction, the four chief kinds of seizings are *round seizings, racking seizings, flat seizings,* and *throat seizings.*

Fig. 153A: To *clap on* a round seizing, heave the two parts together, by means of a Spanish windlass (no. 177) if necessary. Splice a small eye, either a tucked eye (no. 184) or an eye-splice (no. 180), in one end of the seizing stuff. Pass the other end round both ropes and through the eye.

Fig. 153B: Wind the seizing stuff eight or nine times round both ropes, heaving each turn taut with a marlinespike (see no. 132). Bring the working end up under the last turn.

Fig. 153C: Lay on a second series of turns, called *riders* or *riding turns,* one fewer in number, but not so taut as to separate the first series of turns. Stick the working end down through the small eye in the other end.

Fig. 153D: Take *cross turns* or *frapping turns* round the previous turns between the two ropes.

Fig. 153E: Turn the work over.

Fig. 153F: Secure the end by means of a hitch on the two cross turns. This hitch can be formed in several different ways.

Fig. 153G: The completed seizing.

Figs. 153H and 153I: Another way to secure the end, illustrated here, resembles the clove hitch.

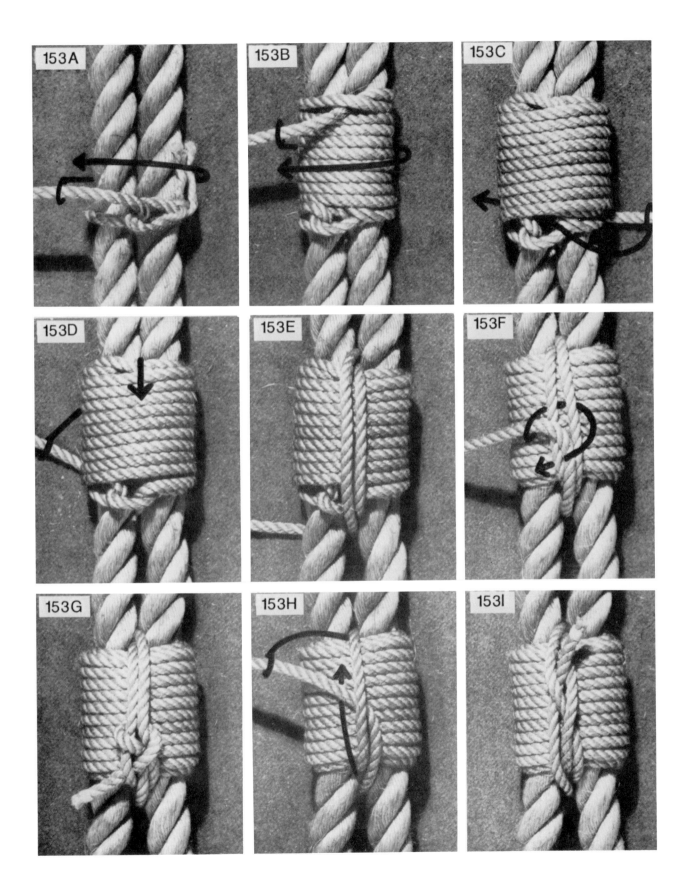

Fig. 153J: A third way to secure the end is to bring it up between the two cross turns and work a wall knot in it.

Fig. 153K: Another way to begin a round seizing is to leave the turns loose, bring the working end back under the loose turns, and stick it up through the small eye in the other end.

Fig. 153L: Heave each turn taut and put on riding turns, as before. Then stick the end down inside the last turn of the first layer and put on cross turns, as described on the preceding page.

154. The Flat Seizing is less strong and permanent than the round seizing. It has cross turns but not riding turns.

155. Stopping resembles no. 154 but is more temporary, sometimes being intended to serve for only a few minutes. The ends may be joined with a reef knot, as here, or disposed of in any of a number of ways. One rope is said to be *stopped* to another when a stopping is put on.

156. The Racking Seizing is sometimes used when unusual strain is expected on one of the ropes.

Fig. 156A: Take ten or twelve figure-eight turns and heave each turn taut.

Fig. 156B: Put riding turns round both ropes between the figure-eight turns.

Fig. 156C: Add cross or frapping turns, as explained on the preceding page under fig. 153D.

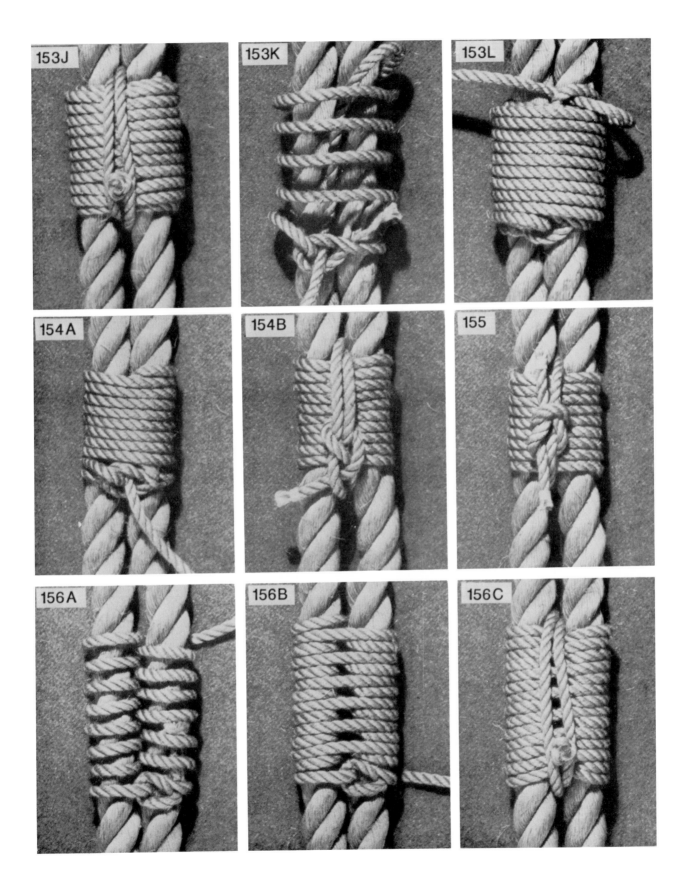

157. A Throat Seizing is similar to a round seizing (no. 153). It has riding turns but not cross turns. It is used in turning in deadeyes hearts, thimbles, and blocks.

158. A Clinch or Monkey's Tail is made with a throat seizing (no. 157) or with a stopping (no. 155). It is used as a stopper to prevent a line from running out through a block.

159. Mousing a Hook. This device is used to prevent a sling from slipping off a hook and, sometimes, to strengthen a hook and prevent it from spreading. It is made somewhat like a round seizing (no. 153), with riding turns but not cross turns. The ends come together in the middle and are tied with a square knot.

160. A Rose Lashing.
First Method

Figs. 160A to 160C: This method is for lashing a fork and two eye-splices to a spar. After the over-and-under turns are put on, the end is passed round in circular fashion until the surplus is exhausted, so that the lanyard will not have to be cut off, but can be used again. A wall knot is tied in the end where it comes up between the turns.

Second Method

Figs. 160D to 160F: This lashing was used to secure the ends of the foot-ropes to the yards.

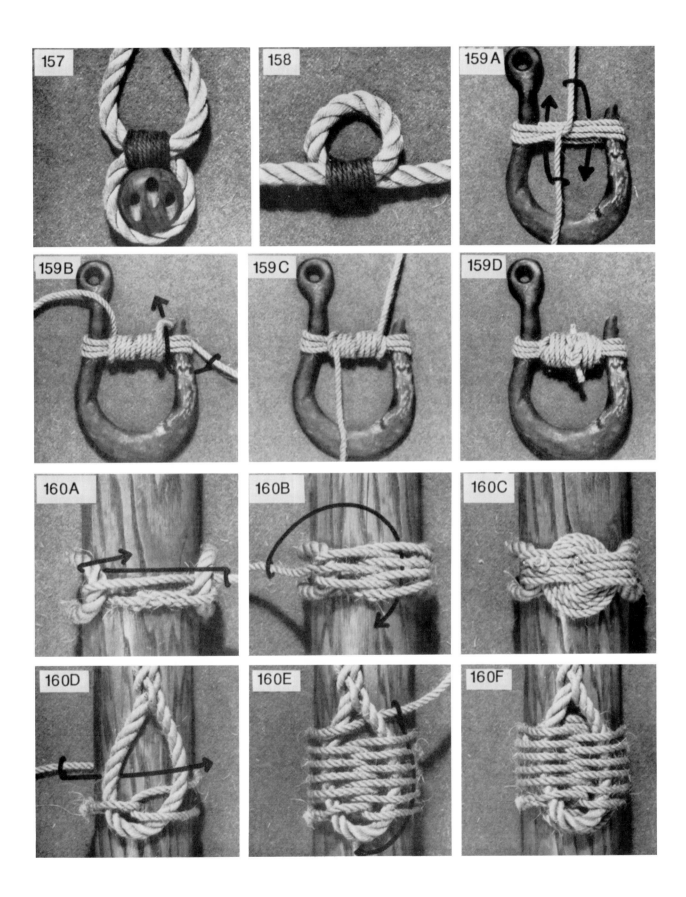

161. Square or Transom Lashing.

Fig. 161A: Start with a clove hitch on the upright. Carry the end up in front of the transom, behind the upright, and down in front of the transom.

Fig. 161B: Continue in this way, keeping inside previous turns on the upright, and outside previous turns on the transom.

Fig. 161C: After three to five turns as described above, conclude with two or three cross turns.

Fig. 161D: Dispose of the end by tying a clove hitch on the transom.

162. Lashing for Shears.
First Method

Fig. 162A: Begin with a clove hitch on one spar and end with a clove hitch on the other. The turns round the parallel spars are not hove taut, because the legs of the shears have to be spread apart. Two cross turns are taken.

Second Method

Fig. 162B: Start with loose turns round both spars, and end with two cross turns and a square knot.

163. Lashing for Gyn or Tripod.
First Method

Fig. 163A: Lay down the spars as illustrated, and begin with a clove hitch on one of them. Take loose turns round all three spars, follow with two cross turns, and conclude with a clove hitch on the middle spar.

Second Method

Figs. 163B and 163C: Begin with a clove hitch on one of the outer spars, and follow with loose racking turns. Conclude with an over-and-under cross turn on each side of the middle spar, and a clove hitch diagonally opposite the first clove hitch.

Fig. 163C: The work has been turned over to show the other side.

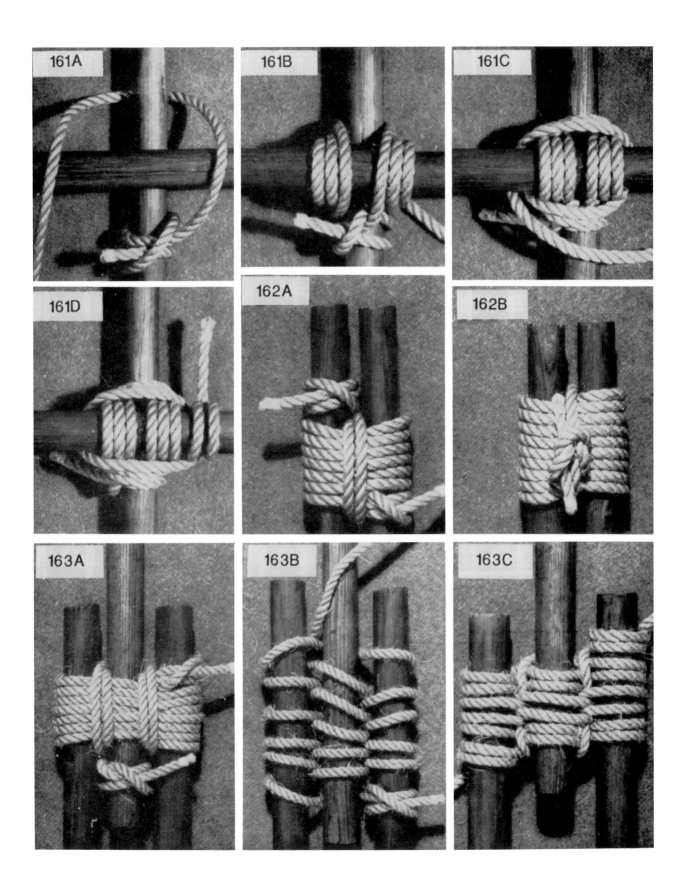

164. A Derrick is a single spar controlled by four guys. For the sake of clarity, only two guys are shown in the illustration. The guys may be secured to the head of the spar by means of clove hitches, with the ends tucked (as in no. 183) and seized. A tackle lashed to the head of the spar will lift a load to any position within a radius equal to one-fifth the height of the derrick.

165. Shears can lift heavier weights than derricks, but only in a vertical plane perpendicular to the plane of the shears, and only to a distance equal to about one-fifth the height of the shears. Placing a strap over the shears is a good way to secure the tackle.

Lever (1819, pp. 17–18) describes how shears were once used for getting in the masts and bowsprit of a ship. "At the head of the Sheers are four ropes, called *Guys;* two leading forwards, and two aft. Also at the upper end of one Spar, a Girtline Block is made fast; and its line reeved through it. At each heel of the Sheers, there is a Tail-tackle, leading aft: and two others are overhauled forwards. . . . The lashing of the sheers is passed like a Throat-Seizing, not too taught; and then the Heels of the Sheers are drawn asunder. . . . When the Sheers are up, they are moved forwards or aft, by Guys, and Heel-ropes."

166. A Tripod, Triangle, or Gyn can raise or lower a load but cannot move it over the ground. Lever (1819, p. 116) pictures a combination triangle and derrick for putting casks into a boat on an open beach. "This method of loading Boats on a beach, was invented by Lieutenant (now Captain) Acklom, of the Royal Navy: and it was first used in Tetuan Bay, for watering his Majesty's Ship Neptune, in the year 1805.—By this contrivance, three hundred and fifty Butts were filled, and sent off to that ship by day-light."

167. The Scaffold Hitch.
Fig. 167A: Take two turns round the plank, and put *A* over *B*.
Fig. 167B: Put *B* over *A* and *C,* and then down under the end of the plank.
Fig. 167C: Join the end and the standing part with a bowline.

168. The Parbuckle is a way of raising or lowering a heavy cylindrical object, such as a cask, a gun, or a spar, without the aid of a tackle. Loop the middle of the rope over a hook or a bollard, and pass the ends round the cask. Haul on the ends of the rope to raise the cask. A skid or plank forming an inclined plane makes the task easier.

Luce (1863, p. 115) describes how parbuckles and "counter parbuckles" made of five-inch hawsers were formerly used to get heavy shear legs aboard a ship when masting without the aid of navy yard facilities.

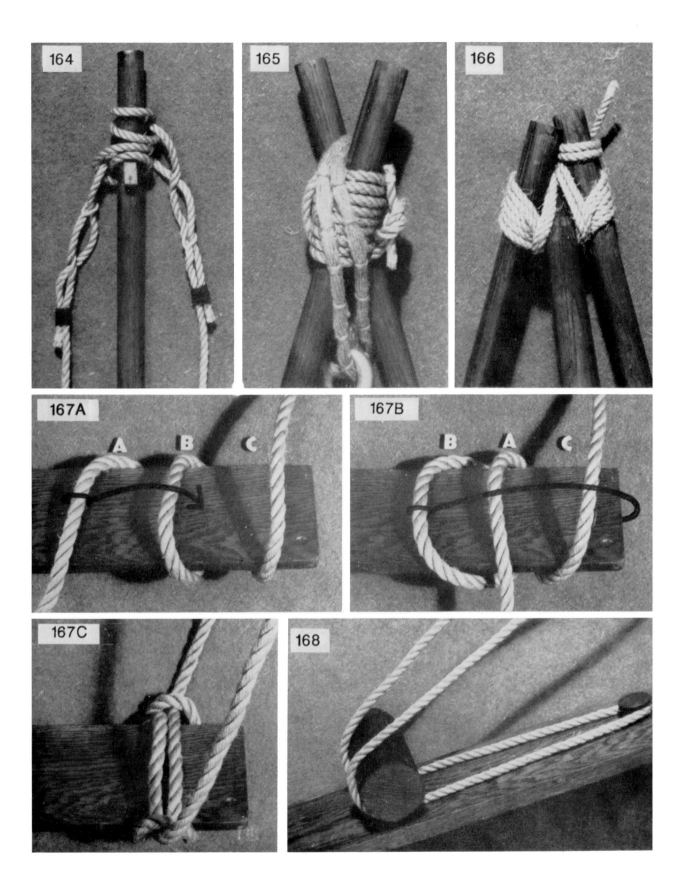

169. The Bale Sling is the same as the lark's head (no. 108). It can be used for bales, sacks, barrels, casks, etc. Compare fig. 116B.

170. This Bale Sling is the same as no. 169, except that it is made with a bowline instead of with a strap.

171. The Barrel Sling (1) is for slinging a barrel with the bung up.

172. The Barrel Sling (2) is for slinging a barrel with the top up.

Fig. 172A: Place the barrel on the rope, and tie the end and the standing part together on top of the barrel with a half-knot. Open the half-knot and spread it out round the barrel.

Fig. 172B: Join the end and the standing part with a bowline knot.

Fig. 172C: Two or more half-knots, if successively opened and spread round the barrel, will give additional security.

173. The Basket Sling, made with two grommet straps, can be used to sling a terra cotta pipe.

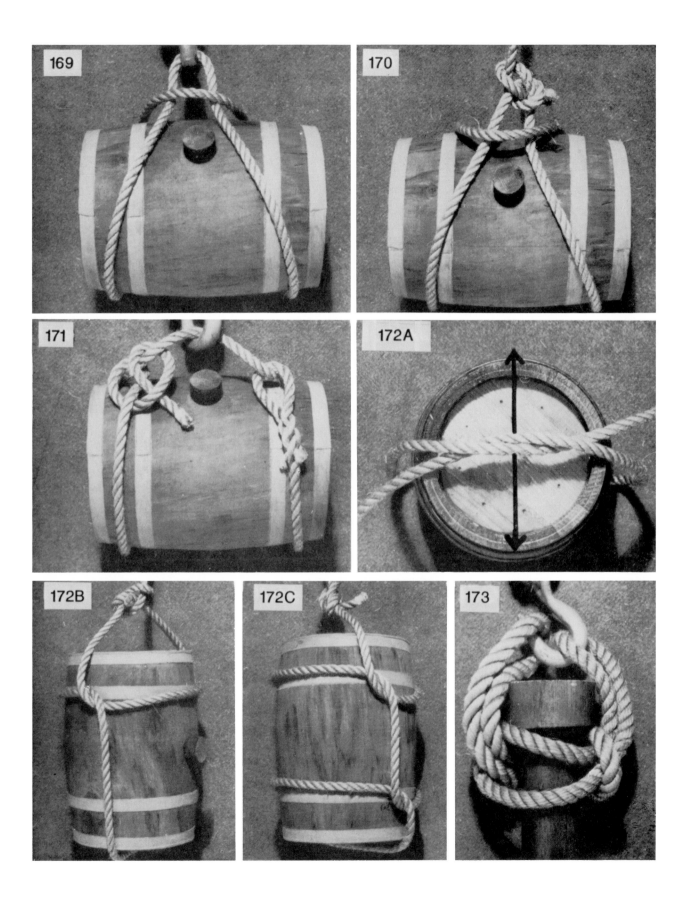

174. Belaying. Halyards, sheets, and running rigging in general are secured to cleats and belaying pins by an operation known as belaying. Figure-eight turns (three or four are ample) constitute the main part of the operation. However, it is possible and sometimes convenient to take an ordinary turn round the cleat or pin, as shown in figs. 174A and 174E, before commencing the figure-eight turns. Or, if it seems easier, the figure-eight turns may be commenced at once, as in figs. 174C, 174D, and 174G. With belaying pins, the halyards may lead either in front of the pin rail, as in fig. 174C, or back of it, as in fig. 174D.

To complete the operation, use a single hitch, as in figs. 174B and 174F. This hitch should always follow the lay of the previous turns; it should not be put on in the lopsided fashion shown in fig. 174I. A final hitch is usually inadvisable when belaying the sheets of small sailboats, or at any time when instantaneous release is important.

Cleats are usually fixed at a slight angle with respect to the lines that are to be belayed on them. The rope is much less likely to jam if it is led to the far end of the cleat, as in figs. 174E and 174G, and not to the near end, as in fig. 174H. Figs. 174H and 174I illustrate practices that should be strictly avoided.

Fig. 174J shows one way of belaying a line on a single bitt with cross-bar or norman.

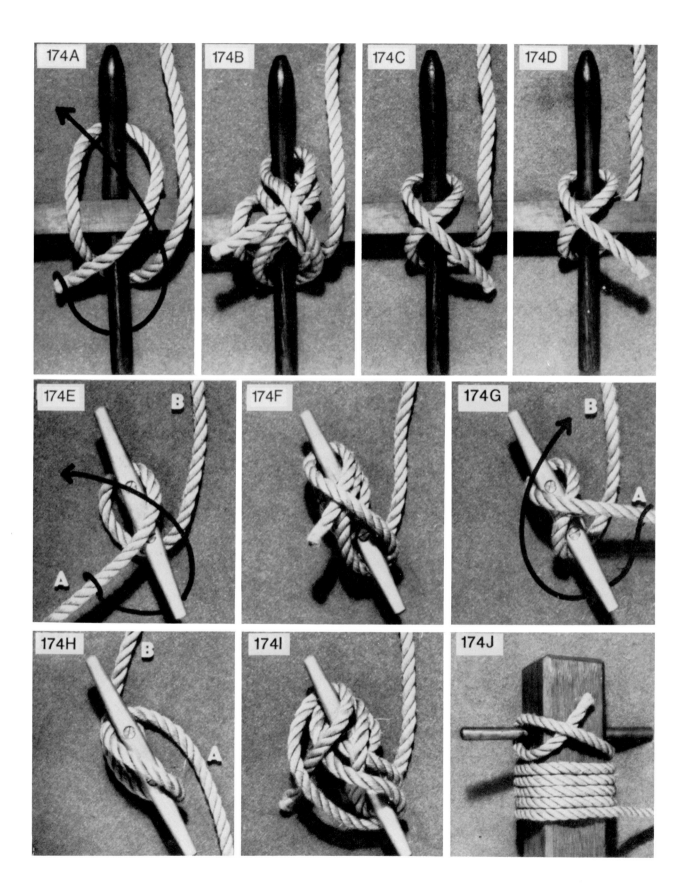

Fig. 174K shows another way to use horizontal figure-eight turns on the cross-bar.

When belaying a line on two bitts, secure the end with a single hitch or with a few turns of marline.

175. Either of two lines can be cast off without disturbing the other line if the eye-splice in the end of the second, before being placed over the bollard, is passed up through the eye-splice in the end of the first.

176. Worming, Parceling, and Serving protect a rope from dampness and chafe.

Fig. 176A: First stretch the rope taut about waist-high. Then, to worm, fill the spiral grooves between the strands with marline, spunyarn, or other stuff of suitable size. In order to work the marline well into the spiral grooves of the rope, pass a soft strand round the rope and secure the end to the handle of the serving mallet. Rotating the mallet heaves the worming taut into the lay. Worming is put on with the lay. Its purpose is to make the rope smooth and cylindrical before parceling and serving.

Fig. 176B: Parceling consists of strips of tarred or waterproof canvas wrapped with the lay over the worming. Parceling is often marled in place (see no. 133).

Fig. 176C: Service is put on against the lay with a serving mallet and marline or spunyarn. Two people are needed, one to pass the ball of marline round the rope, the other to apply the service. (If the mallet is fitted with a reel for the marline, the second person is unnecessary.) The two individuals stand facing each other on opposite sides of the rope, in each case to the right of the rope. The marline is wrapped round the handle of the mallet two or three times, and the mallet is then passed round and round the rope. Each revolution adds one turn to the service. The friction of the marline on the handle of the mallet is the force that determines how taut the service will be, and the amount of friction is determined by the number of times the marline is wrapped round the handle. An old mnemonic couplet goes as follows:

Worm and parcel with the lay;
Turn and serve the other way.

177. The Spanish Windlass is a device for exerting power.

First Method

Fig. 177A: A bar, two marline spikes, and a well-greased line are used to heave the two parts of the rope together when putting on an eye seizing. A timber hitch (no. 107) or a marlinespike hitch (no. 132) can be used to secure the line to the marlinespikes.

Second Method

Fig. 177B: One end of the rope (*C*) is tied to the object that is to be moved, the other end (*D*) to a fixed anchorage, such as a tree. The bar (*B*) is then rotated round the upright (*A*). This device can be used to loosen or start an object that is stuck, but not to pull an object any distance.

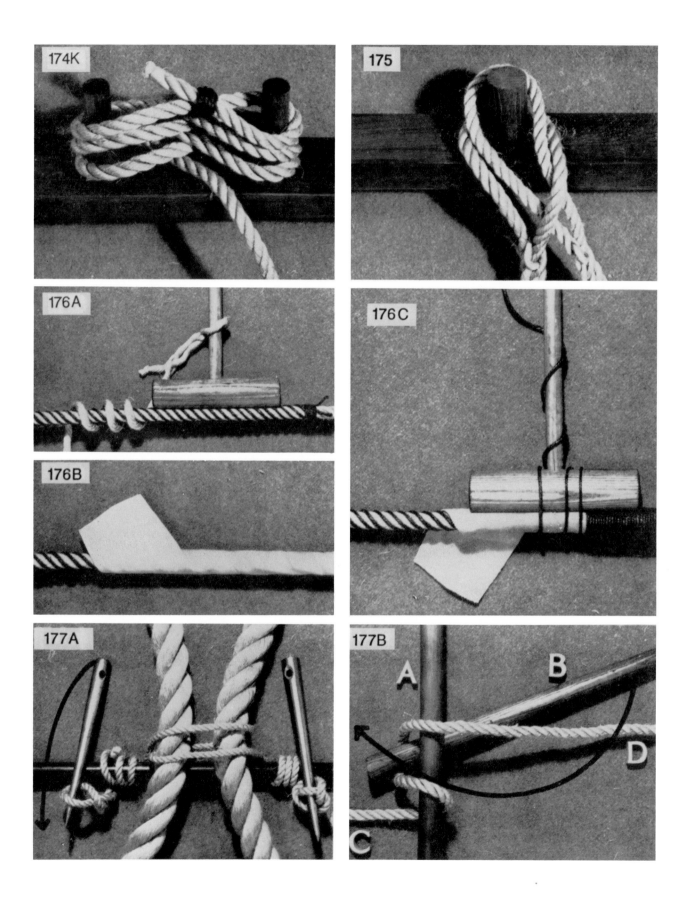

178. The Short Splice is the strongest way to join the ends of two ropes. It is stronger than the long splice, but it increases the diameter of the rope so that the rope cannot be run over a sheave.

Fig. 178A: Unlay the strands a short distance, and *crotch* them or *marry* them. The illustration explains these terms.

Fig. 178B: Hold the strands of one of the ropes in place with the hand, or stop them down temporarily. Then, beginning with any strand of the other rope, tuck it over one strand and under one strand, against the lay. In the same way tuck the two remaining strands.

Fig. 178C: The first tuck is usually comparatively easy, since the ropes are not yet closely joined, and the strands are still open. For subsequent tucks it may be desirable to use a marlinespike or fid to force an opening between the strands.

Fig. 178D: An opening in very small rope can often be made by holding the rope firmly, as illustrated, and untwisting the strands at the desired point.

Fig. 178E: One strand has here been tucked, but not pulled all the way through.

Fig. 178F: With small rope, and especially when the strands are opened, as in fig. 178D, it is often convenient to push a bight instead of the end of the strand through the opening, and then by means of the bight to pull the end through the rest of the way.

Fig. 178G: Three strands have been tucked once each. Remove the temporary stopping and tuck the opposite three strands, once each, against the lay.

Fig. 178H: The strands have been tucked twice each, and the job is finished. Three tucks are sometimes considered desirable. Leave the ends long enough so that they will not tend to work out.

179. The Long Splice does not increase the diameter of the rope appreciably, and therefore the rope can be run over a sheave.

Fig. 179A: Unlay the strands several feet, and crotch them.

Fig. 179B: Unlay *A* a considerable distance farther, and lay up *D* in the spiral groove vacated by *A*. Do the same in the opposite direction with *F* and *B*. Three pairs of strands should now intersect at three different points. (These points should be farther apart than the photograph indicates.) The problem that remains is to dispose of the intersecting pairs of strands; of the several ways to do this, three are described here.

First Method

Fig. 179C: If a slight increase in diameter is unobjectionable, knot each pair of strands with a half-knot.

Fig. 179D: Tuck *each* strand twice against the lay. Halve each strand and tuck once or twice again. (In fig. 179D, each strand of a typical pair has been tucked once.)

Second Method

Fig. 179E: Knot each pair of strands with a half-knot, and tuck with the lay. Tucking with the lay means winding each strand spirally round the opposing strand. This is equivalent to tucking each strand against the lay over one and under *two*. (In fig. 179E, each strand of a typical pair has been tucked once with the lay.)

Fig. 179F: One strand of a typical pair has been tucked twice with the lay, halved, and tucked again. The half-knot joining the two strands is near the right-hand margin of the photograph.

Third Method

Fig. 179G: If the diameter must be as small as possible, halve each strand, and knot half of one strand with half of the other (the two halves at the left in the photograph). Cut off the unused halves later.

Fig. 179H: Tuck the knotted halves several times, either with or against the lay, removing some of the yarns at each tuck. (In fig. 179H, the half-knot is in the center of the picture. The unused halves of the two strands have been cut off. Each strand is tucked with the lay, some of the yarns having been removed at each tuck. The ends of the strands disappear off the edge of the photograph to the left and right.)

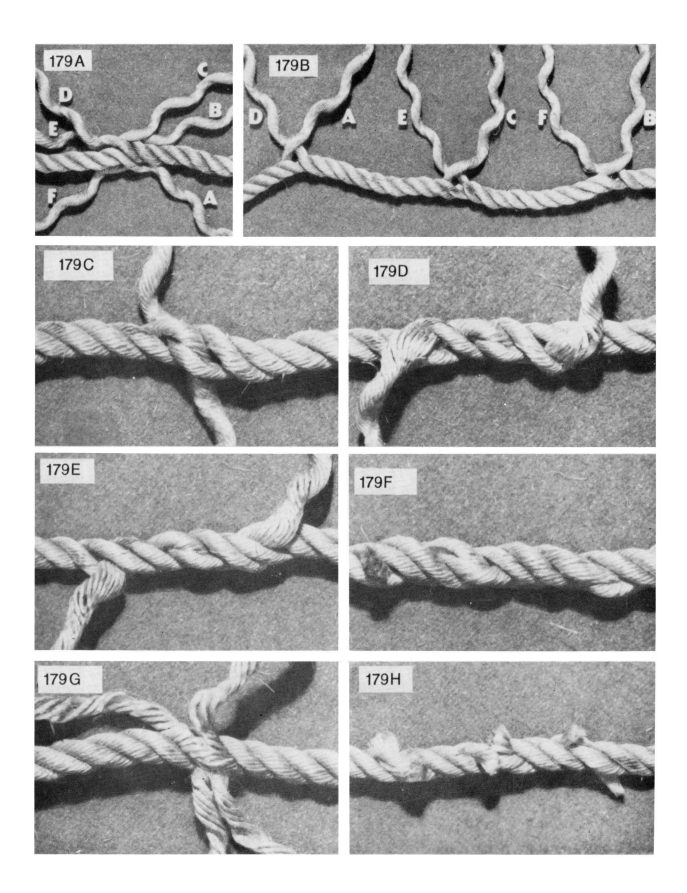

180. The Eye-Splice.

Fig. 180A: Unlay the strands a short distance. Tuck the middle strand (*X*) under one strand, *against* the lay.

Fig. 180B: Tuck *Y* under the next strand.

Fig. 180C: Turn the work over, and tuck *Z* under the remaining strand.

Fig. 180D: Tuck each strand a second time, over one and under one, against the lay.

Fig. 180E: Tuck each strand a third time. (For ordinary purposes two tucks are probably enough, but Henderson and Birdsall's tests show that three tucks are needed if the tension is severe.) The eye-splice can be made directly round a thimble, or a thimble can be inserted after the splice is complete. Do not cut the ends off too close, or they may work out. Figs. 180D and 180E show the two sides of the splice.

Another type of eye-splice, called the *sail-maker's eye-splice,* is made by tucking the strands *with* the lay. That is, each strand is wrapped spirally round the opposing strand, with the lay. This result is attained by tucking each strand over one and under *two,* against the lay. Henderson and Birdsall's tests indicate that the sailmaker's eye-splice has a higher breaking strength than the mariner's eye-splice, but that it is more apt to work loose.

Fig. 180F: With four-strand rope, tuck *X* under one strand and *Y* under one strand. Turn the work over, and tuck the two remaining strands under one strand each. Then proceed as with three-strand rope. According to Henderson and Birdsall, this method is stronger than the *yachtman's eye-splice,* in which *Y* enters beside *X* and is initially tucked under two strands instead of under one.

181. The Artificial, Flemish, Made, or Spindle Eye-Splice.

Fig. 181A: Whip the rope near the end, unlay the strands to that point, and separate the strands into yarns. Divide the yarns into two equal groups, and knot them, one pair at a time, with half-knots, round a spindle or spar the size of the desired eye.

Fig. 181B: Distribute the half-knots at different points round the spindle. With several lengths of marline, bind the knotted yarns in place. This can be done most easily if the lengths of marline are laid out along the spindle before the yarns are knotted.

Fig. 181C: Cut off and scrape down the ends of the yarns, parcel, and serve with marline.

The spindle eye was mentioned by Steel in 1794 and illustrated by Lever in 1808.

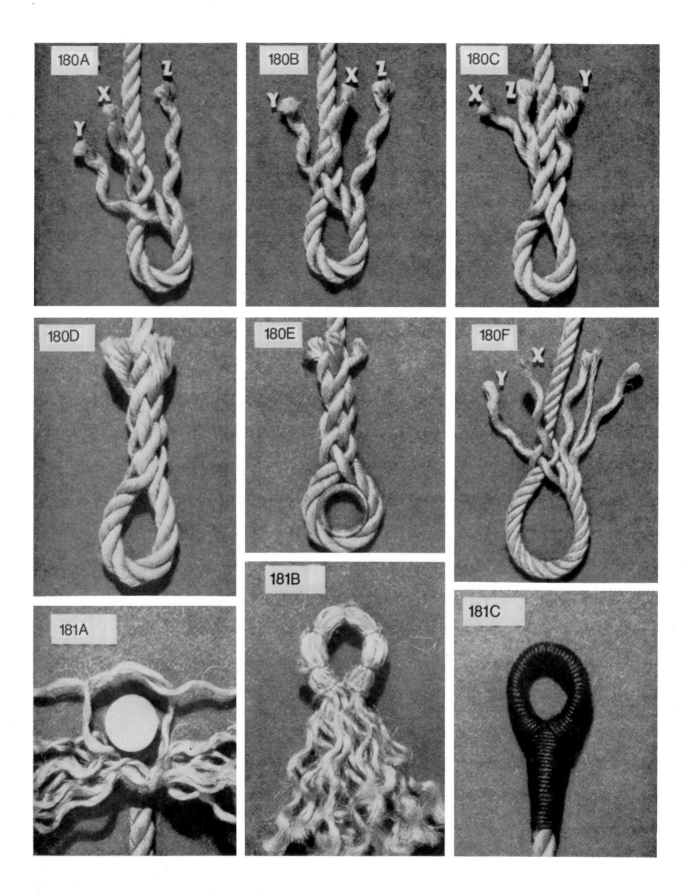

182. The Chain Splice.

Fig. 182A: Unlay the strands a considerable distance. Reeve two of the strands through the end link of the chain. Unlay the third strand a couple of feet farther.

Fig. 182B: Tuck the first or lower strand back under the second or upper strand.

Fig. 182C: Lay up the second strand in the groove vacated by the third strand. When the second and third strands meet, half-knot them together.

Fig. 182D: Tuck the two knotted strands, as in making a long splice (no. 179). Tuck the first strand over and under against the lay two or three times.

183. The Tucked or Marline Splice. Tuck each end twice through the center of the opposite standing part. This splice serves the same purpose as the rope-yarn knot (no. 48).

184. The Tucked or Marline Eye-Splice is analogous to no. 183 and is used in putting on the first turn of a seizing (no. 153).

185. The Grommet or Grummet is made with a single strand, which should be considerably more than three times as long as the circumference of the grommet. Lay up this strand on itself in the form of a circle, and when the ends come together, knot them and tuck them as in making a long splice (no. 179). If the grommet is small, the ends can sometimes be cut off short, after being half-knotted, without being tucked. Grommets are used for chest handles, quoits, straps, etc.

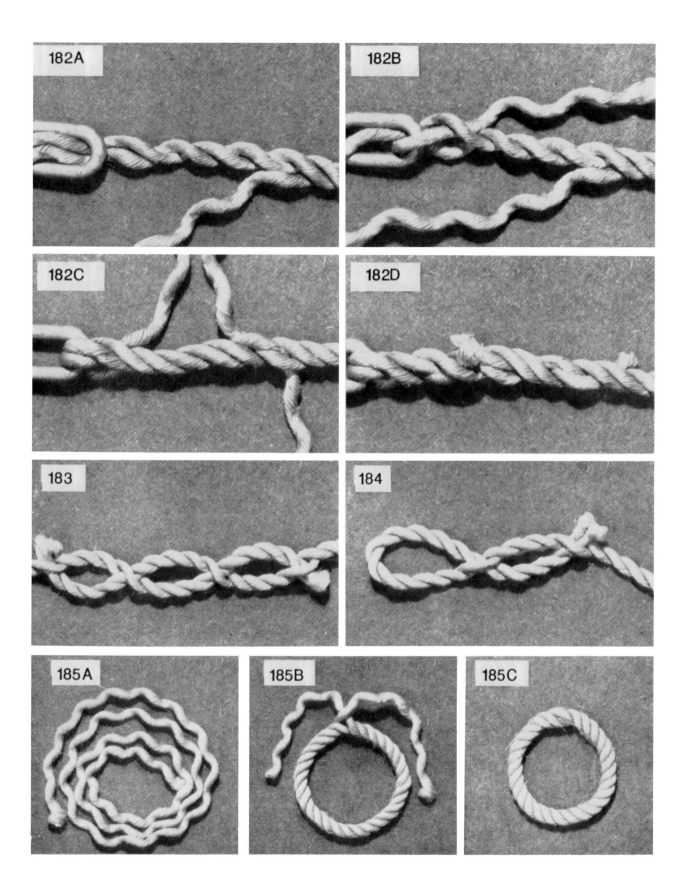

186. The Cringle, like the grommet, is made with a single strand, but it is worked into another rope, such as the bolt-rope of a sail. Captain John Smith spelled the word *creengle* in 1627.

First Method

Fig. 186A: Take a strand of suitable length and stick it under two strands in the bolt-rope (if the bolt-rope has four strands), or under one strand (if the bolt-rope has three strands).

Fig. 186B: Lay up the two ends of the strand on the cringle.

Fig. 186C: When each end has reached the opposite side of the cringle, stick it under one strand of the bolt-rope.

Fig. 186D: Tuck the two ends against the lay, over and under, two or three times.

Second Method

Fig. 186E: To make a cringle round a thimble, reeve the ends of a suitable strand through the eyelet holes in the sail.

Fig. 186F: Lay the ends of the strand up on the cringle, and reeve them through the eyelet holes again.

Fig. 186G: Lay the strands up a second time, until they meet at the top.

Fig. 186H: The cringle should be somewhat smaller than the thimble. Stretch it by hammering a fid into the hole, insert the thimble quickly, and allow the cringle to shrink down on the thimble.

Fig. 186I: Cut off the ends.

186A

186B

186C

186D

186E

186F

186G

186H

186I

187. The Long Splice in Wire Rope. Splicing wire rope is more difficult in practice than in theory. Special tools are needed, such as a rigger's vise, a rigging screw, wire cutters, several steel splicing pins and spikes, and two wooden mallets. The difficulties to be overcome vary with the size of the rope, the kind of steel that the rope is made of, the number of strands and the way they are laid up, and other factors. Only general directions for one of the basic splices are given here.

Fig. 187A: Unlay the strands in pairs (15 or 20 feet for rope half an inch in diameter) and whip them, or dip the ends in solder. (When a blowtorch is used to cut the rope, the ends of the strands are sometimes sealed by the heat of the torch, but this practice has disadvantages.) Crotch the two ropes.

Fig. 187B: Unlay one pair of strands several feet farther, and lay up the opposing pair in the groove vacated by the first pair. Treat two other pairs in the same way, but in the opposite direction. The result will be six pairs of strands meeting at three different points. The illustration shows one of these points.

Fig. 187C: Divide the pairs of strands in similar fashion, until there are twelve separate strands meeting at six different points. The illustration shows one of these points.

To this stage, the method is analogous to the long splice in hemp. But the strands are now disposed of in a different way. A steel spike is inserted at the point where two strands meet, the spike is forced down through the center of the rope, and the manila heart or core is cut in two. The end of the heart protrudes from the opening made by the point of the spike. The spike is now rotated in such a way that it moves along the axis of the rope and forces the manila heart out through the opening in front of the spike.

Fig. 187D: As the heart is removed, the wire strand is laid up in its place in the center of the rope.

Fig. 187E: The manila heart is cut off when the end of the wire strand is reached.

Fig. 187F: The other eleven strands are treated in the same way. The joint between any two strands of a pair is hardly noticeable.

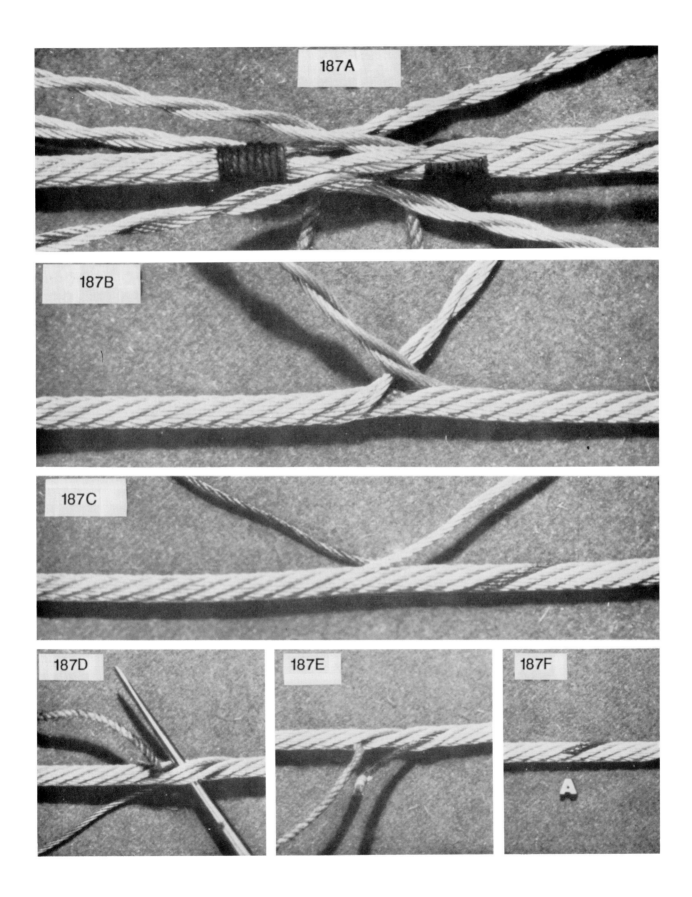

187A

187B

187C

187D

187E

187F

153

188. The Eye-Splice in Wire Rope.

Fig. 188A: Bend the rope round a pear-shaped thimble two or three feet from the end. For this purpose a rigger's vise is essential. Whip the ends of the strands, or dip them in solder, and unlay them as far as the thimble. Tuck the first strand, *H,* under three strands. (In the illustration, *N* is the fiber heart or core.)

Fig. 188B: Tuck *I* under two strands, entering between the same two strands as *H.*

Fig. 188C: Tuck *J* under one strand, entering between the same two strands as *H* and *I.*

Fig. 188D: Turn the rope over, replace it in the vice, and tuck *K* under one strand.

Fig. 188E: Tuck *L* under one strand.

Fig. 188F: Tuck *M* under one strand. All six strands have now been tucked once each, and should come out between six different pairs of strands in the standing part.

Each strand is now tucked two or three times more, tapered, and tucked two or three times again. Tucks are made with the lay, a process that consists, essentially, of winding each strand spirally round a corresponding strand in the standing part. Except when *H, I,* and *J* are tucked for the first time, the strands should be untwisted once or twice at each tuck, so that they may lie flat and become one with the strands about which they are wrapped. The steel spike, when an opening is forced, should not be inserted at the point where the tuck is desired, but some distance along the rope, away from the thimble. In this way the strand can be pulled through more easily, and at once falls into place when a rotating pressure is exerted on the handle of the spike. Before it is possible to force an opening in large rope, it is usually necessary to untwist the whole rope to some extent by means of a bar or other form of leverage.

Fig. 188G: Each strand has been tucked twice.

Fig. 188H: Each strand has been tucked three times whole, then tapered and tucked, and tapered and tucked again. In tapering, about a third of the wires are removed before each tuck. The final tucks should be made carefully, for the splice is most likely to fail at this point. The finished splice should be hammered into symmetry, beginning at the point nearest the thimble and working toward the standing part. However, the wires must not be hammered or pried too far out of shape, lest the rope be weakened. In splicing large rope, there is bound to be a good deal of distortion and consequent weakening, so that, according to John Cutter, of the John A. Roebling Sons Company, a 2½-inch wire rope with an eye-splice in it may be only about 50 percent efficient. Very small rope, spliced, may be 95 percent efficient.

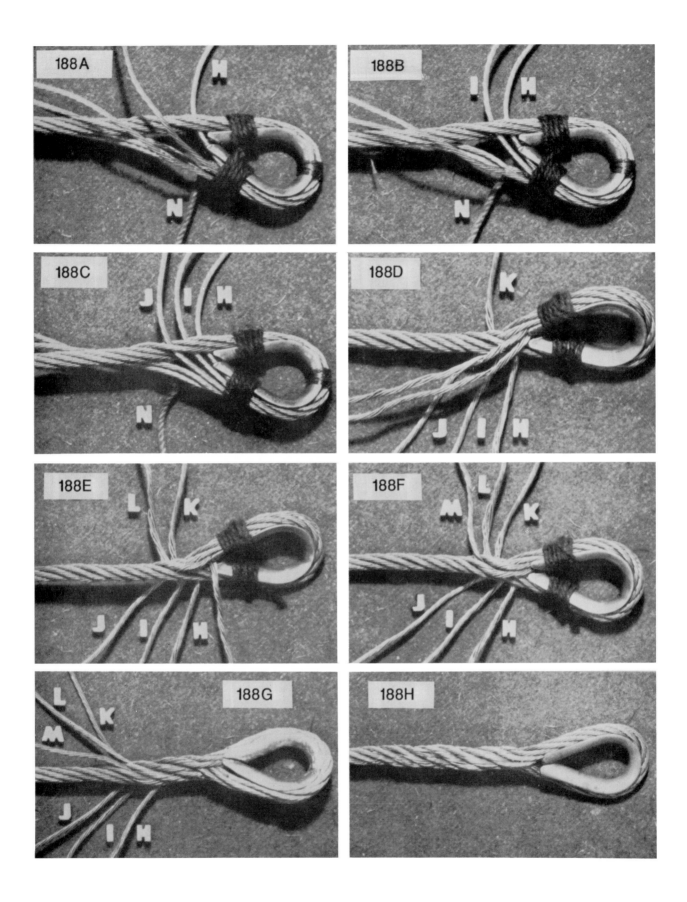

189. The Swage Eye-Splice or Mechanical Eye-Splice in Wire Rope. The Nicropress method of swaging wire rope is demonstrated here.

Fig. 189A: Pictured are two types of Nicropress tool presses. The top press is a multipurpose tool, used for four different sizes of wire rope. The bottom tool is designed for use with ¼-inch wire rope and is the tool used in figs. 189D and 189E. Select the correct tool press and correct size Nicropress sleeve for the size of wire rope being swaged. Before the job is begun, the press should be closed without the sleeve in it; a preload should be felt. If there is no preload, the manufacturer's instructions for adjusting the tool should be followed.

Fig. 189B: To begin the eye-splice, insert the wire rope carefully into the sleeve while turning the sleeve in the same direction as the lay of the wire rope. This helps prevent the wire rope from unlaying. Pull an excess of the wire rope through the sleeve. Any other accessories, such as a thimble (as illustrated) or a shackle, can now be positioned in the loop. Carefully insert the end back through the sleeve, again twisting in the direction of the lay. While some literature states that the loop can be any size, it is recommended that a thimble be used to reduce abrasion on the inside wires of the wire rope.

Fig. 189C: Pulling an excess of the wire rope through the sleeve makes it easier to adjust the wire rope round the thimble. This is accomplished by pulling the standing part of the wire away from the sleeve with one hand while maintaining enough pressure on the wire/sleeve with the other hand so as not to pull the bitter end of the wire rope back out of the sleeve.

Fig. 189D: Position the center of the sleeve in the groove in the Nicropress tool and close the tool just enough to hold the sleeve securely. The rounded sides of the sleeve must fit into the grooves of the press properly, and the sleeve must be positioned as in fig. 189D. Make the final adjustment of the loop size by again pulling on the standing part of the wire rope. Leave at least one-eighth of an inch of the bitter end protruding out of the sleeve. Then compress the tool slowly and completely, making the first press into the sleeve. It may be helpful, when using a large tool press, to position one handle of the tool on the floor or deck. Operate the tool's other handle with one hand, leaving one hand free to adjust and position the wire rope and sleeve.

Fig. 189E: After the first press is made, rotate the wire and sleeve 180 degrees and reposition it in the grooves of the Nicropress tool. The rotation helps prevent the sleeve from becoming bent or "bananaing" during the process. It is important not to position the grooves of the press flush with the end of the sleeve. When the wire is properly positioned, compress the tool slowly and completely again to put in the second press. The third press can be applied near the opposite end of the sleeve without rotating the wire rope.

Fig. 189F: The completed Nicropress swage.

Fig. 189G: A "go-gauge," sized for the wire rope, should be used to make sure the tool has compressed the Nicropress sleeve the proper amount. Another method is to measure the diameter of the sleeve, again from round edge to round edge, with calipers. The diameter must fall within the tolerances in table 6.

Table 6. Tolerances for Compressed Wire Rope

Diameter of Wire Rope (in inches)	After-Press Diameter (in inches)		Number of Compressions
	Minimum	Maximum	
¹⁄₁₆	.174	.182	2
³⁄₃₂	.236	.263	2
⅛	.335	.351	3
⁵⁄₃₂	.371	.388	3
³⁄₁₆	.450	.473	3
¼	.550	.583	3
⁵⁄₁₆	.680	.718	3

Source: *Instructions for UniGrip Tools and Sleeves.*
Table courtesy of Universal Wire Products, Inc.

Each compression should be checked. If the "go-gauge" will not pass over the sleeve, or the measurements fall outside of the tolerances, the press tool must be adjusted.

190. The Lap Splice is used to join two bitter ends of a wire rope, or the bitter ends of two different wire ropes. Making a full-strength lap splice generally requires using two Nicropress sleeves. Follow the same basic steps as for the swage eye-splice (no. 189), working on one sleeve at a time. A short gap should be left between the two sleeves.

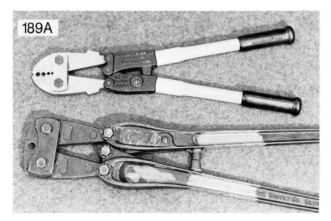

189A

189B

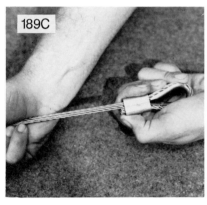

189C

189D

189E

189F

189G

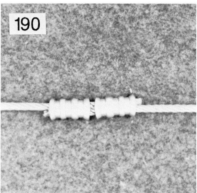

190

157

191. The Tail Splice, for splicing hemp or manila rope tails to flexible wire running rigging, is used on sailing yachts and is said to have been originated by Nat Herreshoff.

Fig. 191A: Whip the ends of the strands with sail twine, and unlay the strands to point *E*. Whip the rope at *E*, and lay up the alternate strands *M, N,* and *O* as far as point *F*. Whip these three strands at *F*.

Fig. 191B: Lay the wire rope in the groove between any two of the strands in the hemp rope, as far as point *E*.

Fig. 191C: Bring the alternate strands *J, K,* and *L* out from the center of the hemp rope, in each case between a different pair of hemp strands.

Fig. 191D: Lay the wire rope farther along in the same groove, as far as point *F*. At *F* bring strands *M, N,* and *O* out from the center of the rope, in each case between a different pair of hemp strands. The result is a hemp rope with a wire heart, with three strands of the wire heart protruding at each of two different points, namely, *E* and *F*.

To dispose of these six ends, a special tubular needle is required. With the aid of this needle each wire strand is stitched right through the opposing hemp strand, instead of being tucked over and under the hemp strands. The wire strands may be stitched either with or against the lay, but in either case they disappear completely from view. After each strand has been stitched from four to eight times, the ends are cut off close. At the points where the ends are cut off, the hemp rope is served with sail twine. The ends of the hemp rope are combed out, tapered, marled, and served with sail twine.

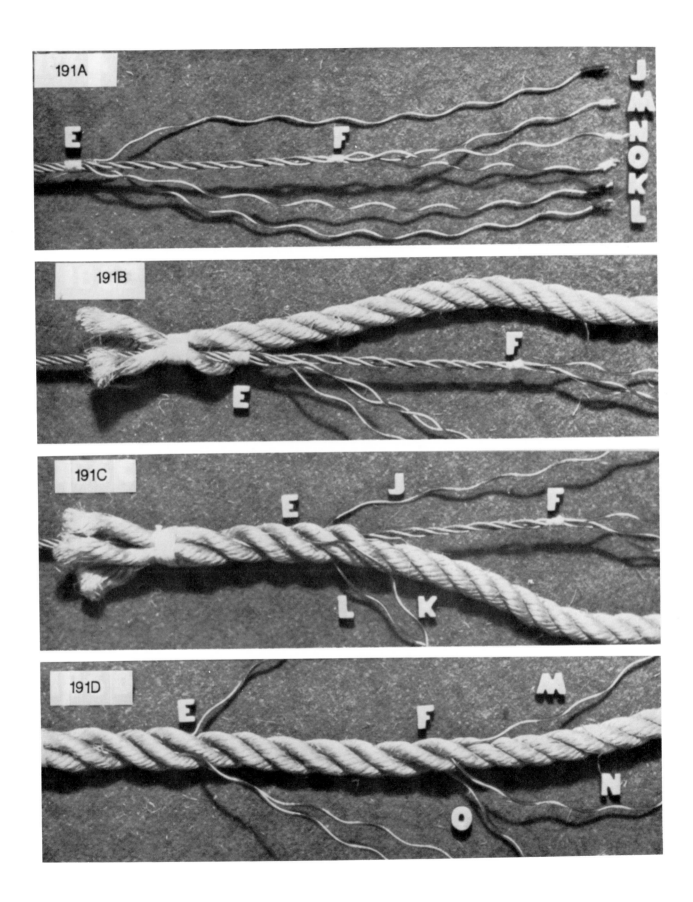

192. Double-Braid Splices. Splicing double-braided synethetic ropes can be easily accomplished. The construction of double-braid splices uses the same theory that holds Chinese handcuffs together. Nos. 193 to 197 are suitable splices for double-braided synthetic ropes.

In fig. 192 are pictured some of the common tools and materials for splicing double-braided lines. Included are sail twine and needles, electrical tape, sail wax, a pusher, a hollow fid, three tubular fids of different sizes, a pair of scissors, and two marking pens.

193. The Basic Eye-Splice.

Fig. 193A: Secure the end of the line with tape. Mark the line *O* one tubular fid length from the bitter end. The size of the fid must be appropriate for the size of the line. Starting from point *O*, make a loop the size required, then mark the other end of the loop *X*. From *X*, measure off four or more fid lengths and tie a slip knot in the line.

Fig. 193B: Fold the line at point *X* and pry out the core using a pusher. As the core first comes out of the cover, mark it *I*.

Fig. 193C: Pull out the remainder of the core, and tape its end.

Fig. 193D: Slide the cover off the core toward the slip knot. From point *I*, measure one short fid length (which is marked on the fid), and mark that point *II*. From point *II*, measure one full fid length and one short fid length, and mark that point *III*.

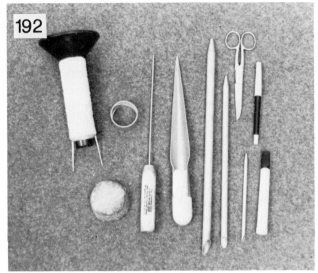

192

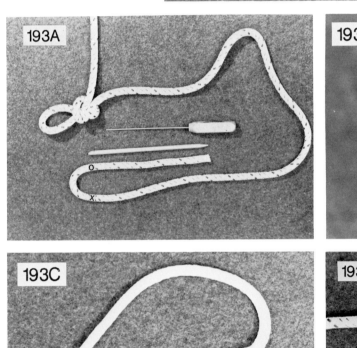

193A

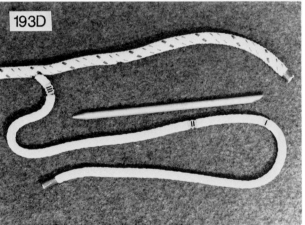

193B

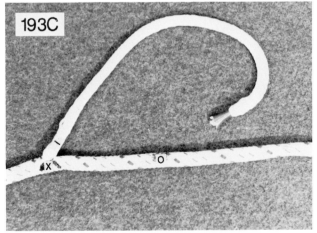

193C

193D

Figs. 193E and 193F: If it is desirable to have a shackle or thimble with ears in the eye, now is the time to place it on the cover. Fig. 193E shows a shackle being spliced in. Insert the fid into the core at point *II* and out at point *III*. Insert the end of the cover into the fid and push it out through point *III,* as in fig. 193F. (Cutting across part of the taped end of the cover at an angle may facilitate its insertion into the fid.)

Figs. 193G to 193I: Insert the fid into the cover at point *O* and out at point *X*. To minimize the possibility of cutting the core too short during the last step and ending up with one side of the splice collapsed, as illustrated in fig. 193S, keep the core inside the cover until 1–2 inches past point *X*. Then bring it out. All remaining steps are then done as illustrated. Put the end of the core through the shackle and into the fid. Push the fid out through point *X,* as in fig. 193H. Then pull the shackle over the cover and place it between points *O* and *X*. Now pull the core out of point *X*. Then pull tightly on both the core and the cover to tighten the crossover. See fig. 193I.

Fig. 193J: Remove the tape from the end of the cover and unravel the braid.

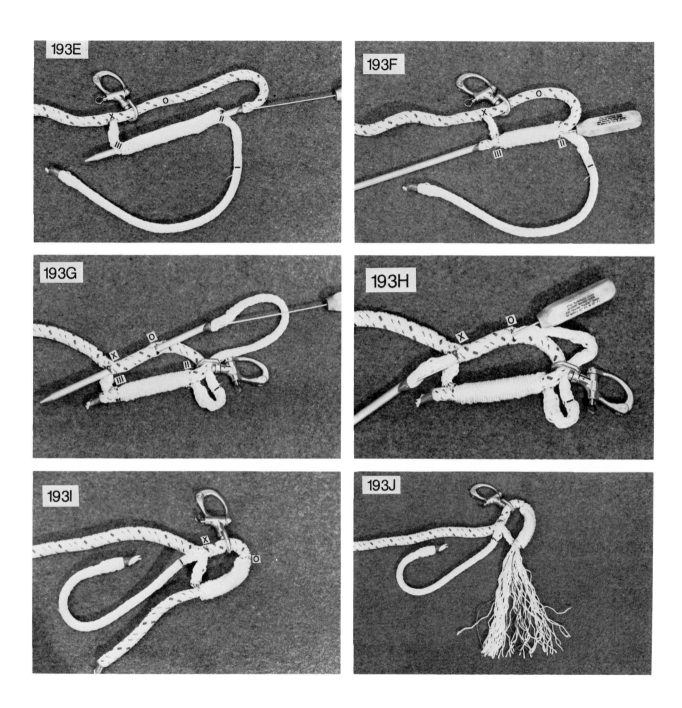

Fig. 193K: Cut off groups of strands at different intervals to form a tapered end.

Figs. 193L to 193N: Hold loop at crossover and pull both sides away from crossover to smooth out loop. See figs. 193M and 193N. Tapered tail should disappear from view.

Fig. 193O: Hold rope at slip knot and slide or "milk" cover firmly toward eye.

Fig. 193P: The crossover will bury itself inside the cover. The crossover must become completely covered. If bunching occurs at the crossover, smooth it out and pull again sharply.

Figs. 193Q to 193S: Cut off the core tail ⅜ of an inch from point X. The ⅜-inch tail will disappear into the splice when put under a load. The eye will collapse on one side when put under a load, as in fig. 193S, if the ⅜-inch tail is not left and the core is cut too short. To secure the splice, whip it near the throat. Some riggers prefer to lock-stitch the throat rather than whip it. If a thimble with ears was used in the eye, soak the splice in boiling water for several minutes to secure the thimble. (The use of thimbles with ears is highly recommended with synthetic lines, because regular thimbles tend to fall out of the splice after the line has been put under a load several times.) Untie the slip knot.

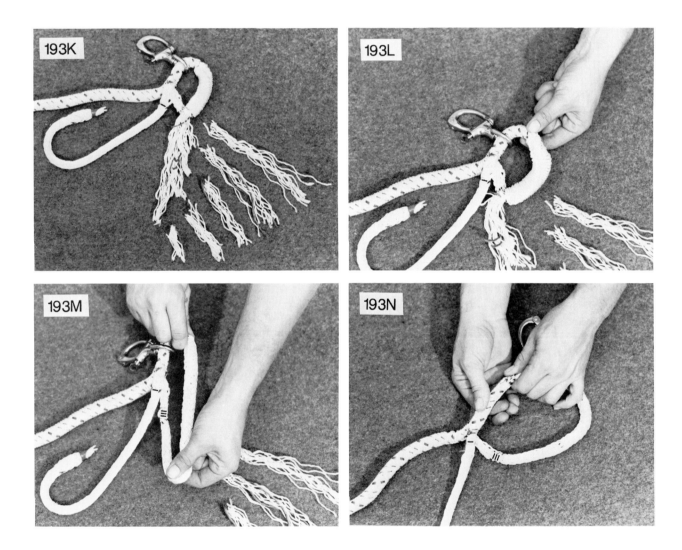

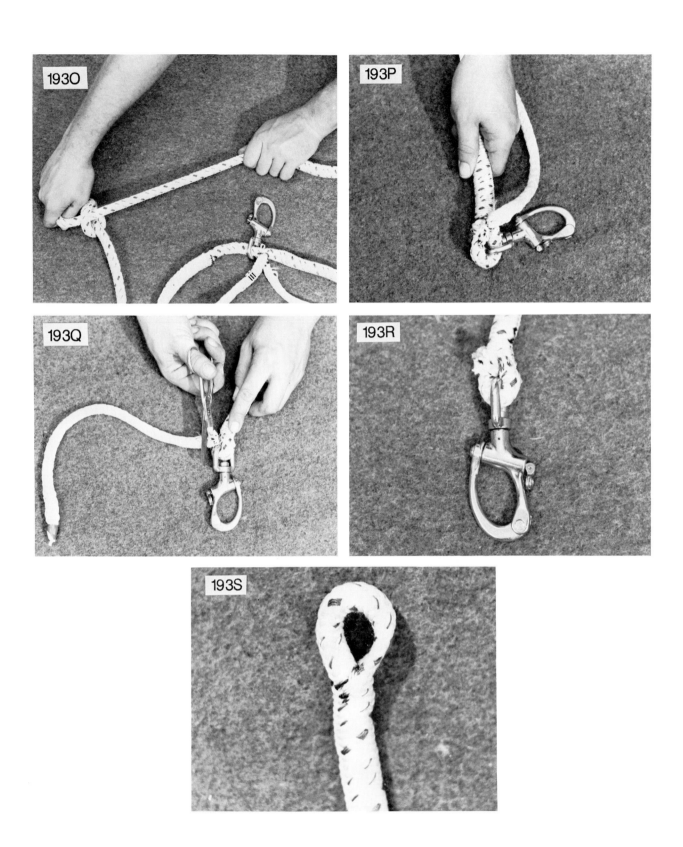

194. The Back Splice can be tapered to reduce bulk, and the length can be adjusted by adjusting the measurements.

Fig. 194A: Mark the line *X* one tubular fid length from the bitter end. Tie a slip knot in the line five or more fid lengths from point *X*.

Fig. 194B: Bend the line sharply at point *X* and pry out the core with a pusher. Mark the core at this point *I*. Pull out the remainder of the core, and tape its end.

Fig. 194C: Slide the cover off the core toward the slip knot. From point *I*, measure one short fid length, and mark that point *II*. From point *II*, measure one full fid length and one short fid length, and mark that point *III*.

Figs. 194D and 194E: Insert the fid into the core at point *II* and out at point *III*. Insert the cover into the fid and push it out through point *III*, as in fig. 194E.

Fig. 194F: Remove the tape from the end of the cover and unravel three-quarters of the cover. Then trim strands to form a taper to avoid blunt ends.

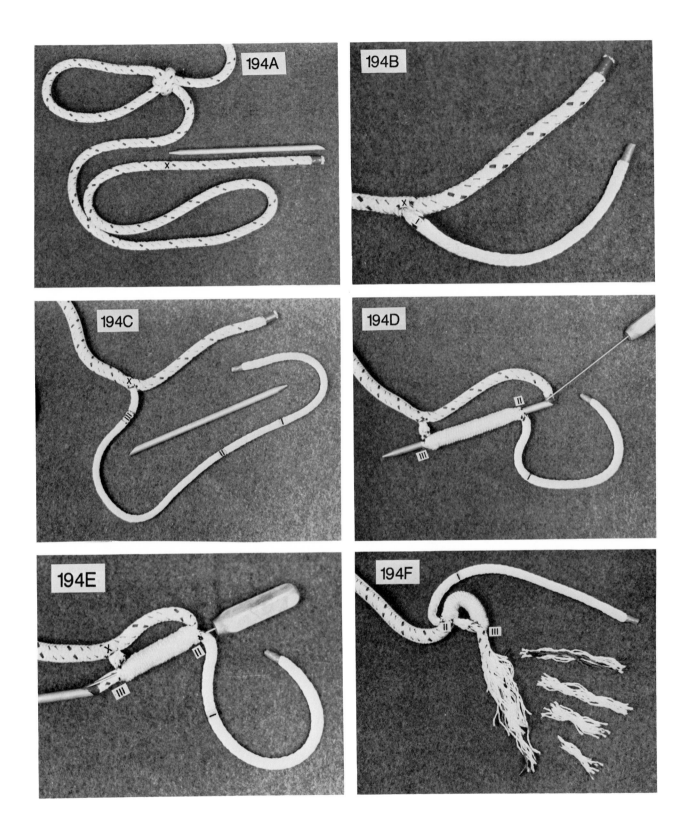

Fig. 194G: Smooth out core from point *II* toward point *III* until the cover just disappears inside the core. Hold the core at point *III* and smooth toward point *II* until a gradual taper is achieved between points *III* and *II*.

Figs. 194H and 194I: Hold the line at the slip knot and "milk" the cover toward splice. The cover will slide over the core at point *X* until all excess is out and point *X* (lump) is well inside the cover. See fig. 194I. Flexing the splice loosens the strands and may help covering. It may also be necessary to secure the slip knot to a fixed object, such as a doorknob or cleat, to assist "milking" in the core.

Figs. 194J and 194K: Cut the core off close to the cover and "milk" the cover to enclose the core end completely. Untie the slip knot.

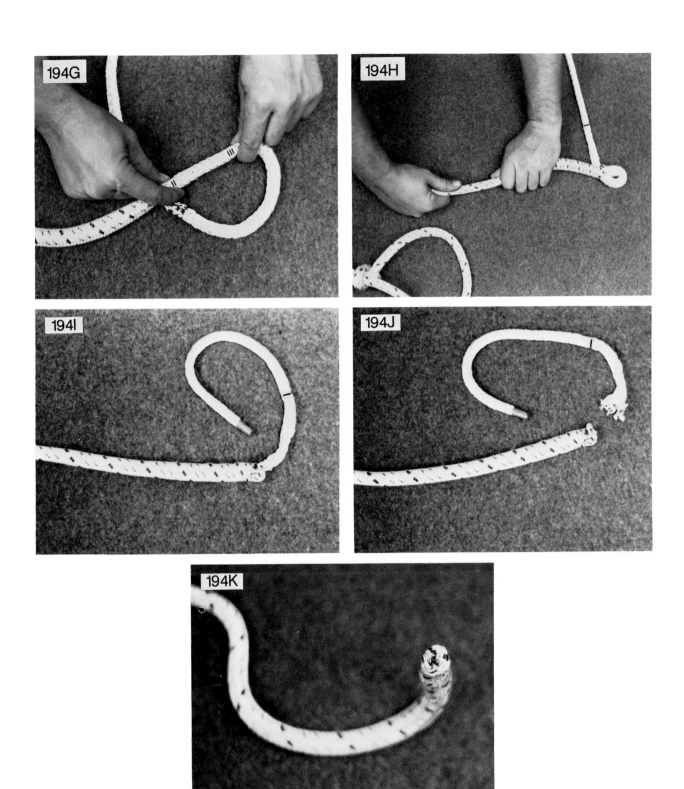

195. The End-for-End Splice can be used to join two double-braid lines or to join two ends of the same double-braid line. A minimum length of 14 fid lengths is required to join the two ends of the same line; this allows 4 fid lengths for the splice itself.

Fig. 195A: Tape the end of each line to be spliced and lay the ends side by side. One tubular fid length from each bitter end, mark the cover point *O*. One short fid length from point *O*, mark the cover point *X*. When joining the ends of two separate lines, tie a slip knot in each five or more fid lengths from point *X*.

Fig. 195B: Bend the lines and extract the cores at point *X*. As the cores first come out of the covers, mark them point *I*. Pull out the remainder of the cores, and tape their ends. Smooth out the lines.

Fig. 195C: Slide the covers off the cores. From point *I*, measure one short fid length, and mark that point *II*. From point *II*, measure one full fid length and one short fid length, and mark that point *III*. Perform the procedure on both lines.

Fig. 195D: Beginning at point *O*, note that the strands are in pairs going to the right and to the left. Starting from the center of point *O* and moving toward the bitter end, mark the eighth pair of strands *T*.

Fig. 195E: Starting at point *T*, mark every second right-hand pair of strands for a total of six marks. Repeat on second line.

Fig. 195F: Again starting at point *T*, mark every second left-hand pair of strands for a total of six marks. Repeat on second line.

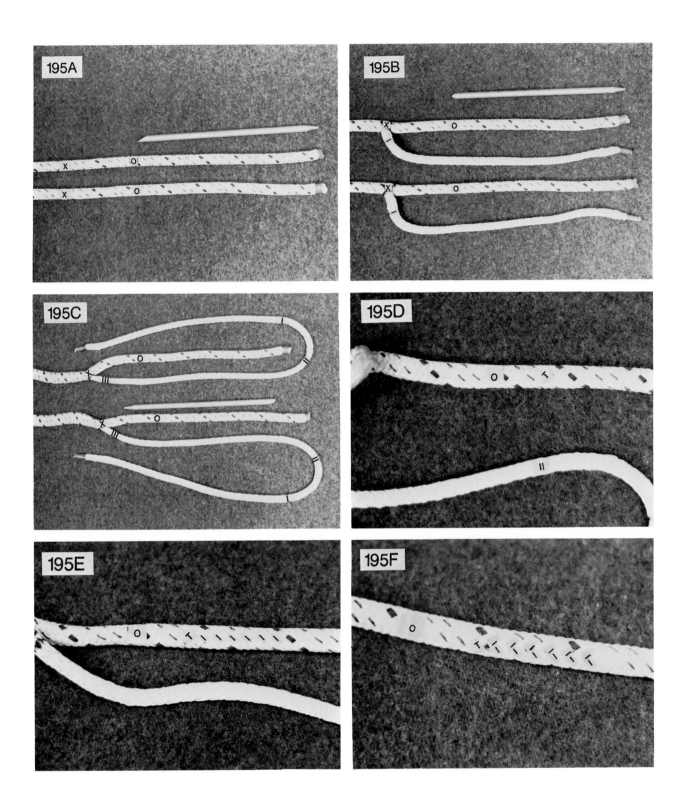

Fig. 195G: Begin cutting the marked strands, cutting the pair closest to the bitter end first. Cut all the marked strands and pull them out. Do not go past point *T*. Repeat on second line.

Fig. 195H: Reposition lines as pictured. Note how the cover of one line is paired with the core of the other line. Avoid twisting.

Figs. 195I to 195K: Insert the fid into the core of one line at point *II* and out at point *III*. Insert the cover of the other line into the fid and push the cover through the core until *T* on the cover meets point *II* on the core. See fig. 195J. Repeat procedure with opposite core and cover. See fig. 195K.

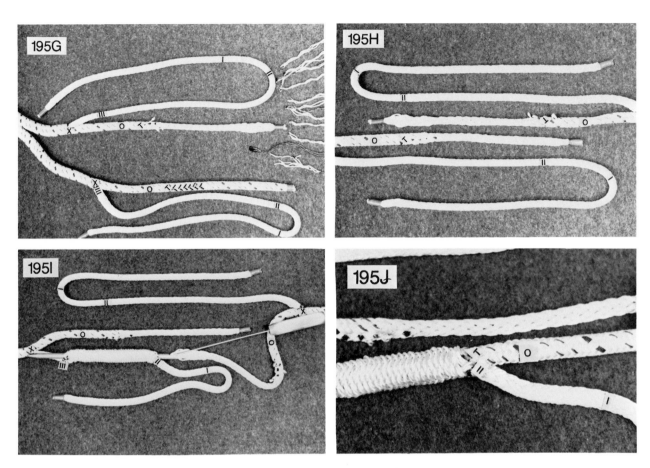

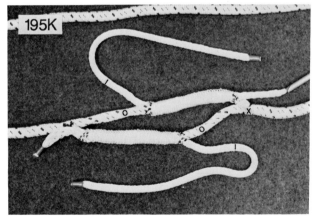

Figs. 195L to 195N: Insert fid into the cover at point *T* and out at point *X*. Insert the core into the fid and push it through. See fig. 195M. Repeat procedure with other line. See fig. 195N.

Fig. 195O: Remove tape from the ends of the covers. Trim the ends of tapered covers at an angle to remove blunt ends. These ends will disappear into the cores at point *III*. Bring up crossovers tightly by pulling up cores and covers.

Fig. 195P: Hold crossover tightly and smooth out braid away from crossover on each line.

Fig. 195Q: Cut core tails off on an angle close to point *X* on each line.

Fig. 195R: Hold the line at the slip knot (or the center, if joining the two ends of the same line) and "milk" cover toward splice and over crossover. Repeat on both sides until all slack in the covers is gone.

Fig. 195S: Both sides of the splice should be of equal length. If they are not, recheck all steps. Untie the slip knots (there are no slip knots if the two ends of the same line were joined).

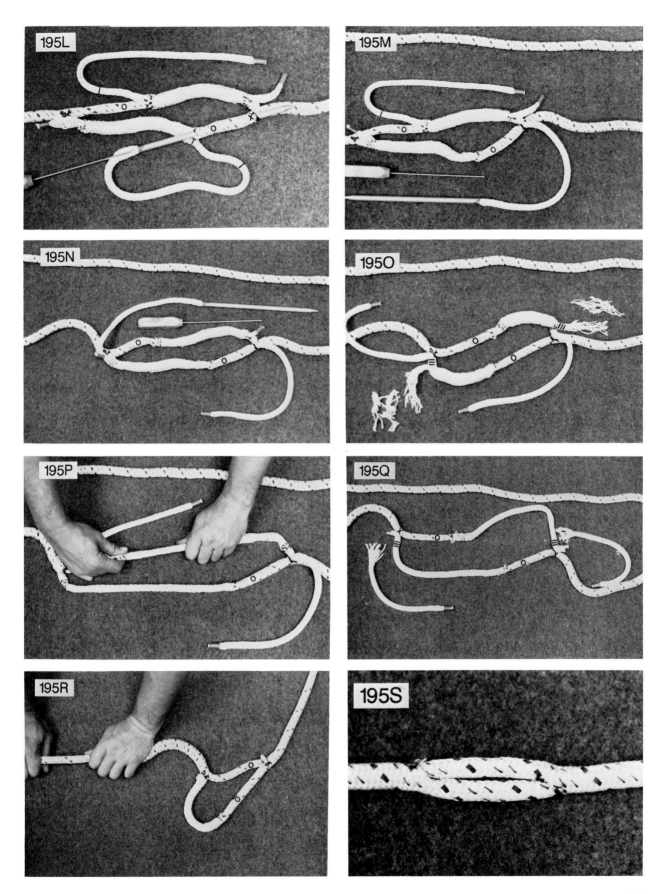

195L

195M

195N

195O

195P

195Q

195R

195S

175

196. The Brummel Splice is a quick and easy splice that is generally used to make Jib or Genoa sheets for sails with the use of only one shackle or Brummel hook.

Fig. 196A: Place shackle or Brummel hook on center of line when making sheets, or where desired if both ends are not to be of the same length. Use a tubular fid twice normal splicing size and insert it perpendicularly through the line at the point where the eye is desired. Tape the end of the line and insert it into the fid. Push the fid and the end of the line through.

Fig. 196B: Pull on the line to make the size eye desired.

Fig. 196C: Insert the fid perpendicularly through the line just pulled through, approximately half an inch from where it exited the first line. Insert the other taped end of the line into the fid and push it through.

Fig. 196D: Pull the line up tightly. This will interlock the splice. (The illustration shows a much shorter line than is required for sheets.)

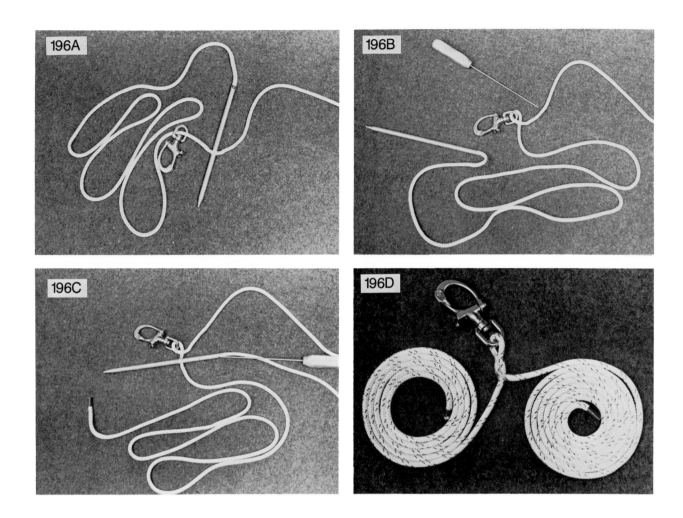

197. The Double-Braided Rope-to-Wire Splice. In splicing double-braided rope to wire, the size guidelines in table 7 should be followed.

Table 7. Size Guidelines, Splicing Double-Braided Rope to Wire

Rope Size (in inches)	Wire Size (in inches)
¼	³⁄₃₂
¼ or ⁵⁄₁₆	⅛
¼, ⁵⁄₁₆, or ⅜	⁵⁄₃₂
⅜ or ⁷⁄₁₆	³⁄₁₆
⅜, ⁷⁄₁₆, or ½	⁷⁄₃₂
⁷⁄₁₆ or ½	¼
½ or ⅝	⁵⁄₁₆

Fig. 197A: Tie a slip knot four to five feet from the end of the rope to be spliced. Slide the cover off the core and mark the core *I* 15 inches from the bitter end. Temporarily tape the end of the core. Now cut 9 inches off the core and tape the end.

Figs. 197B and 197C: Taper the end of the wire for 18 inches. To accomplish this, wrap the wire with plastic electrical tape 18 inches from the end. Unravel and cut the first strand at that point. (Tape the wire at each point where a strand is to be cut to prevent the wire from unravelling.) Unravel and cut the second strand 15 inches from the end. Unravel and cut the third strand 12½ inches from the end. Unravel and cut the fourth strand 10¼ inches from the end. Unravel and cut the fifth strand 8¼ inches from the end. Unravel and cut the sixth (and final) strand 7 inches from the end. To prevent unravelling and chafing, use silver solder (best method), metal furrles, or swedge sleeves on each cut, or wrap plastic electrical tape around the entire wire taper. (In fig. 197C, electrical tape has been used.) Frequently silver solder, swedges, and metal furrles require taping to prevent chafing. Wires with a core should extend 7 inches beyond the taper.

Fig. 197D: Using tape, mark the wire 18 inches from the beginning of the taper.

Fig. 197E: Slide the tapered wire into the center of the core of the rope until the 18-inch mark on the wire is even with the end of the core. (Taping a small fid to the end of the wire may make this step easier. Slide the cover back far enough to recover the small fid when the wire is inserted into the core at proper depth.)

Fig. 197F: Slide back the cover and tape the core tightly 1 to 3 inches in front of the start of the wire taper. (The wire taper should be palpable through the core.)

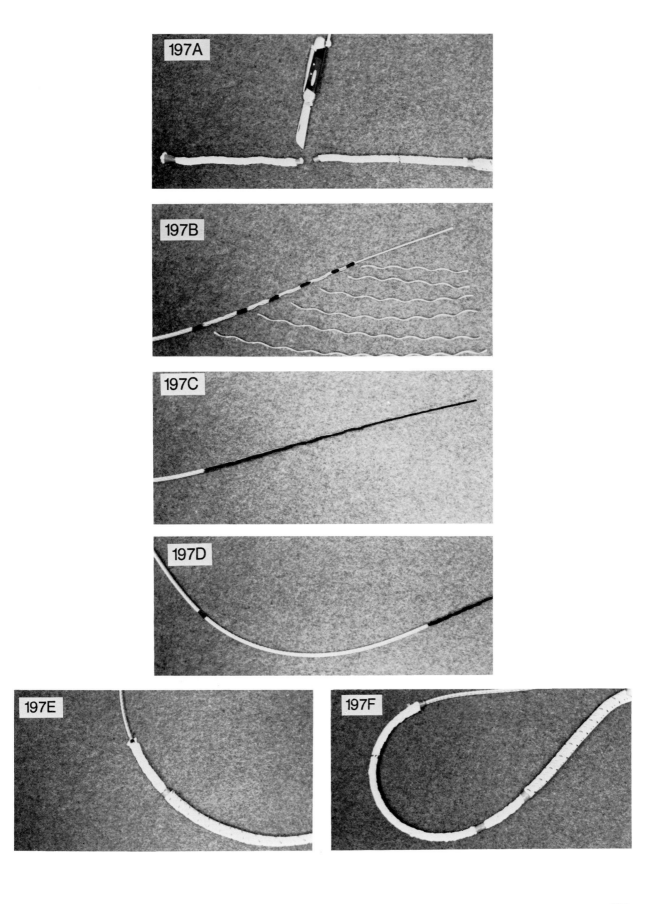

Fig. 197G: Unravel the rope core from the end to the tape. Divide the strands into three equal groups and tape the ends.

Fig. 197H: Separate the wire strands with a hollow fid and wrap one group of rope core strands twice, tightly, round two wire strands. Repeat the wraps with each rope-core strand group, pulling each group of strands up and out to tighten. Wrap strands on right-hand twist wire clockwise, and on left-hand twist wire counterclockwise. After each rope-core strand group has been wrapped twice around two wire strands, cut out one-third of the strands consistently and close to the wire. Repeat this procedure, wrapping and cutting, twice more. Each rope-core strand group will be wrapped around the same two wire strands a total of six times. The wrapped section should also be at least three inches long. The rope-core strand groups must stay with the same wire strand groups for all wraps. In small wire, if the wire core tries to pop out, wrap the wire core along with a group of wire strands. After the sixth wrap, cut off the excess strands close to the wire.

Fig. 197I: "Milk" the cover over the core splice. Make sure that all the slack is out of the cover. Tape the cover tightly over the smallest part of the tapered core splice.

Fig. 197J: Remove the tape from the end of the cover. Unravel the cover from the end to the taped section. Divide the strands into three equal groups and tape the ends. Now repeat the procedure in fig. 197H with the core strands. In this case, the rope-cover strand groups will be wrapped and cut.

Fig. 197K: After splicing the rope-cover strand groups to the wire, remove the tape from the cover. Untie the slip knot and heat the splice slightly, being careful not to burn the rope. Heating the splice will shrink it. Rub the splice with sail wax and heat again, soaking the wax into the rope fibers to help prevent fraying.

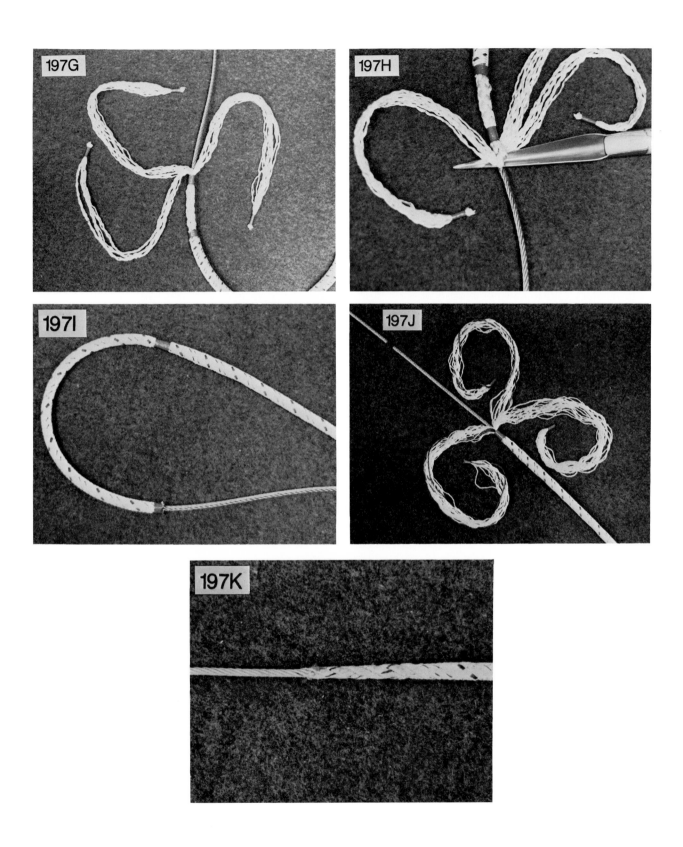

181

198. The Western-Union Splice (see the War Department's *Basic Field Manual* FM24–5) is for splicing two solid conductor insulated wires.

Fig. 198A: Remove the insulation for about 8 inches, and twist the wires together by hand for about 2½ inches.

Fig. 198B: Bend the two ends at right angles to the wire.

Fig. 198C: Wind the ends five or six times round the wire, and cut off the ends. Wrap friction tape round the splice to insulate it.

199. The Lineman's Splice, as shown me by Leon W. Case, is similar to no. 198, but neater.

Fig. 199A: Grip the two ends of the wire with a pair of pliers. (Linemen's pliers are well adapted to this purpose.) Wind the ends at right angles round the standing parts, either in opposite directions, as in no. 198, or in the same direction.

Fig. 199B: The finished splice when the ends are wound in opposite directions.

Fig. 199C: The finished splice when both ends are wound in the same direction. A similar splice is made by machine on barrels, bales, etc. Moses C. Smith patented one such machine in 1876 (U.S. patent no. 178,388), and a splice, or bale-tie, as he called it, in 1878 (U.S. patent no. 206,362).

200. The Field-Wire Splice is for joining flexible wire of several small strands. In the illustrations, the manila rope represents the flexible field wire and the cotton rope represents a piece of solid wire, called the seizing wire, 6 to 8 inches long.

Fig. 200A: Remove the insulation, and tie the ends together with a square knot (no. 24). The square knot should be about a quarter of an inch from the rubber insulation. The braided outside insulation should be removed from the inner, or rubber, insulation for a distance of about half an inch. Insert the seizing wire through the center of the square knot.

Fig. 200B: Wind the seizing wire round the field wire on both sides of the square knot, in the directions shown. Take four or five turns on the bare wire, and two or three turns on the rubber insulation. (The illustrations do not attempt to show the insulation.) Cut off the ends and wrap them with friction tape.

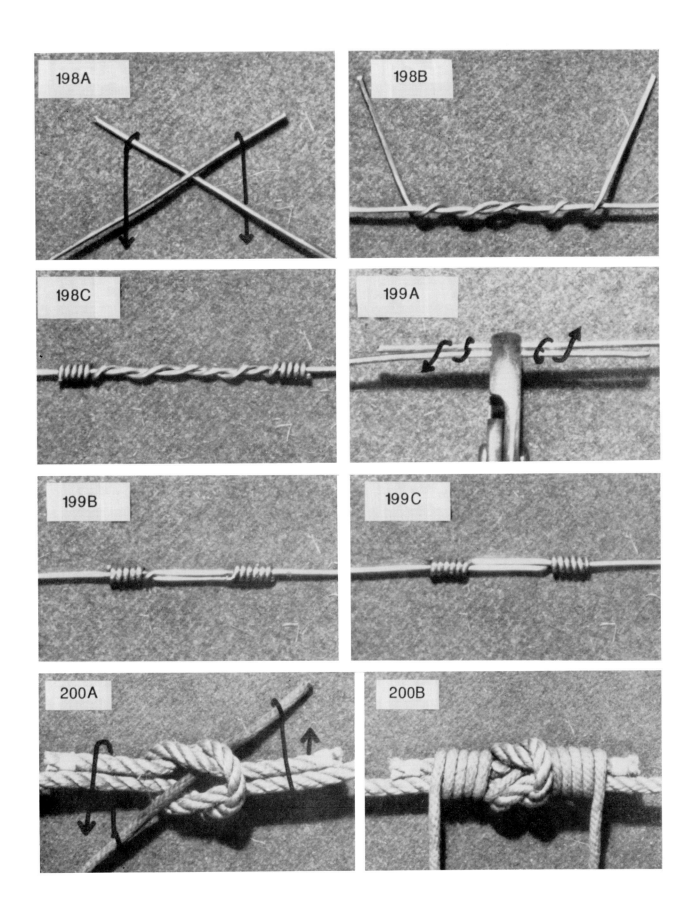

201. The Monkey's Fist is a knob used to weight the end of a heaving line.

Fig. 201A: Form two (or three) loops, as illustrated. Three are preferable, but for the sake of clarity, two are shown in the illustrations. Pass the end *A* twice round the first two loops.

Fig. 201B: Pass *A* twice round the second set of loops.

Fig. 201C: Work the loops taut.

Fig. 201D: Splice the end and standing part together.

Fig. 201E: This specimen has all the parts tripled, instead of doubled, as described above. A metal weight, not so heavy as to be dangerous, can be inserted inside the ball before the turns are worked taut. The parts are sometimes quadrupled.

202. This terminal knot for the heaving line is from Ashley's articles in the magazine *Sea Stories,* 1925, p. 109.

203. This terminal knot, called the *doughnut* by Ashley, was also published in *Sea Stories,* 1925, p. 111.

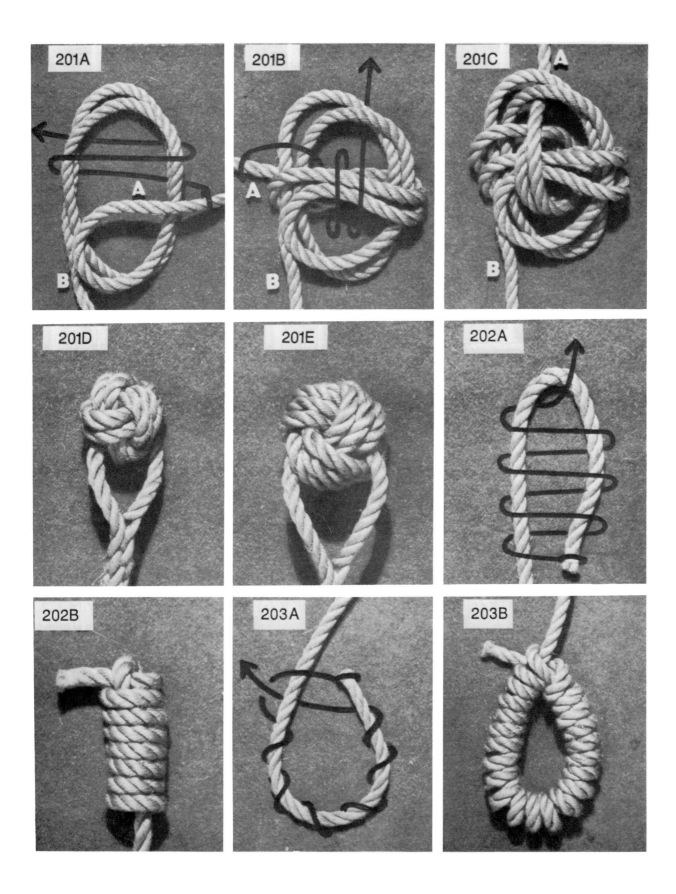

204. The Crown Knot is the first of several so-called *multistrand knots* that will now be described.

Fig. 204A: Unlay the strands a short distance, and form a bight with strand *A*.

Fig. 204B: Form a bight with strand *B* over the end of strand *A*.

Fig. 204C: Form a bight with strand *C* over the end of strand *B*, and stick the end of *C* down through the bight of *A*.

Fig. 204D: Each strand now comes down through the bight of the next strand.

Fig. 204E: The crown knot is seldom if ever used alone.

Fig. 204F: The end of a rope, however, is sometimes finished off by means of a crown knot, with the ends tucked two or three times against the lay. This device (an unattractive and clumsy device, in my opinion) is called a *crown knot*, an *end splice*, or a *back splice*.

205. The Wall Knot is the converse of the crown knot. That is, each strand comes *up* through the bight of the next strand, instead of *down* through the bight of the next strand.

Fig. 205A: Make a bight in *A*, and bend *B* down over *A*.

Fig. 205B: Bend *C* round *B* and up through the bight of *A*.

Fig. 205C: Each strand now comes up through the bight of the next strand, and the strands may be worked taut, as illustrated in figs. 205D and 205E.

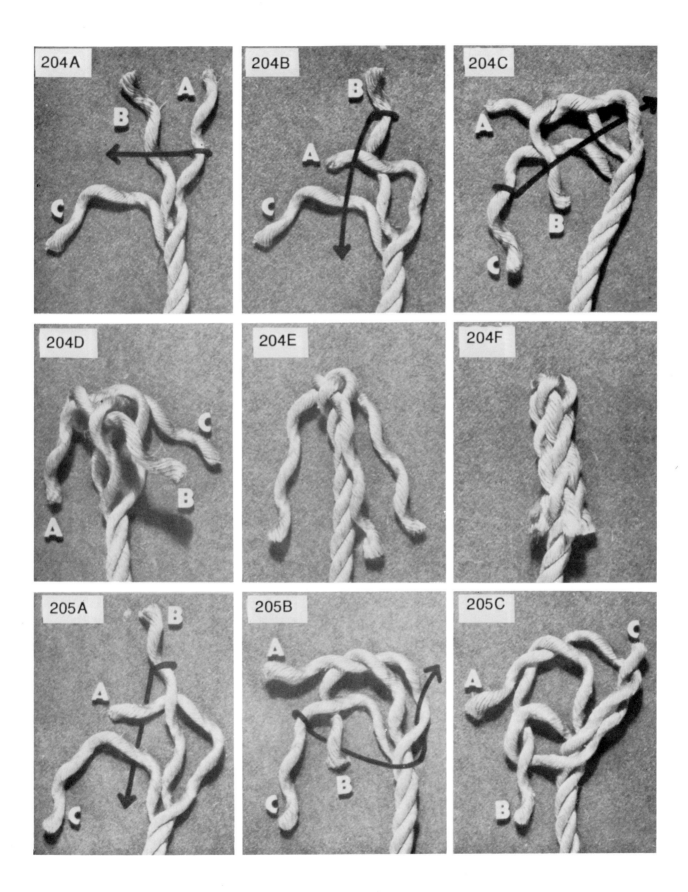

Fig. 205D: When the strands have been drawn taut, the wall knot looks like this.

Fig. 205E: The strands are now laid up again above the knot, whipped, and cut off.

Fig. 205F: Most multistrand knots, including the wall knot, can also be tied against the lay, as illustrated here.

206. The Stopper Knot is intermediate between a wall and a double wall. The method of tying it seems to have been first illustrated by Mason (1928). It is pictured but not explained in several old manuals of seamanship.

Fig. 206A: Start with a wall knot, and then bring each end up through the next bight, as shown by the arrow.

Fig. 206B: This is another view of the same process. The arrow shows how each strand is tucked.

Fig. 206C: The stopper knot has a large diameter and a thin profile.

207. The Double Wall Knot. In doubling a multistrand knot, the end of each strand is said to *follow the lead,* which means that each strand, as it is tucked, lies beside the adjacent strand, so that the adjacent strand is, as it were, doubled. Sometimes the lead is followed *below* the adjacent strand (see the arrow in fig. 207A), and sometimes *above* the adjacent strand (see the arrow in fig. 207B). In these two illustrations, *N* is the strand adjacent to *L*.

Fig. 207C: The arrow points to the adjacent strand, or, in other words, to the strand that should be followed in doubling.

The double wall knot has three forms, which were first distinguished in print by Ashley (1944). They differ in the way the strands are tucked.

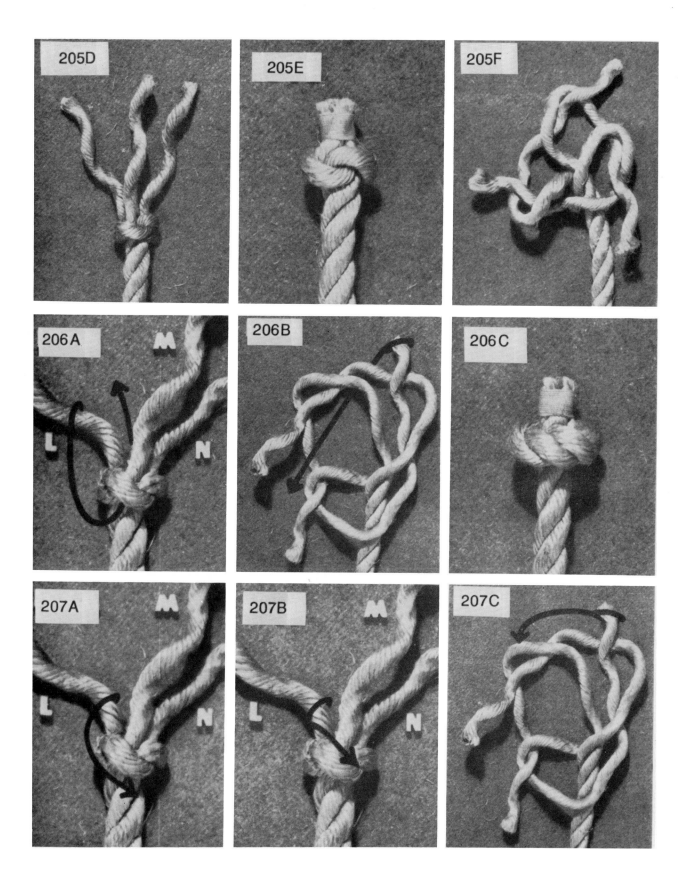

Figs. 207D and 207E: In this form the lead is followed *above* the adjacent strand.

Figs. 207F and 207G: In this form the lead is followed *below* the adjacent strand.

Figs. 207H and 207I: The lead is followed *below* the adjacent strand, and each strand is given an additional tuck.

208. The Diamond Knot differs from the wall knot in that each strand comes up, not through the bight of the next strand, but through the bight of the next strand but one.

Fig. 208A: To tie the diamond knot, stop the strands down to the standing part, and stick each strand up round the next strand and through the bight of the next strand but one. The arrow shows how to do this. (*A* is tucked through the bight of *C,* and so on.)

Fig. 208B: The completed knot.

209. The Double Diamond Knot. Start with a diamond knot; follow the lead with each strand (either above or below the adjacent strand) until all the strands are doubled and the ends come out on top of the knot.

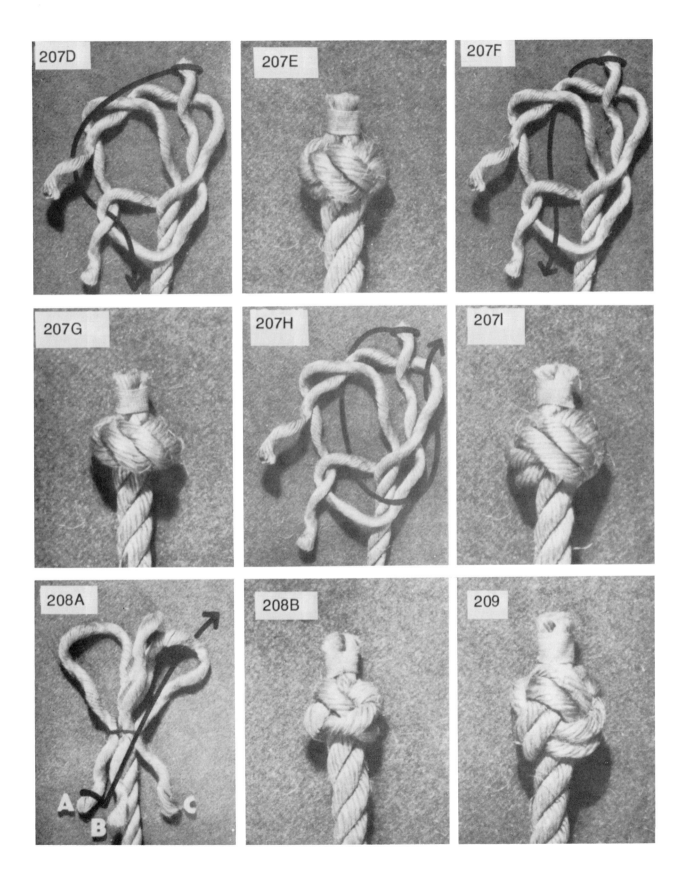

210. The Footrope Knot is from *The Ashley Book of Knots* (1944). It is exactly like a diamond knot tied upside down, but it is a better knot, because the ends come out closer together on top of the knot.

Figs. 210A and 210B: To tie it, crown the rope and then wall it under the crown. Then tuck the ends up through the center, as shown by the arrows. These two illustrations show different views of the same operation.

Fig. 210C: The completed knot.

Ashley cites the following mnemonic couplet:

First a crown, then a wall;
Tuck up, and that's all.

211. The Double Footrope Knot is also from Ashley (1944).

Fig. 211A: Tie a crown knot with a wall knot under it, as described above (no. 210). Then follow the lead of the crown above the adjacent strand.

Fig. 211B: Follow the lead of the wall above the adjacent strand, and bring the ends out on top, at the center of the knot.

Fig. 211C: The completed knot.

212. The Matthew Walker Knot is one of the most attractive of the multistrand knots.

Fig. 212A: Tie a wall knot with strands *A* and *B* around strand *C*. Then pass *C* round *A* and up through the bights of both *B* and *A*, as shown by the arrow.

Fig. 212B: This illustration shows the structure of the knot before the strands have been worked taut.

Fig. 212C: The completed knot.

In this knot, each strand comes up through the bights of the next two strands. Another way to tie it, therefore, is to start with a wall knot, and then to stick each strand successively up through one more bight. This method is convenient when there are four or more strands.

The first reference to the Matthew Walker knot in the *New English Dictionary* dates from 1860 (*All Year Round,* no. 66, p. 382): "Which Knot?" asked Toby. "Single or double wall, single or double diamond, Matthew Walker, spritsail sheet, stopper, or shroud?"

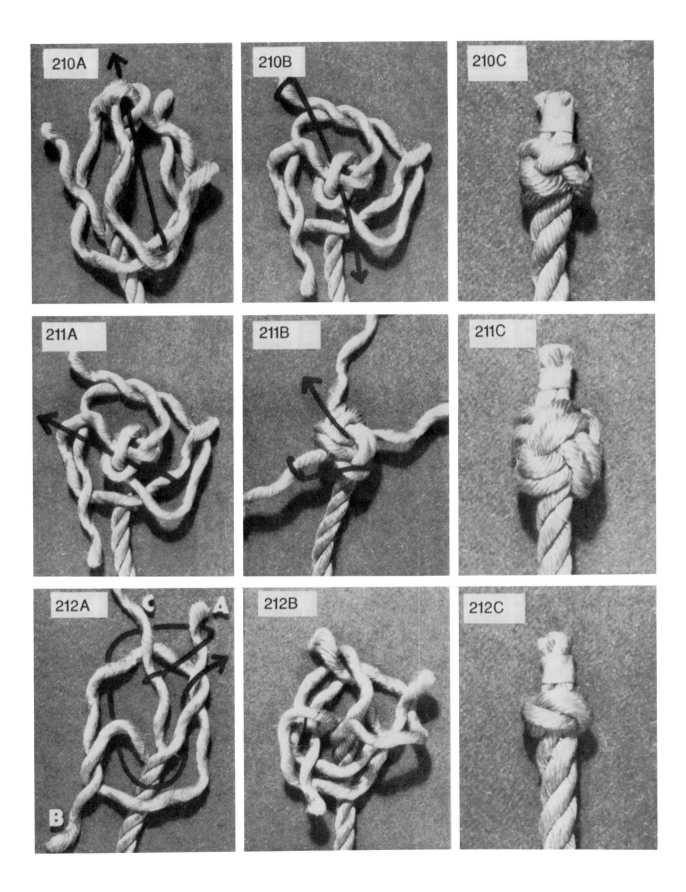

210A 210B 210C

211A 211B 211C

212A 212B 212C

213. The Double Matthew Walker Knot. In this knot, each strand comes up through all three bights, including (in three-strand rope) its own.

Fig. 213A: Bring *A* round the standing part and up through its own bight.

Fig. 213B: Bring *C* round the standing part and up through its own bight and the bight of *A*.

Fig. 213C: Bring *B* round the standing part and up through all three bights.

Figs. 213D and 213E: Two views of the double Matthew Walker before the strands have been worked taut.

Fig. 213F: The completed knot.

214. The Double Wall-and-Crown or Manrope Knot. Start with a wall-and-crown, and then, to double the strands, follow the lead of the wall above the adjacent strand, and then follow the lead of the crown.

The late George H. Taber, of Pittsburgh, supplied me with the following mnemonic couplet:

First a wall, then a crown;
Now tuck up, then tuck down.

The manrope knot is a knob in the end of a rope. Since it is a multistrand knot, it is grouped here with nos. 204 to 213, but it should not, like them, be used as a stopper knot (see the Glossary). It is important to note that a single wall-and-crown, i.e., a wall knot with a crown knot on top of it (figs. 214A and 214B), does not constitute a complete knot and is not given separate treatment here. It is only after the strands of a wall-and-crown have been doubled (fig. 214C) or tripled (not shown) that a complete knot is produced.

Manrope knots were formerly tied in the ends of elaborate manropes, which were often coach whipped (no. 234), painted, fringed, tasselled, decorated with Turk's heads, and otherwise dressed up. Manropes hung from stanchions in the rails and provided a handhold for the captain and for visitors coming aboard the ship. They were generally tied in four-strand, rather than in three-strand, rope.

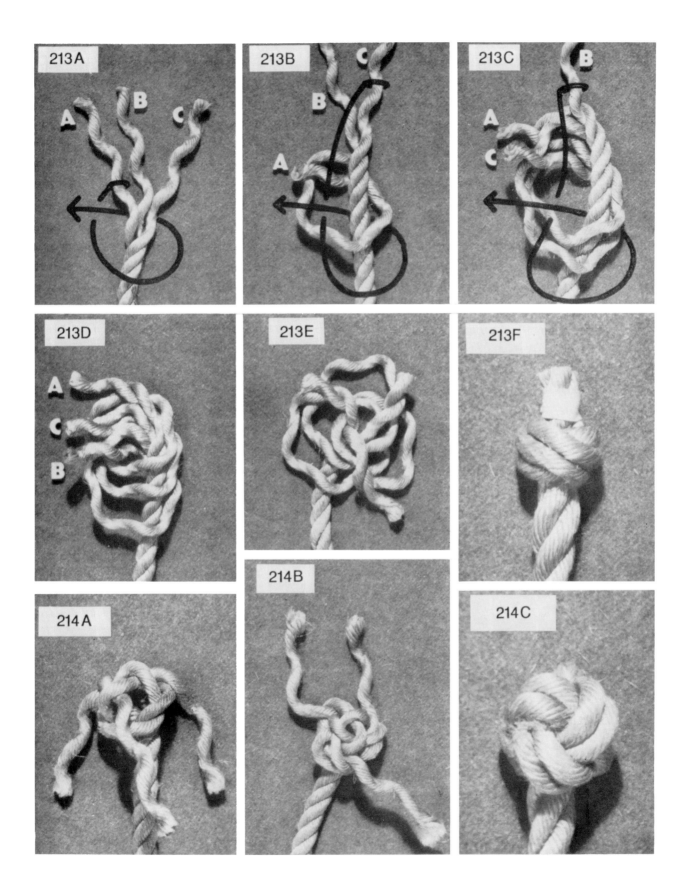

215. The Electrician's or Underwriter's Knot is a two-strand wall knot tied in electric-light wire. Its purpose is to relieve the strain that would otherwise come on the ends of the wire in a light fixture.

Figs. 215A and 215B: Since wire is stiffer than rope, the knot should be tied as shown here. In this way it can easily be pulled up taut.

Fig. 215C: The completed knot.

A two-strand wall knot is the same in structure as a what knot (no. 30).

216. The English Diamond Knot was formerly used by sailors on the draw cords of their clothes bags.

Fig. 216A: To tie the English diamond knot, join the ends of a length of cord by means of a carrick bend (no. 51), and stick the ends down through the center of the knot, as shown by the arrows.

Fig. 216B: The finished knot.

217. The Lanyard Knot is a Matthew Walker knot of four strands. The lanyards used in setting up the shrouds in the days of the deadeye were made of four-strand rope. A lanyard knot was tied in the end of the lanyard to prevent it from unreeving.

218. The Spritsail Sheet Knot is a sort of double wall-and-crown knot of six strands. Steel (1794) gives a clear description of how to tie it, and Lever (1808) says that it was used as a stopper knot in the merchant service.

Fig. 218A: Unlay the ends of a length of three-strand rope, and wall the six ends together, either with or against the lay. Fold *D* to the right, and *A* to the left, across the top of the wall.

Fig. 218B: Tuck *B* and *C* over *D* and *A,* and tuck *E* and *F* over *A* and under *D.*

Figs. 218C and 218D: Follow the wall and then the crown until all the strands are doubled.

The appearance of the knot is slightly different if the initial wall knot is made against the lay.

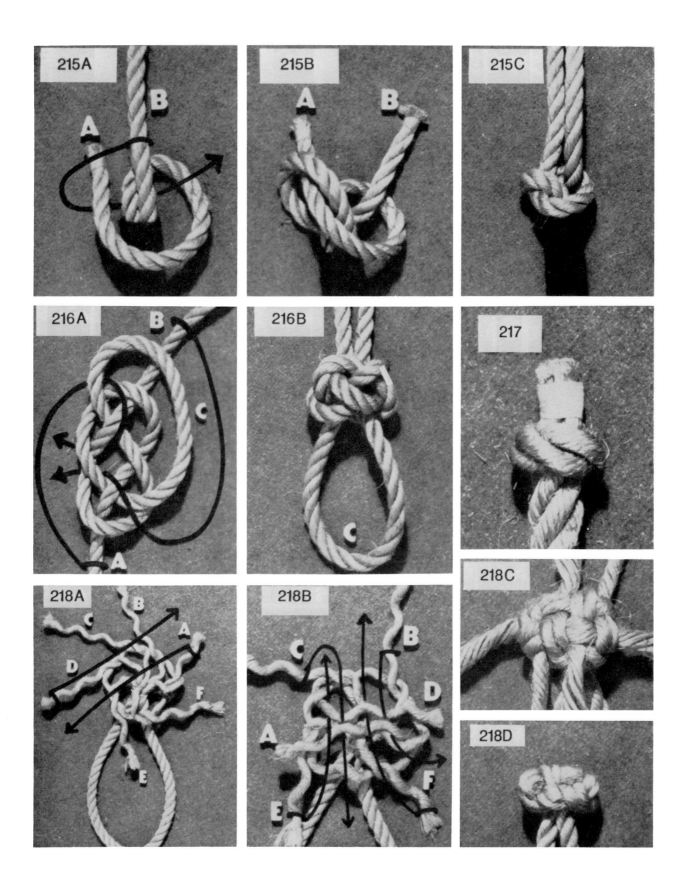

215A B A

215B A B

215C

216A B C A

216B C

217

218A B C D A E F

218B C B A D E F

218C

218D

219. The Shroud Knot was formerly used to repair hemp shrouds that had been shot away in battle.

Fig. 219A: Unlay the strands a short distance, and crotch them. With each set of strands, tie a wall knot (no. 205) round the opposite rope, against the lay. The two wall knots, under tension, pull up very tight, with their backs against each other.

Figs. 219B and 219C: To dispose of the ends, scrape and taper the strands, and then marl, parcel, and serve them.

There are several other ways to dispose of the strands. One way (not illustrated) is to tuck them over and under, against the lay, as in splicing.

A large number of shroud knots, most of them quite useless, have been devised. The French shroud knot, illustrated in *Sailors' Knots* (1935), collapses in the testing machine and is not included in this book. On the other hand, the stopper knot (no. 206) makes a strong and attractive shroud knot.

The shroud knot is weaker than the short splice and, contrary to the usual impression, it requires as much rope as the short splice does—in fact, probably more. Its chief advantage appears to be that it was quicker and easier to tie than the short splice when an emergency repair had to be made in the standing rigging. The parceling and serving took time, of course, but could be put on later.

220. The Footrope Knot or Standing Turk's-Head.

Fig. 220A: *Side-splice* a length of small stuff of suitable diameter into the middle of another length of the same stuff. (A *side-splice* is made in the same way as an eye-splice, no. 180.) Stick these small strands through the strands of the larger rope, or footrope, in such a way that the splice is in the middle and one end comes out between each pair of strands. (With four-strand rope, merely stick two lengths of smaller rope between the strands.)

Fig. 220B: Make a wall knot and then a crown knot round the larger rope.

Fig. 220C: Follow round the wall and then round the crown until all the strands are tripled.

A diamond knot (no. 208), instead of the wall-and-crown shown in fig. 220B, gives a similar result.

221. The Long Footrope Knot or Standing Turk's-Head.

Fig. 221A: Tie a diamond knot (no. 208) with the three small strands round the larger rope. (See no. 220 for an explanation of the three small strands.)

Fig. 221B: Tie another diamond knot facing the first in such a way that the ends come out in the middle.

Fig. 221C: Follow the lead until all the strands are tripled.

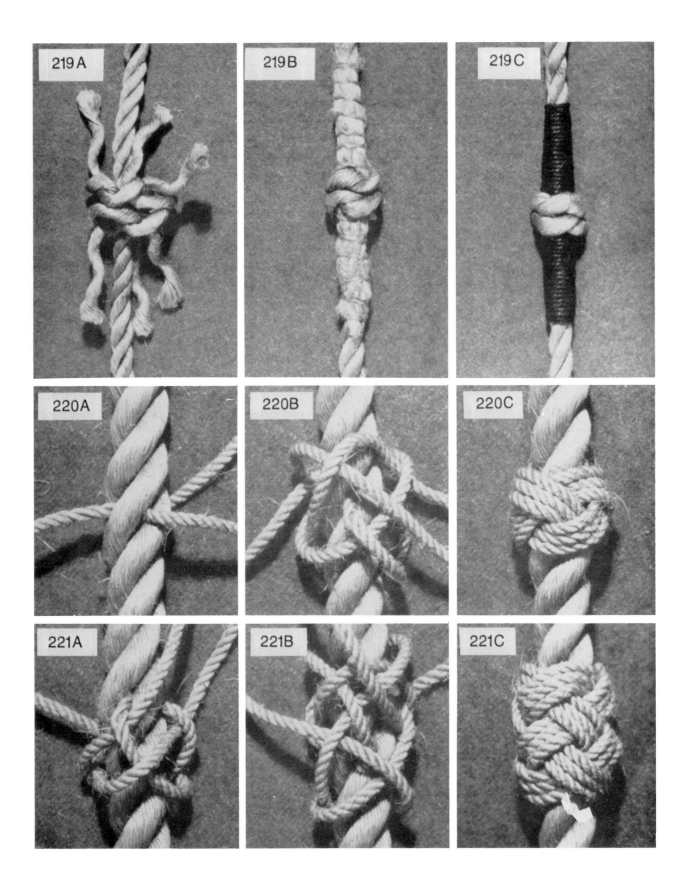

222. The Turk's-Head of Three Leads. The size of a Turk's-head depends on its circumference and its width. The circumference is measured by the number of *bights* or *scallops* on the rim or edge. The width is measured by the number of times the end is passed round before the doubling or tripling begins (as explained below). These complete turns are called *leads, strands,* or *parts.* Following Ashley, I will call them *leads.* L. G. Miller's system of notation, indicated in parentheses, uses Roman numerals to represent the leads and Arabic numerals to represent the bights.

Three Leads, Two Bights (III.2)

Fig. 222A: Take a turn round the fingers or round the object to be contained. Then pass the end round again, and tuck it over and under and over, as shown by the arrow. This is the smallest possible Turk's-head. It is shown complete in fig. 222I, after the process of doubling and tripling the leads has been explained.

Three Leads, Five Bights (III.5)

Fig. 222B: After the end has been tucked, as explained above, rotate the top of the knot toward you until the crossing of the leads becomes visible. Then tuck the end to the right, under and over, beyond the crossing.

Fig. 222C: Pull a bight to the right, under the right-hand lead.

Fig. 222D: Tuck the end to the left, under and over. The Turk's-head of three leads and five bights (III.5) is now complete, and all that remains is to double or triple the leads.

Fig. 222E: To do this, bring the two ends together, and tuck the working end under and over, under and over, etc., parallel to the inert end. Fig. 222E shows the first tuck in this process.

Fig. 222F: This illustration shows the second tuck in the doubling process.

Fig. 222G: After all the leads have been doubled, the Turk's-head of three leads and five bights (III.5) looks like this.

Fig. 222H: It is more usual to triple the leads, as shown here. This is probably the most common of all Turk's-heads.

Fig. 222I: The Turk's-head of three leads and two bights (III.2), described above (fig. 222A), is shown here with the leads tripled.

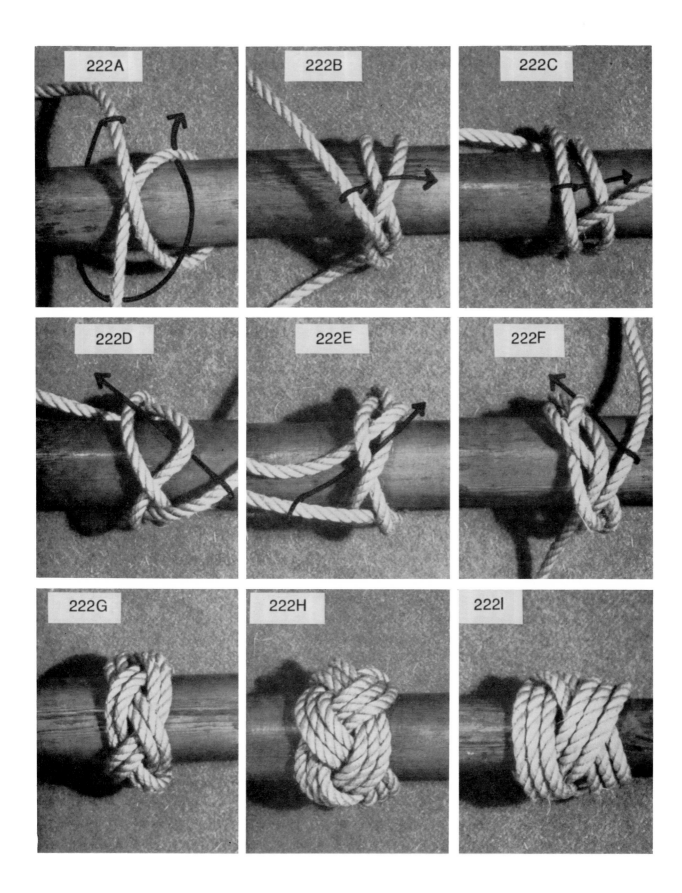

Three Leads, Eight Bights (III.8)

Fig. 222J: To make this Turk's-head, start with fig. 222E, and repeat the steps shown in figs. 222B, 222C, and 222D. This will enlarge the circumference by three bights, but it will not increase the width. The circumference can be enlarged in this way indefinitely, to 8, 11, 14, 17 bights, etc.

Three Leads, Four Bights (III.4)

Fig. 222K: Take a turn round the fingers or round the object to be contained, pass the end round again, and tuck it over and under, as shown by the arrow.

Fig. 222L: Rotate the top of the resulting structure toward you.

Fig. 222M: Pull a bight to the right *over* the right-hand lead.

Fig. 222N: Tuck the end to the left, over and under, as shown by the arrow.

Fig. 222O: This shows the finished Turk's-head, before the doubling or tripling of the leads begins.

Fig. 222P: This shows the Turk's-head of three leads and four bights (III.4) after the leads have been tripled.

Three Leads, Seven Bights (III.7)

Fig. 222Q: The circumference of the foregoing knot can be increased, without increasing the width, by starting with fig. 222O and repeating figs. 222K to 222N. The resulting knot, shown here, has three leads and seven bights (III.7). Each time figs. 222K to 222N are repeated, the circumference is increased by three bights, so that three-lead Turk's-heads of 7, 10, 13, 16, 19 bights, etc., can be made by this method.

Fig. 222R: It is sometimes convenient to make a Turk's-head on the fingers, as shown here, and then to place it round the object to be contained.

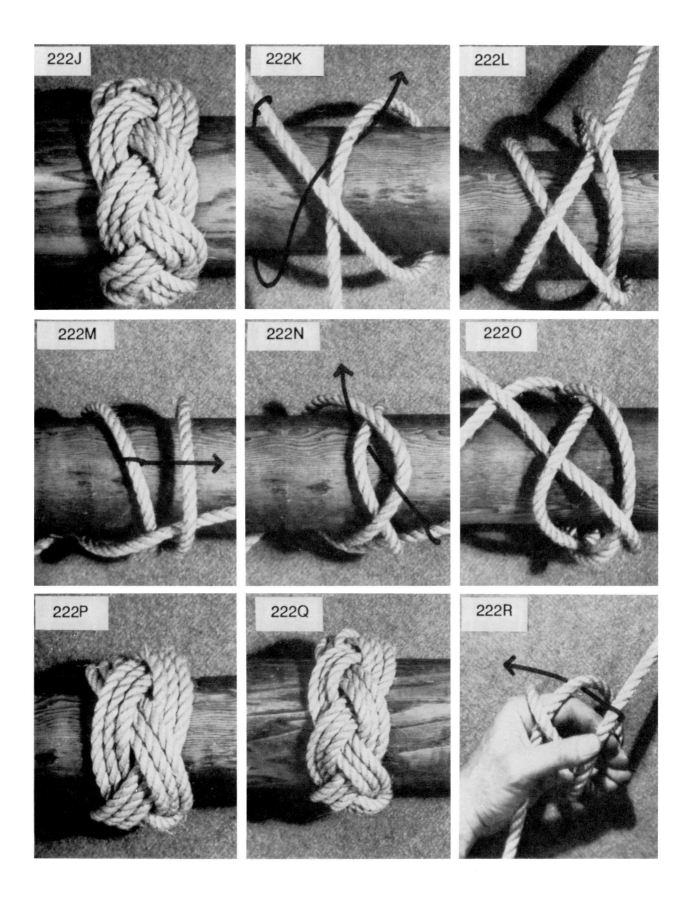

223. The Turk's-Head of Four Leads. By the *law of the common divisor,* independently discovered by C. W. Ashley, G. H. Taber, and L. G. Miller, Turk's-heads of any number of leads and any number of bights are possible, provided the two numbers are prime to each other, or, in other words, have no common divisor. In the case of three-lead Turk's-heads, we have seen how knots of 2, 5, 8, 11, 14 bights, etc., can be made by one method, and knots of 4, 7, 10, 13, 16 bights, etc., by a second method. Three-lead Turk's-heads of 3, 6, 9, 12, 15 bights, etc., are impossible.

According to this law, four-lead Turk's-heads of any odd number of bights (3, 5, 7, 9, etc.) are possible, but four-lead Turk's-heads of any even number of bights are impossible.

Four Leads, Three Bights (IV.3)

Fig. 223A: Tie an overhand knot, pass the end round again, and tuck it *to the left* through the center of the overhand knot, as shown by the arrow.

Fig. 223B: Pass the end round once more, and tuck it over and under to the right, as shown by the arrow.

Fig. 223C: Rotate the top of the structure toward you, and tuck the end to the left, over, under, and over.

Fig. 223D: Triple all the leads, as explained under no. 222.

Four Leads, Five Bights (IV.5)

Fig. 223E: Tie an overhand knot, pass the end round again, and tuck it *to the right* through the center of the overhand knot.

Fig. 223F: Rotate the structure, and tuck the end to the left, over and under.

Fig. 223G: Pass the end round again, and tuck it to the right, as shown.

Fig. 223H: Tuck the end to the left, as shown.

Fig. 223I: The Turk's-head of four leads and five bights (IV.5).

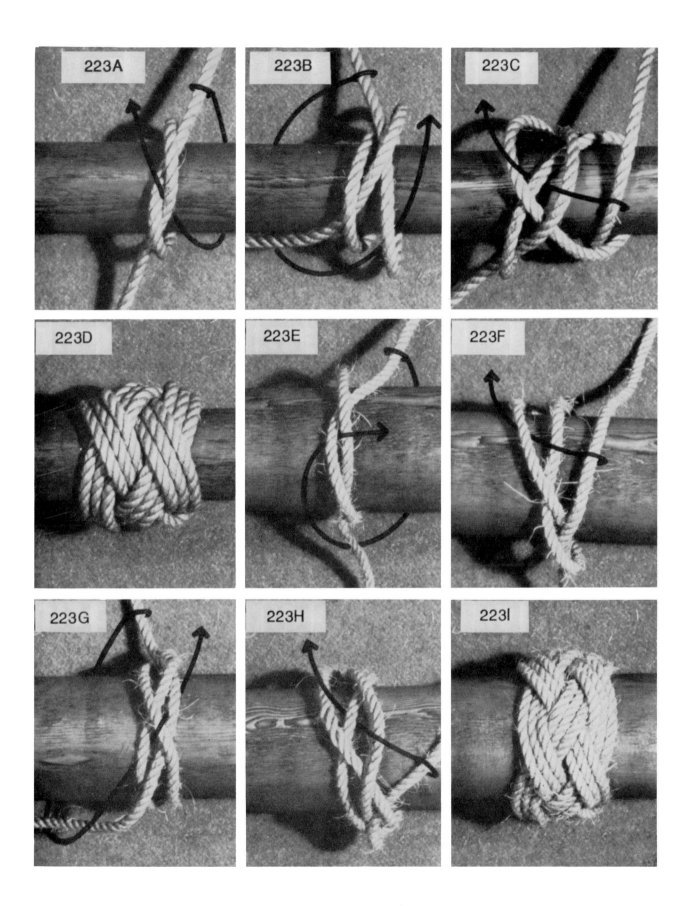

Four Leads, Seven Bights (IV.7)

Fig. 223J: Start with a double overhand knot, pass the end round again, and tuck it through the knot, *left, right,* and *left,* as shown by the arrow.

Fig. 223K: Pass the end round once more, and tuck it to the right, over and under. Compare fig. 223B.

Fig. 223L: Rotate the structure, and tuck the end to the left, over and under and over. Compare fig. 223C.

Fig. 223M: Rotate, and tuck to the right. This is a repetition of fig. 223K.

Fig. 223N: Rotate, and tuck to the left. This is a repetition of fig. 223L.

Fig. 223O: Triple the leads. The method of making IV.7 is analogous to the method of making IV.3.

Four Leads, Nine Bights (IV.9)

The student should be able to work this knot out for himself, by analogy with IV.5. It starts with a double overhand knot, and the end is then passed round again, and tucked through the knot, *right, left, right.* Thereafter the procedure is like figs. 223E to 223H.

In like manner, IV.11 and IV.13 start with a triple overhand; IV.15 and IV.17 start with a four-fold overhand; IV.19 and IV.21 start with a five-fold overhand; and so on. The smaller knot in each pair is made like IV.3, and the larger knot like IV.5, as described above.

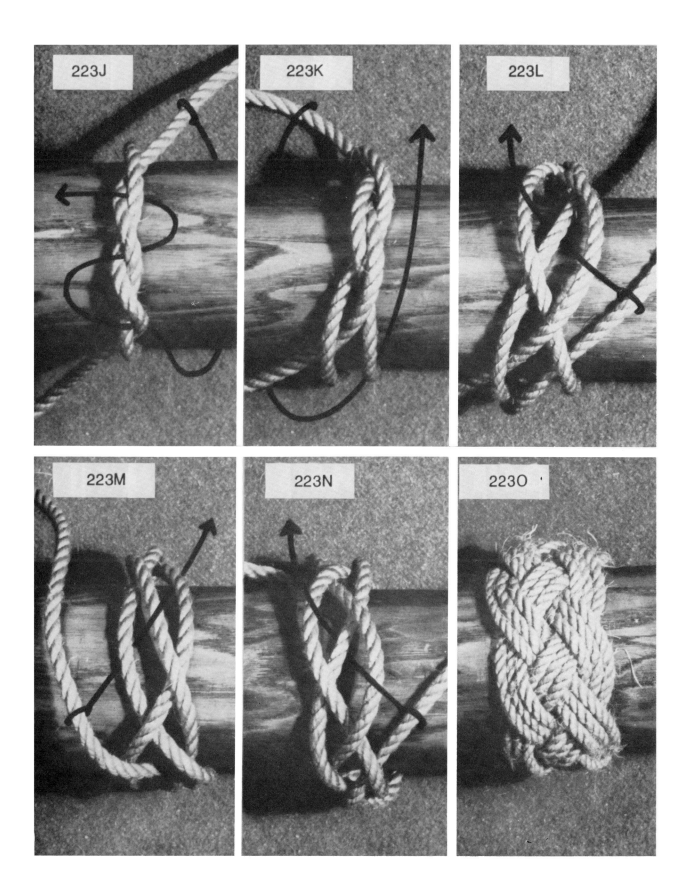

224. The Turk's-Head of Five Leads. By the law of the common divisor, Turk's-heads of five leads can be made with any number of bights except 5 and multiples of 5. It so happens, however, that V.4 and V.9 are the most convenient sizes, since they start with three-lead Turk's-heads and are *raised* to five leads by easily remembered methods. Five-lead knots of 2, 3, 6, 7, or 8 bights are made directly. These knots are made more easily with the use of a diagram, which the reader can sketch on a piece of paper.

Five Leads, Four Bights (V.4)

Fig. 224A: Start with a Turk's-head of three leads and two bights (III.2).

Fig. 224B: Pass the end round and tuck it to the right, under and over, as shown by the arrow. In other words, begin the process of doubling the leads of a three-lead, two-bight knot (III.2).

Fig. 224C: Do not continue the process of doubling the lead. Instead, tuck the end to the left, over and under, as shown by the arrow.

Fig. 224D: Pass the end round, and tuck to the right, over and under and over.

Fig. 224E: Rotate the top of the structure toward you, and tuck to the left, under, over, under, and over.

Fig. 224F: Triple all the leads.

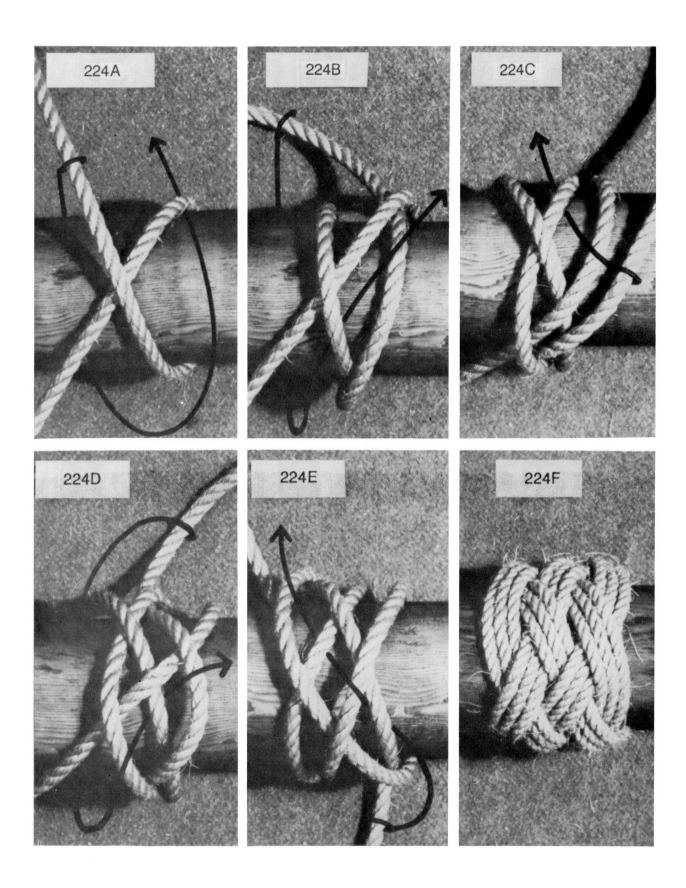

Five Leads, Nine Bights (V.9)

Fig. 224G: Begin with a three-lead, five-bight Turk's-head (III.5), as illustrated in fig. 222E. Double *one* lead.

Fig. 224H: After one lead has been doubled, and the working end has joined the inert end again, stop doubling, and tuck to the right, splitting the previously doubled lead, as shown by the arrow.

Fig. 224I: Pull a bight to the right, under the right-hand part.

Fig. 224J: Pull a bight to the left, over the left-hand part.

Fig. 224K: With the parts arranged as illustrated, tuck to the left, under, over, under, and over, again splitting the doubled lead.

Fig. 224L: Rotate the top of the structure toward you, and tuck to the right, under, over, under, and over.

Fig. 224M: Pull bights from the doubled part to the right and left, as before.

Fig. 224N: Tuck to the left, under, over, under, and over.

Fig. 224O: Triple all the leads.

L. G. Miller has developed a set of mathematical formulas by which Turk's-heads of any size can be solved on paper before being tied. By means of these formulas, he solved XVII.15 in my presence in a few minutes.

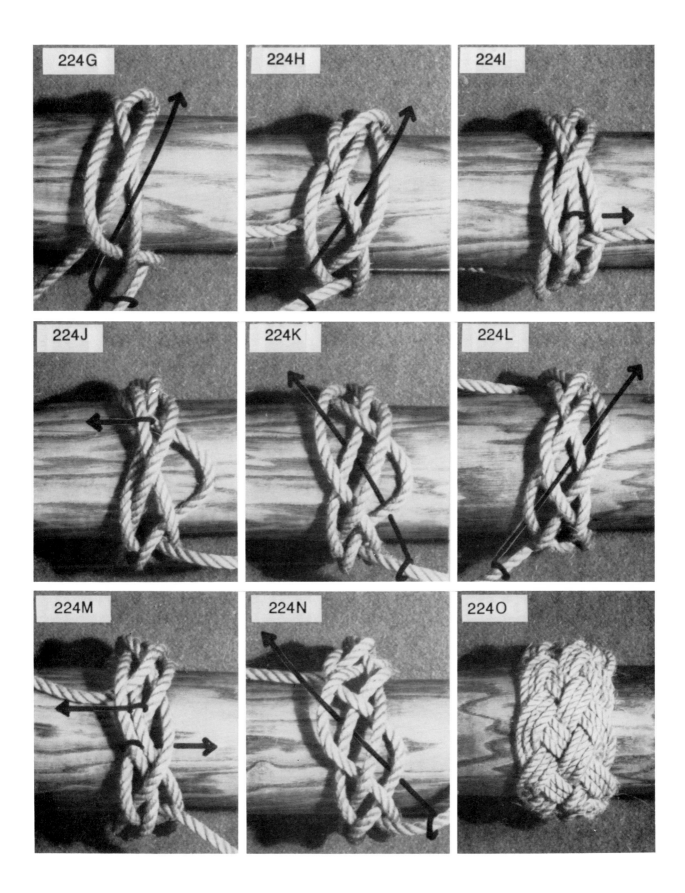

224G 224H 224I

224J 224K 224L

224M 224N 224O

225. The Turk's-Head of Six Leads and Five Bights (VI.5).

Fig. 225A: Start with a Turk's-head of four leads and three bights. (Fig. 225A is the same as fig. 223C after the end has been tucked as there illustrated.) In fig. 225A, follow the lead, as in doubling, under, over, and under, to the right.

Fig. 225B: Rotate the work, and continue to follow the lead, as in doubling, but first tuck the end *under* the lead that is being followed.

Fig. 225C: Rotate the work, and split the doubled part by tucking to the right, over, under, over, and under.

Fig. 225D: Rotate the work, and tuck to the left, over, under, over, under, and over.

Fig. 225E: Triple all the leads. This is a knot of six leads and five bights (VI.5). When *raised* by this method, a Turk's-head always has one more lead than bights and is called a square Turk's-head.

226. The Turk's-Head of Seven Leads and Six Bights (VII.6).

Fig. 226A: Begin with a knot of five leads and four bights (V.4), and double one lead. In the illustration the doubling process has already been begun, the end having been tucked once, to the right. Continue this process to the left, but first cross it *over* the lead that is being followed. Then tuck to the left, as shown by the arrow in fig. 226A.

Fig. 226B: Rotate the work, and split the doubled lead by tucking to the right, over, under, over, under, and over.

Fig. 226C: Rotate, and tuck to the left, under, over, under, over, under, and over.

Fig. 226D: Triple all the leads. This is a knot of seven leads and six bights (VII.6).

Square Turk's-heads can be *raised* or enlarged indefinitely by repeating one or the other of the two methods shown on this page. However, they soon become too unwieldy to be of any practical use.

227. A Long Turk's-Head with Four Bights can be made with the aid of eight nails or tacks set in a cylinder the desired distance apart, four at each end. Let the tacks at the left be numbered 1L to 4L, and the tacks at the right 1R to 4R.

Fig. 227A: Wind the cord to the right, from 1L to 1R, and then back to the left, from 1R to 2L, over all previous turns.

Fig. 227B: Wind the cord to the right, from 2L to 2R, over all previous turns.

Fig. 227C: Wind the cord to the left, from 2R to 3L, under, over, under, over, under, over—that is, alternating with the strand that goes from 1R to 2L.

Fig. 227D: Wind the cord to the right, from 3L to 3R, under, over, under, over, under, over—that is, alternating with the strand that goes from 2L to 2R.

Fig. 227E: Wind the cord to the left, from 3R to 4L, over one, under one, over two, under one, over two, under one, over one—that is, alternating with the strand that goes from 2R to 3L.

Fig. 227F: Wind the cord to the right, from 4L to 4R, over one, under one, over two, under one, over two, under one, over one—that is, alternating with the strand that goes from 1L to 1R.

Fig. 227G: Wind the cord to the left, from 4R to 1L, under, over, under, over, under, over.

Fig. 227H: The strands may now be doubled or tripled, and the Turk's-head will be complete.

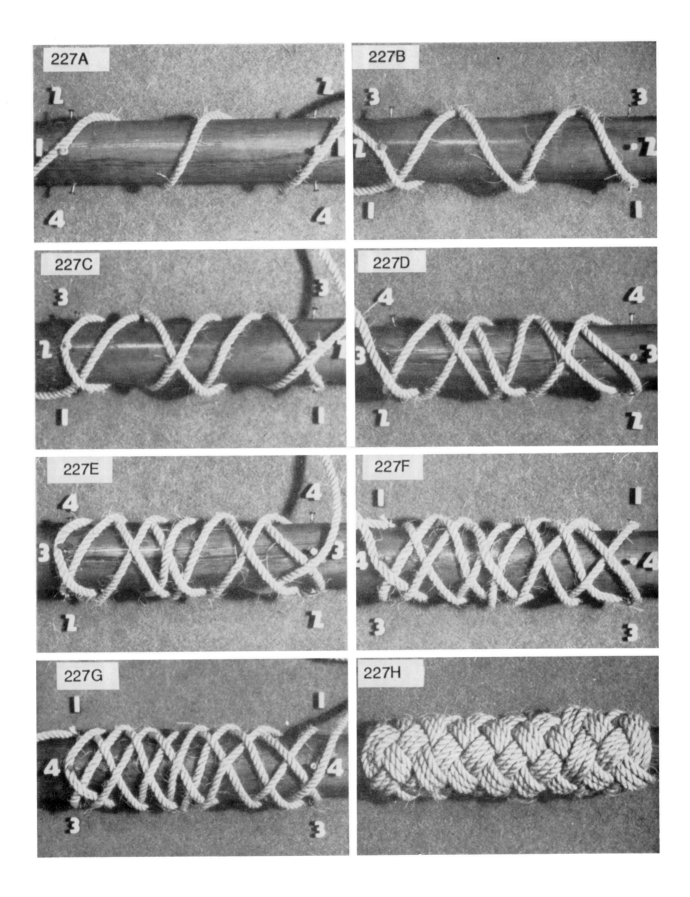

228. A Long Turk's-Head with Two Bights can be made with the aid of four nails or tacks set in a cylinder the desired distance apart, two at each end. Let the tacks at the left be numbered 1L and 2L, and the tacks at the right 1R and 2R.

Fig. 228A: Wind the cord to the right, from 1L to 1R, and then back to the left, from 1R to 2L, over all previous turns.

Fig. 228B: Wind the cord to the right, from 2L to 2R, over all previous turns.

Fig. 228C: Wind the cord to the left, from 2R to 1L, under, over, under, over, under, over.

Fig. 228D: The strands may now be doubled or tripled, and the Turk's-head will be complete.

229. The Long Standing Turk's-Head is made with several strands instead of with one strand.

Fig. 229A: Lash the strands at one end A, wind them spirally to the left round the rope or spar, lash them again at B, and crown them.

Fig. 229B: Tuck the ends spirally to the right, alternately over and under the previous turns. Tuck each strand in turn, one tuck at a time.

Fig. 229C: When the starting point A is reached, wall the other ends of the strands.

Fig. 229D: Double or triple all the strands, scattering the ends throughout the finished Turk's-head.

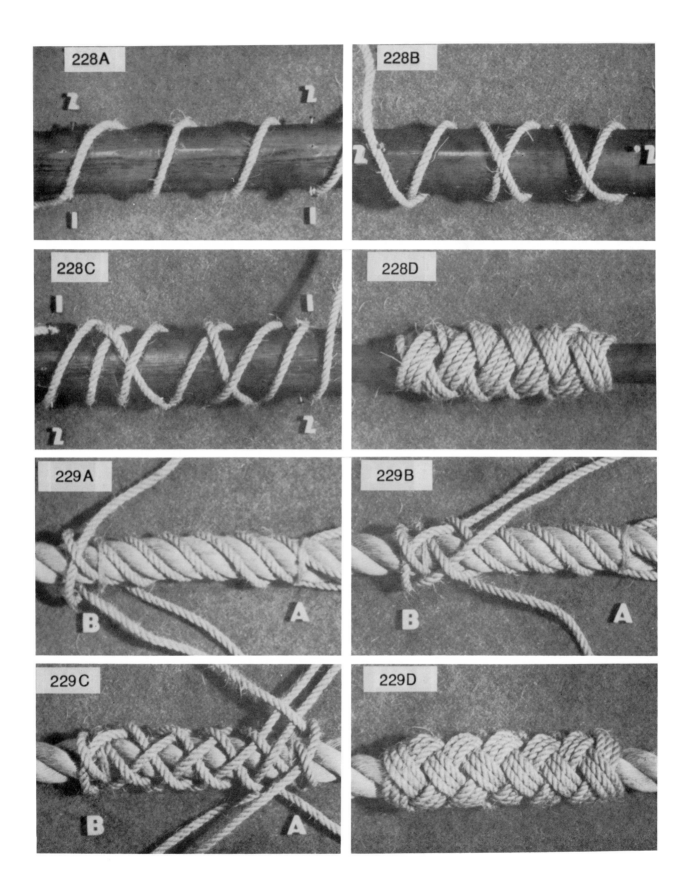

230. Plain Sennit is made with any number of strands, the principle being the same regardless of the number.

Fig. 230A: To make plain sennit of three strands, cross *C* over *B* and lay it beside *A*.

Fig. 230B: Cross *A* over *C*, and lay it beside *B*.

Fig. 230C: Cross *B* over *A*, and lay it beside *C*. This process is continued until the specimen is long enough.

Fig. 230I(*A*): A completed specimen. Plain sennit of three strands is like ordinary braid.

Fig. 230D: To make plain sennit of five strands, divide the strands into two unequal groups, *AB* and *CDE*. Cross *E*, the outside strand of the larger group, over *CD*, and lay it beside *AB*.

Fig. 230E: Group *ABE* is now the larger group. Cross *A* over *BE* and lay it beside *CD*. Continue in the same way, always laying the outside strand of the larger group over beside the smaller group.

Fig. 230I(*B*): A completed specimen. Plain sennit of seven strands is made in similar fashion.

Fig. 230F: To make plain sennit of an even number of strands, such as four, arrange the strands in two groups, and cross *D* over *B* to the left.

Fig. 230G: Cross *A* to the right under *C* and over *D*.

Fig. 230H: Cross *B* over *A* to the left. As the work continues, the right-hand strand is always crossed over one, and the left-hand strand is always crossed under one and over one.

Fig. 230I(*C*): A completed specimen.

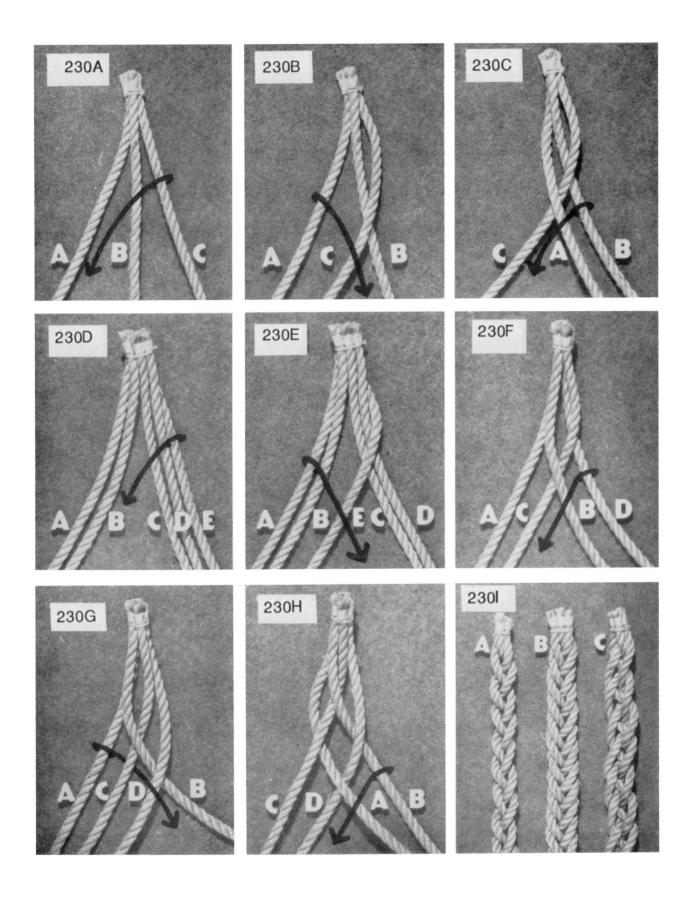

230A   A   B   C

230B   A   C   B

230C   C   A   B

230D   A   B   C   D   E

230E   A   B   E C   D

230F   A   C   B   D

230G   A   C   D   B

230H   C   D   A   B

230I   A   B   C

219

231. Square Sennit is made with any multiple of four strands.

Fig. 231A: To make four-strand square sennit, separate the strands into two groups and cross *B* to the right over *C*. Pass *A* back, over *B* and down beside *C*.

Fig. 231B: Pass *D* back, over *A,* and down beside *B.*

Fig. 231C: Pass *C* back, over *D,* and down beside *A.*

Fig. 231F(*A*): A completed specimen.

Fig. 231D: To make eight-strand square sennit, divide the strands into four groups, and cross *CD* to the right over *EF.* Pass *A* back, over *CD,* and down beside *EF.* Move *E* over beside *B.* (Strand *A* having been removed, the outside group of two strands on the left now consists of *B* and *E.*)

Fig. 231E: Pass *H* back, over *FA,* and down beside

CD. Move *D* over beside *G.* (Strand *H* having been removed, the outside group of two strands on the right now consists of *G* and *D.*) Alternate in this manner between the two outer strands.

Fig. 231F(*B*): A completed specimen.

232. Flat Sennit can be made with any number of strands, odd or even.
First Method
Fig. 232A: Pass the outer strand alternately under and over the other strands.

Fig. 232B: Treat the second strand in the same way.

Fig. 232C: Continue until sufficient length is attained.

A second way to make flat sennit, sometimes called French sennit, usually employs an odd number of strands.

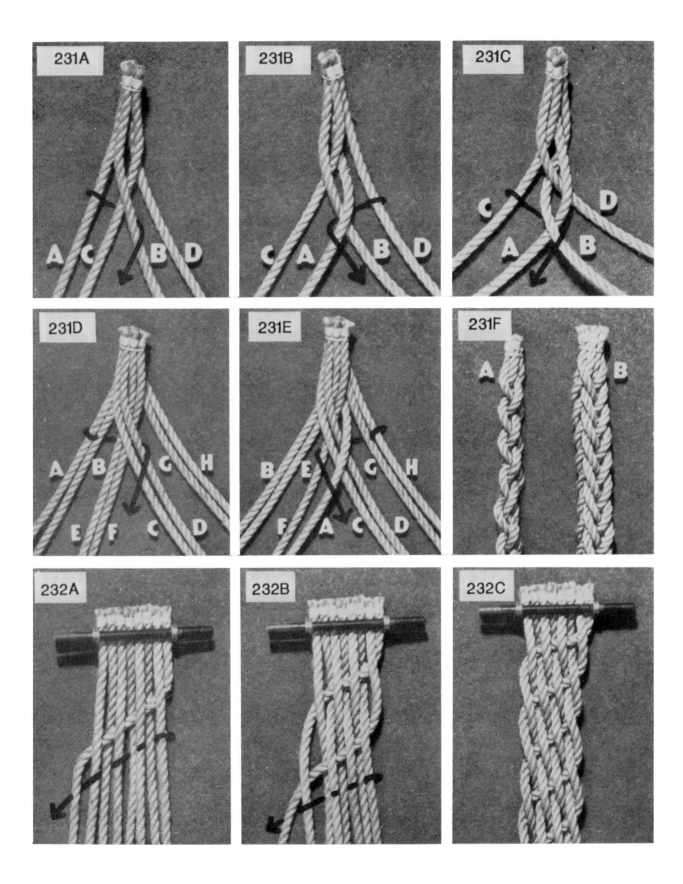

Second Method

Fig. 232D: Divide the strands into two groups, with one more strand in one group than in the other. Pass the outer strand in the larger group under and over (to the left in fig. 232D), and place it with the smaller group. Then, as shown by the arrow, pass the outer strand of the second group (which is now the larger group) under and over, and place it with the first group.

Fig. 232E: Pass the outer strand of the right-hand group over and under to the left, and place it with the left-hand group.

Fig. 232F: The finished product is similar in construction to fig. 232C on the preceding page, but it does not look like it because of the stiffness of the material out of which the specimen is made.

233. Round Sennit is made with any even number of strands above two. Round sennit of four strands is structurally like square sennit of four strands. The method of making round sennit is illustrated here by a six-strand specimen.

Fig. 233A: Bend up every other strand (*A*, *C*, and *E*) to the right, under *B*, *D*, and *F* respectively. Then bend *B*, *D*, and *F* up to the left, and *A*, *C*, and *E* down to the right.

For the sake of clarity, the arrows show how to treat only one pair of strands in each illustration (figs. 233A to 233C).

Fig. 233B: Bend *A*, *C*, and *E* up to the right, and *B*, *D*, and *F* down to the left.

Fig. 233C: Bend *B*, *D*, and *F* up to the left, and *A*, *C*, and *E* down to the right.

Fig. 233D: Four- and six-strand round sennit (*A* and *B* respectively) are illustrated. With eight strands and over, round sennit is usually made round a heart or core.

234. Coach Whipping or Cross Pointing is exactly like round sennit in structure, but it is generally made with two or more strands in each lead, and it is always made round a central cylinder or core.

Fig. 234A: The start of a specimen of four doubled strands.

Fig. 234B: The finished specimen. The ends are often concealed and held in place by means of Turk's-heads.

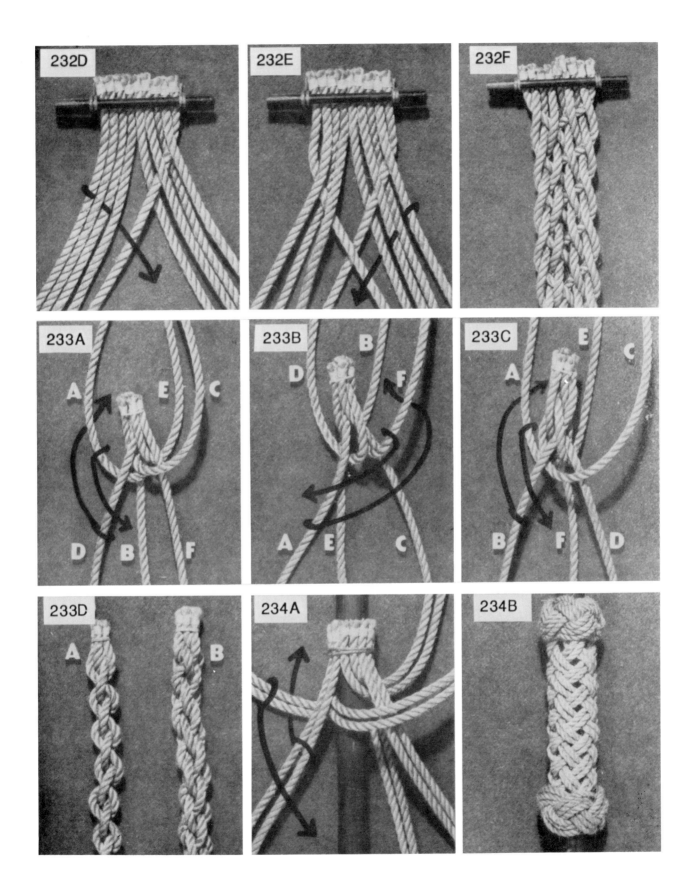

Bibliography

Knot Books and Pamphlets

Aldridge, A. F. *Knots.* New York: Rudder Publishing Co., 1918. P. 160.

Anonymous. *Cordage and Tackle (Knotting and Splicing, and the Use of Spars and Tackle).* Post Office Engineering Department, Technical Instructions 15. London: His Majesty's Stationery Office, 1911. P. 36.
Another edition, 1926. P. 34.

————. *Fiber Rope.* Safe Practices Pamphlet no. 6. Chicago: National Safety Council, 1941. P. 8.
(Earlier editions differ in content and are titled *Knots, Bends, Hitches, and Slings.*)

————. *The Girl Guide Knot Book.* See Gibson, J.

————. *How to Splice Wire Rope, and Catalogue.* New York: American Steel & Wire Co., 1923. Pp. 65–84.

————. *How to Tie Knots.* New Bedford: New Bedford Cordage Co., 1936. P. 20.

————. *Impiego delle Funi e Macchine di Circostanza.* Rome: Istituto Poligrafico Dello Stato, 1940. Pp. viii, 107. (First published in 1928.)

————. *Knots and How to Tie Them.* New Bedford: New Bedford Cordage Co., 1936. P. 20.

————. *Knots and How to Tie Them.* New York: John Simmons Co., [1912]. P. 24.

————. *Knots and How to Tie Them.* New York: Boy Scouts of America, 1942. P. 53.

————. *Knots, Bends, Hitches, and Slings.* Safe Practices Pamphlet no. 6. Chicago: National Safety Council, 1927. P. 7.
(Probably first published in 1917. Another issue or edition was copyrighted in 1936.)

————. *Knots, Hitches, and Bends.* Philadelphia: C. W. Hunt Co., 1916.

————. *Knots the Sailors Use.* New York: Whitlock Cordage Co., n.d. P. 8 (folder).
(Probably first issued as early as 1925. An expanded edition was copyrighted in 1939.)

————. *Manual of Useful Knots, Hitches, and Splices.* Dundee: McLeod, 1943.

————. *Punokset ja Solmut.* Helsinki: Otava Oy., 1944. P. 110.

————. *Reglement for Tougsvaerksarbeider . . . for 1ste Ingenieurbataillon.* Copenhagen, 1868. P. 52.

————. *Rope for the Boatman.* North Plymouth: Plymouth Cordage Co., 1931. P. 29.

————. *Rope Knowledge for Scouts.* Auburn, N.Y.: Columbian Rope Co., 1933. P. 32.

————. *Rope on the Farm.* North Plymouth: Plymouth Cordage Co., n.d. P. 23.

————. *Rope Splicing.* Milwaukee: Caspar, Krueger Dory Co., ca. 1935.

————. *Ropes, Useful Knots, and Hitches.* Bulletin no. 193, revised issue. New Zealand Department of Agriculture, 1947. P. 8.
(Publisher and place of publication not specified. Reprinted from the *New Zealand Journal of Agriculture.*)

————. *Das Spleissen der Hanf- und Drahtseile.* Berlin: Berg & Schoch, 1927. P. 115.

————. *The Splicing of Wire Rope.* Trenton: John A. Roebling's Sons Co., 1917. P. 49.
(Other editions, differing in content, were published in 1932 and 1936.)

————. *Tōke Musubi-hō Roku* ("Record of the Method of Knotting in My Family"). (Early-nineteenth-century MS. in the Boston Museum of Fine Arts.)

————. *Use, Care, and Maintenance of Manila Rope and Blocks.* Bell System Practices. American Telephone and Telegraph Co.; 1931. P. 63.

————. *Useful Hitches and Splices.* Chicago: J. C. Dorn, n.d.

————. *Useful Knots and How to Tie Them.* North Plymouth: Plymouth Cordage Co., n.d. P. 16.
Another edition, 1940. P. 23.
Another edition, 1946. P. 30.

————. *Useful Knots, Hitches, and Splices.* Racine: Johnson Smith & Co., [1935]. P. 31.
(Probably first issued as early as 1922; revised and reissued several times.)

Ashley, Clifford W. *The Ashley Book of Knots.* New York: Doubleday, Doran & Co., 1944. Pp. x, 620.
(The definitive encyclopedia of knots: authoritative, systematic, complete, readable.)

————. *"The Sailor and His Knots." Sea Stories,* July–Dec. 1925.
(Six articles in a periodical that is now rare and hard to find.)

Barnes, Stanley. *Anglers' Knots in Gut and Nylon*. Birmingham: Cornish Brothers, [1947]. P. 158.
Second edition, much enlarged, 1951. P. 266.

Belash, Constantine A. *Braiding and Knotting for Amateurs*. Boston: Beacon Press, 1936. Pp. viii, 126.
Another edition, Boston: C. T. Branford, 1952. Pp. viii, 133.

Biddle, Tyrrel E. *How to Make Knots, Bends, and Splices as Used at Sea*. London: Norie & Wilson, n.d. [before 1879]. Pp. [ii], 17, [v].
Another edition, London: C. Wilson, late Norie & Wilson, n.d. [1879?]. P. 16.
Another edition, [19--?]. P. 18.

Bineau, René. *Le Manuel du Gabier*. Paris: Éditions SPES, [1946?]. P. 94.

Blandford, P. W. *Rope Splicing*. Glasgow: Brown, Son & Ferguson, 1950. Pp. vii, 78.

Blauser, Israel P. *Uses of Rope on the Farm*. Circular 301. Urbana: College of Agriculture and Agricultural Experiment Station, University of Illinois, 1925. P. 56.
Another issue, 1943.

Bocher, Emmanuel. *Les Cordes, Tresses, Noeuds*. Vol. 4 of a 5-volume work titled *Manuel des Travaux à l'Aiguille*. Paris: Edouard Rahir, successor to Damascène Morgand, 1914. P. 267.
(A handsome folio volume, superbly illustrated.)

Boitard, Pierre. *Nouveau Manuel du Cordier*. Paris, 1839. P. 294.

[Bowling, Tom, pseud.]. *The Book of Knots*. London: Robert Hardwicke, 1866. Pp. vii, 21.
Other editions, by various publishers, in 1870, 1876, 1882, 1886, 1890, 1899, 1904.
(This is probably the first knot book. It is sometimes ascribed to Frederick Chamier [1796–1870], presumably because he published *Tom Bowling*, a novel, in 1841. It is ascribed to Paul Rapsey Hodge, fl. 1840–45, in the catalogs of the British Museum and Library of Congress. It has had an influence out of proportion to its merit.)

Brainard, Frederick R. *Knots, Splices, Hitches, Bends, and Lashings*. New York: Practical Publishing Co., 1893. P. 76.

Brown's Knots and Splices. See Jutsum, J. Netherclift.

Burger, A. A. *Rope and Its Uses*. Iowa Boys' and Girls' Club, course A. Ames: Agricultural Extension Department, Iowa State College, 1914–15. P. 48.
Another edition, revised by W. A. Buchanan, was published as Extension Bulletin 24 in 1917. P. 46.
Other issues and editions in 1920, 1922, 1923, 1927, 1932, 1937, and 1945.
Reprinted as Extension Service Circular 144, North Dakota Agricultural College, Fargo, 1936. P. 32.
Reprinted in *Nature and Outdoor Life*, New York, The University Society, 1927. Pp. 203–48.
(The 1932 and subsequent editions have only 32 pages.)

Burgess, Joseph Tom. *Knots, Ties, and Splices*. London: George Routledge & Sons, [1884]. Pp. viii, 101.
Another edition, revised by John Irving, 1934. Pp. v, 122.

Bush, C. R. *Rope Book: Knots, Hitches, and Splices. Iowa Agriculturist* 11, no. 11 (1911): 22.

Cahoon, Kenneth E. *Practical Knots and Splices*. Annapolis: United States Naval Institute, 1942. Pp. viii, 69.

Clerckx, H. *Knoopen, Steken, Lengen, Stroppen*. Antwerp: Veiligheidsmuseum, n.d. [ca. 1950]. Folio, no pagination.

Comét, N. R. *Sjömansknopen*. Malmo, 1908.
Second edition, Stockholm, 1923. P. 72.

Dana, H. J., and Pearl, W. A. *The Use of Ropes and Tackle*. Engineering Bulletin no. 8. Pullman: State College of Washington, 1922. P. 68.

Davis, F., and Van de Water, M. *Knots and Rope*. Washington, D.C.: Infantry Journal Press, 1946. P. 96.

Day, C. L. *Sailors' Knots*. New York: Dodd, Mead & Co., 1935. Pp. xv, 163.
Another edition, London: Sidgwick & Jackson, 1936.
———. *The Art of Knotting and Splicing*. New York: Dodd, Mead & Co., 1947. Pp. xv, 229.
———. *Knots and Splices: A Handbook of Sailors' Knots*. Southampton: Adlard Coles, 1953. P. 64.

Dent, J. Grant. *Rope Work*. St. Paul: by the author, 1925. P. 43.
———. *Ropework: Practical Knots, Hitches, and Splices*. Special Bulletin 192. St. Paul: Agricultural Extension Division, University of Minnesota, 1937. P. 28.

Drew, James M. *Some Knots and Splices*. Extension Bulletin no. 33. St. Paul: Department of Agriculture, University of Minnesota, 1912. P. 16.
(Reprinted in the *Irrigation Age* 28 [May 1913]: 212–20.)
———. "Rope and Cordage." Chap. 12, pp. 202–54, in Lester Griswold's *Handicraft*, Colorado Springs, 1931.
———. *Ropework: Knots, Hitches, Splices, Halters*. St. Paul: Webb Book Publishing Co., 1936. Pp. [iii], 66.
Another edition, 1942. Pp. [iii], 58.

Faber, M. E. *Knots and Braids in Handicraft*. Waupun, Wis.: The Handcrafters, 1941. P. 29.

Fehre, Hans. *Seemännische Handarbeiten*. Hamburg, 1925.

Frear, J. B. *Rope and Its Use on the Farm*. Bulletin 136. St. Paul: Agricultural Experiment Station, University of Minnesota, 1915. P. 74.

Gibson, J. *The Boy Scout Knot Book*. Glasgow: Brown, Son & Ferguson, 1933. Pp. [vi], 72.
(First published in 1916; almost identical to *The Girl Guide Knot Book*.)

Gilbert, A. C. *Gilbert Knots and Splices*. New Haven: A. C. Gilbert Co., 1920. Pp. 3–66.

[Gilcraft, pseud.]. *Knotting*. London: C. Arthur Pearson, 1929. P. 108.

Graeser, Max, and Fischer, Hildegarde. *Knüpfen und Flechten*. Leipzig: H. Beyer, [1941]. P. 50.

Grant, Bruce. *Leather Braiding*. Cambridge, Md.: Cornell Maritime Press, 1950. Pp. xviii, 173.
———. *How to Make Cowboy Horse Gear*. Cambridge, Md.: Cornell Maritime Press, 1953. Pp. xiv, 108.

Graumont, Raoul. *Handbook of Knots*. New York: Cornell Maritime Press, 1945. Pp. xiv, 194.

(Reprinted, with alterations, from Graumont and Hensel, *Encyclopedia*.)

Graumont, Raoul, and Hensel, John. *Encyclopedia of Knots and Fancy Rope Work.* New York: Cornell Maritime Press, 1939. Pp. xv, 615.
Second edition, 1942. Pp. xv, 629.
(Much of the historical introduction is derived, with verbal alterations, from Day, *Sailors' Knots,* 1935.)
———. *Square Knot, Tatting, Fringe, and Needle Work.* New York: Cornell Maritime Press, 1943. Pp. xii, 113.
(Reprinted, with alterations, from Graumont and Hensel, *Encyclopedia*.)
———. *Splicing Wire and Fiber Rope.* New York: Cornell Maritime Press, 1945. Pp. xiv, 114.
(Reprinted, with alterations, from Graumont and Hensel, *Encyclopedia*.)

Graumont, Raoul, and Wenstrom, Elmer. *Fisherman's Knots and Nets.* New York: Cornell Maritime Press, 1948. Pp. xv, 203.

Griswold, Lester. *Handicraft.* Colorado Springs, 1931.
(Reprinted many times. The eighth edition, enlarged, appeared in 1942.)

Gucker, Fritz. *Kleine Knotenfibel.* Heidenheim: A. Halscheidt, [1953]. P. 55.

Hadfield, J. W. *Rope: Its Use and Care on the Farm.* Farmers' Bulletin no. 61. Sydney, New South Wales: Department of Agriculture, 1912. P. 19.

Hardy, Evan A. *Ropes, Knots, and Hitches.* Agricultural Extension Bulletin no. 29. Saskatoon: College of Agriculture, University of Saskatchewan, 1925. P. 20.

Hasluck, Paul Nooncree. *Knotting and Splicing Ropes and Cordage.* London: Cassell and Co., 1905. P. 160.
Revised by Eric Franklin, 1952. Pp. xii, 140.
(Reprinted, with alterations, from a series of articles titled "Knotting, Splicing, and Working Cordage," by Lancelot L. Haslope (pseudonym?), in *Work: An Illustrated Magazine,* 1891–92, of which Hasluck was editor. An American edition was published by McKay in Philadelphia.)

Hegenson, J. C., and Humphries, L. R. *Farm Appliances, Including Handicraft Work.* Extension Circular 4. Logan: Utah Agricultural College, 1916. P. 22.

Hodge, P. R. See [Bowling, Tom].

Holden, P. G., and Carroll, C. M. *Making Things.* Chicago: International Harvester Co., 1919. Pp. 31–72.

Houdini, Harry. *Magical Rope Ties and Escapes.* London, n.d.

Hubin, V. *Knoopen in Gebruik bij 't Leger.* Wilryck, n.d. P. 56.

Hull, Burling G. G. *Thirty-Three Rope Ties and Chain Releases.* New York: American Magician Corp., 1916. P. 40.

Hunter, W. A. *Fisherman's Knots and Wrinkles.* London: A. & C. Black, 1927. P. 73.
Other editions in 1928, 1932, 1936. Norwegian edition in 1934.

Irving, John. *Bends, Hitches, Knots, and Splices.* London: Seeley Service & Co., [1953]. P. 66.

Ise Ansai. *Musubi no Ki* ("A Note on Knots"). Seiyudo, 1840.
(A Japanese book in the Boston Museum of Fine Arts.)

Jarrow. *Rope Magic.* North Plymouth: Plymouth Cordage Co., 1941. P. 20.

Jones, M. M., and Clark, M. W. *Farm Handicraft I: Rope Work.*
4-H Club Circular 51. Columbia: College of Agriculture, University of Missouri, 1937. P. 44.

Jorgensen, T. *Den Lille Tovvaerkslaeri.* Esbjerg: Esbjerg Tovvaerksfabrik, 1950. P. 51.

Jutsum, J. Netherclift. *Knots, Bends, Splices.* Glasgow: Brown & Son, 1907. P. 70.
Another edition, 1912. Pp. vii, 86.
Another edition, Glasgow: Brown, Son & Ferguson, 1929.
The editions of 1943 and 1945 bear the title *Brown's Knots and Splices.*

[KAA, pseud.]. *Noeuds.* Les Manuels Techniques no. 9. Louvain, 1938. P. 88.
Third edition, 1947.

Kendall, E. W., and Stevenson, L. *Knots and Splices: The Use of Rope on the Farm.* Bulletin 327. Toronto: Ontario Department of Agriculture, 1927. P. 14.
Another edition, by Kendall and E. G. Webb, 1942. P. 20.

Kunhardt, C. P. *Ropes: Their Knots and Splices.* New York: Forest and Stream Publishing Co., 1893. P. 48.

Latter, Lucy. *Knotting, Looping, and Plaiting.* London, n.d.

Laurent, G. *Nouveau Manuel Complet du Cordier.* Paris, 1911. P. 397.

Le Blanc, H. *The Art of Tying the Cravat.* Second edition. London: Effingham Wilson, 1828. P. 72.

Ledoux, R. *Tresses et Noeuds Décoratifs.* Courbevoie, 1939. P. 95.

Leeming, Joseph. *Fun with String.* Philadelphia: J. B. Lippincott Co., 1940. Pp. xii, 161.

Leland, H. A., Harrington, W. C., and Pushee, G. F. *Rope and Its Uses on the Farm.* Extension Leaflet no. 139. Amherst: Massachusetts State College, 1931. P. 35.
Revised edition, 1937. P. 36.

Lopez Osornio, Mario A. *Al Tranco.* Buenos Aires: Comisión Nacional de Cultura, 1936. P. 121.
———. *El Cuarto De Las Sogas.* Buenos Aires: Rosso, 1935. P. 140.
———. *Trenzas Gauchas.* Buenos Aires: Rosso, 1936. P. 120.
Another edition. Chascomús: Baltar, 1938. P. 120.
———. *Trenzas Gauchas.* Buenos Aires: El Ateneo, 1943. P. 365.
(This is a collected edition of the three preceding works.)

Macdonald, E. M. *Cord Knotting.* Leicester: Dryad Handicrafts, 1945. P. 16.

McCalmont, J. R. *Care and Use of Rope on the Farm.* Farmers' Bulletin no. 1931. Washington, D.C.: U.S. Department of Agriculture, 1943. Pp. ii, 17.

Miatt, George. *How to Hold on to a Rope.* New York, 1905. P. 4.

Milburn, George. *How to Tie All Kinds of Knots.* Little Blue Book no. 501. Girard, Kans.: Haldeman-Julius, 1927. P. 64.

Morley, René. *Les Pionniers: 1. Noeuds et Passerelles.* Courbevoie, 1938. P. 117.
Fourth edition, Paris, 1946.

[Nauticus, pseud.]. *The Splicing of Ropes (Cotton and Wire).*
London: Technical Publishing Co., 1912. P. 32.

Niece, H. T. *Rope and Its Uses on the Farm.* Agricultural Extension Bulletin 28. Pocatello: University of Idaho, 1919. P. 16.

Noordraven, T. J. *Schiemanswerk.* Fourth edition. Revised by S. P. De Boer. Amsterdam: J. F. Duwaer & Sons, 1950. P. 93.

Norman, C. A. *Practical Knots, Hitches, and Splices.* Agricultural Extention Bulletin no. 88. Lafayette, Ind.: Purdue University, 1920. P. 16.

Öhrvall, Hjalmar. *Om Knutar.* Stockholm: Albert Bonnier, 1908. Pp. iv, 115.
Second edition, enlarged, 1916. Pp. v, 262.
(In many ways the best book on knots that has thus far been published.)
———. *De Viktigaste Knutarna.* Stockholm: Albert Bonnier, 1912. P. 32.
Another edition, 1922. P. 36.

Osborn, E. H. *Rope Work.* Sauk Center, Minn.: Herald Print, [1915]. P. 40.

Osugawa Kyūho. *Tama no Asobi* ("A Collection of Family Knots"), 1901.
(A Japanese book in the Boston Museum of Fine Arts.)

Overholt, Virgil. *The Use of Rope on the Farm.* Bulletin no. 5, vol. 12. Columbus: Agricultural Extension Service, Ohio State University, 1916. P. 48.
(Revised edition published in 1928 as Bulletin no. 82. Reprinted 1932, 1934, 1936, 1939, 1940. Reprinted 1917 as chap. 28 of H. C. Ramsower, *Equipment for the Farm and for the Farmstead.* Reprinted 1922, 1933, 1936 as Extension Circular 700 of the Nebraska Agricultural College Extension Service. A total of 86,000 copies of Overholt's pamphlet were printed by 1940.)

Paskins, T. F. *Splicing and Socketing of Wire Ropes.* Musselburgh: Bruntons, ca. 1920. P. 52.

Popple, Leonard. *Marline-Spike Seamanship: The Art of Handling, Splicing, and Knotting Wire.* Glasgow: Brown, Son & Ferguson, 1946. Pp. xii, 82.

Pringle, H. S. *Rope Work, Power Transmission, Soldering.* Cornell 4-H Club Bulletin 60. Ithaca: New York State College of Agriculture, 1941. P. 52.

Renner, C. *Knoten, Spleissen, und andere seemännische Handarbeiten.* Berlin: von Klasing, 1926. P. 61.
Third edition, 1933. Pp. vii, 80.

Riley, H. W. *Knots, Hitches, and Splices.* The Cornell Reading Courses, Rural Engineering Series no. 1, vol. 1, no. 8. Ithaca: New York State College of Agriculture, 1912. Pp. 46–88.

Riley, H. W., Robb, B. B., and Behrends, F. G. *Hitches, Knots, and Splices.* Cornell Extension Bulletin no. 62. Ithaca: New York State College of Agriculture, 1923. P. 76.
———. *Tying Knots and Splicing Rope.* Cornell Junior Extension Bulletin 13. Ithaca: New York State College of Agriculture, 1925. P. 24.
Revised edition, 1928. P. 26.

Robb, B. B., and Behrends, F. G. *Knots, Hitches, and Splices.* New York: John Wiley & Sons, 1924. Pp. ix, 65.
(A reprint of chap. 2 of *Farm Engineering,* 1924, by the same authors. Based on Riley's admirable 1912 pamphlet for farmers.)

Roehl, Louis. *Rope Work.* Milwaukee: Bruce Publishing Co., [1921]. P. 47.
(A reprint of chap. 16 of *The Farmer's Shop Book,* 1921, by the same author.)

Ropponen, Martta E. *Solmukirja.* Porvoo, Finland: Werner Söderström, 1931. P. 129.

Saito, Yen. *Knots and Paper Folding.* Tokyo, 1918.

Saugman, Axel. *Tovvaerksarbejder.* Aarhus, Denmark: De Unges Forlag, 1923. P. 96.

Schömann, A. *Das Tauwerk.* Berlin: Beuth Verlag, 1925. P. 36.

Scoates, Daniels. *Laboratory Exercises in Farm Mechanics for Agricultural High Schools.* Farmer's Bulletin 638. Washington, D.C.: U.S. Department of Agriculture, 1915. p. 26.

Shaw, George Russell. *Knots Useful and Ornamental.* New York: Houghton Mifflin Co., 1924. Pp. vi, 109.
Second edition, enlarged, 1933. Pp. x, 194.

Sherrill, C. O., and Marshall, G. C. *Notes on Cordage and Tackle.* Fort Leavenworth: State College Press, 1909. Pp. ii, 25.

Skirving, R. Scot. *Wire Splicing for Yachtsmen.* Glasgow: Brown, Son & Ferguson, 1931. P. 34.
———. *Wire Splicing.* Glasgow: Brown, Son & Ferguson, 1932. Pp. vii, 48.
Another edition, 1943. Pp. vii, 49.

Smith, Hervey Garrett. *The Marlinspike Sailor.* New York: Rudder Publishing Co., 1949. Pp. vii, 51.
Second edition, enlarged, 1952. Pp. ix, 115.
———. *The Arts of the Sailor.* New York: D. Van Nostrand Co., 1953. Pp. viii, 233.

Smith, J. Macgregor. *Rope Knots and Hitches.* Department of Agriculture, Province of Saskatchewan, ca. 1919. P. [8].
———. *Ropework for the Farm.* Bulletin no. 9. Edmonton: College of Agriculture, University of Alberta, 1924.
Second edition, 1927. P. 33.
Fifth edition, 1940. P. 44.

Sondheim, Erich. *Knoten, Spleissen, Takeln.* Bielefeld: Klasing, 1953. P. 168.

Spencer, Charles L. *Knots, Splices, and Fancy Work.* Glasgow: Brown, Son & Ferguson, 1934. Pp. xiv, 138.
Second edition, 1935.
Third edition, 1938. Pp. xviii, 193.

Reprinted with supplement, 1939. Pp. xviii, 193, 8. (American editions published by Dodd, Mead & Co.)

Stanyon, P. J. *Great Paper and String Tricks*. London: Stanyon & Co., 1904. P. 16.

Stopford, P. J. *Cordage and Cables*. Glasgow: James Brown & Son, 1925. Pp. vii, 108.
Second edition, Brown, Son & Ferguson, 1940. Pp. vii, 116.

Svensson, Sam. *Handbok i Sjömansarbete*. Stockholm: Kooperativa Förbundets Bokförlag, 1950. P. 132.

Tossijn, Philip. *Knoopenproblemen*. Louvain: De Pijl, 1942. P. 64.
———. *Knoopen*. Second edition. Louvain: De Pijl, 1944. P. 104.
Third edition. Brussels: De Pijl, 1946. P. 64.
———. *Sierknoopen*. Louvain: De Pijl, 1942. P. 141.
Second edition. Brussels: De Pijl, 1946. P. 128.
———. *Touw- en Veterwerk*. Louvain: De Pijl, 1942. P. 168.
Second edition. Brussels: De Pijl, 1946. P. 164.

Van Uffelen, J. *Koorden en Knoopen*. Antwerp, 1933. P. 45.

Verrill, A. Hyatt. *Knots, Splices, and Rope Work*. New York: Norman W. Henley Publishing Co., 1912. P. 104.
Fifth edition, revised and enlarged by E. A. McCann, 1944. P. 146.

White, E. A. *The Care and Use of Rope on the Farm*. P. 64.
(Proof sheets of a pamphlet, apparently never published, in the Library of the U.S. Department of Agriculture in Washington, D.C. Some of the cuts seem to have been used by Blauser in his knot pamphlet dated 1925.)

White, W. R. *Knots and Splices*. Circular 194. State College: Agricultural Extension Service, Pennsylvania State College, 1938. P. 22.
Another edition, revised, 1942.

Woollard, Leslie. *Knotting and Netting*. London: W. & G. Foyle, 1952. P. 87.

Knot Tests (Listed Chronologically)

Anonymous. *Report of the Special Committee on Equipment for Mountaineers*. London: Alpine Club, 1892. (Also bound with vol. 15 of the *Alpine Journal*.)

Scovel, J. C., Jr. "Comparative Strength of Various Knots in Manila Rope." Undergraduate thesis, Massachusetts Institute of Technology, 1896. Published, in part, under the title "Results of Tests Made in the Engineering Laboratories," *Technology Quarterly* 9 (June–Sept. 1896): 234–35.

Miller, E. F. "Testing the Strength of Materials: 2. Rope Tests." *Machinery* 6 (Mar. 1900): 198–99.

Hunt, C. W. "Working Loads for Manila Rope." *Transactions of the American Society of Mechanical Engineers* 23 (1901–02): 125–30.

Eckenstein, Oscar. "Knots with the Lay." *Climbers' Club Journal* 11, no. 44 (1909): 144.

Anonymous. "Manila Rope Fastenings." *Engineering Record* 70, no. 26 (1914): 706.

Farrar, J. P. See G. W. Young, *Mountain Craft,* London, 1920.

Dent, J. G. *Rope Work*. St. Paul, 1925.

Lobo, G., Jr., and Bodden, F. A. "The Effect of the Size of Fiber Rope on the Strength of Knots." Master's thesis, Massachusetts Institute of Technology, 1927.

Wright, C. E. I., and Magowan, J. E. "Knots for Climbers." *Alpine Journal* 40 (1928): 120–40, 340–51.

Dent, J. G. "Strength Tests of Knots, Hitches, and Splices." *Agricultural Engineering* 10, no. 8 (1929): 261–62.

Barron, H. Letter to *Field and Stream,* Jan. 1931, pp. 70–71.

Day, C. L. *Sailors' Knots*. New York, 1935.

Drew, J. M. Unpublished tests reported in letter to C. L. Day, 25 May 1935.

Trumpler, P. R. "The Strength of Rope Knots." Master's thesis, Lafayette College, 1936.

Henderson, J. B., and Birdsall, B. B. "Strength of Eye Splices in Manila Rope." Master's thesis, Massachusetts Institute of Technology, 1937.

Ashley, C. W. *The Ashley Book of Knots*. New York, 1944.

McClane, A. J. "Fishing." *Field and Stream,* Nov. 1949, pp. 90–94.

Barnes, Stanley. *Anglers' Knots in Gut and Nylon*. Second edition. Birmingham, 1951.

Miscellaneous Titles (Listed Chronologically)

Zabaglia, Nicola. *Castelli e Ponti*. Rome, 1743.

Duhamel Du Monceau, H. L. *Traité Général des Pesches*. Paris, 1769–72. 4 vols.

Falconer, William. *An Universal Dictionary of the Marine*. London, 1769.

Lescallier, Daniel. *Traité Pratique du Gréement des Vaisseaux*. Paris, 1791.

Steel, David. *The Elements and Practice of Rigging and Seamanship*. London, 1794. 2 vols.
(Often reprinted in whole or in part; modern edition published by Foyle, London, 1932.)

Lever, D'Arcy. *The Young Officer's Sheet Anchor*. Leeds, 1808.
(Enlarged edition, 1819; revised 1843 by G. W. Blunt; modern edition published by Lauriat, Boston, 1930 and 1938.)

Brady, William N. *The Naval Apprentice's Kedge Anchor; or Young Sailor's Assistant*. New York, 1841.
(Often reprinted as *The Kedge Anchor; or, Young Sailor's Assistant*.)

Alston, A. H. *Seamanship*. London, 1860.
(Revised 1871 by R. H. Harris; 1902 by T. P. Walker.)

Nares, George S. *The Naval Cadet's Guide*. London, 1860.
(Second edition, 1862, titled *Seamanship*; sixth edition, 1882, revised by A. C. B. Bromley; seventh edition, 1897, revised by T. P. Walker.)

Luce, Stephen B. *Seamanship*. Newport, 1863.
(Revised 1884 by Aaron Ward; 1898 by W. S. Benson.)

Todd, John, and Whall, W. B. *Practical Seamanship*. New York, 1890.

Knight, Austin M. *Modern Seamanship*. New York, 1901. (Ninth edition, revised 1930 by H. A. Baldridge; tenth edition, revised 1937 by the Officers of the Department of Seamanship and Navigation, U.S. Naval Academy.)

Henderson, Wilfred. *Seamanship*. Portsmouth, 1907.

Anonymous. *Manual of Seamanship*. London, 1908–09. 2 vols. ("By the Authority of the Lords Commissioners of the Admiralty." Often revised and reprinted.)

Riesenberg, Felix. *Standard Seamanship*. New York, 1922.

The History and Folklore of Knots

Bourke, J. G. "The Medicine Men of the Apache." *Ninth Annual Report of the Bureau of Ethnology to the Secretary of the Smithsonian Institution 1887–88*. Washington, D.C., 1892. Pp. 443–617.

Day, C. L. "Knots and Knot Lore: A Study in Primitive Beliefs and Superstitions." *Western Folklore* 9 (July 1950): 229–56.

Dilling, W. J. Hastings' *Encyclopaedia of Religion and Ethics*, vol. 7 (1915), s.v. "knots."

Frazer, J. G. *The Golden Bough*, vols. 1, 3, and 9 (1911–13).

Gandz, Solomon. "The Knot in Hebrew Literature, or from the Knot to the Alphabet." *Isis* 14 (1930): 189–214.

Heckenbach, J. *De Nuditate Sacra Sacrisque Vinculis*. Giessen, 1911.

Keyssner, Karl. *Paulys Real-Encyclopädie der Classischen Altertumswissenschaft*, vol. 17, s.v. "nodus."

Locke, L. L. "A Peruvian Knot Record." *The American Anthropologist* 14 (1912): 325–32.

———. *The Ancient Quipu or Peruvian Knot Record*. New York, 1923.

———. *A Peruvian Quipu*. New York, 1927.

Miller, L. G. "The Earliest (?) Description of a String Figure." *American Anthropologist* 47 (July–Sept. 1945): 461–62.

Murray, M. A. "Knots." *Ancient Egypt*, pt. 1 (1922), pp. 14–19.

Nordenskiöld, Erland. *Calculations with Years and Months in the Peruvian Quipus*. Oxford, 1925.

———. *The Secret of the Peruvian Quipus*. Oxford, 1925.

Öhrvall, Hjalmar. *Om Knutar*. Second edition, Stockholm, 1916.

———. "Något om knutar i antiken, särskildt hos Oreibasios." *Eranos* 16 (1916): 51–81.

Oribasius. *Oeuvres d'Oribase*. Greek text with parallel French translation by Bussemaker and Daremberg. Paris, vol. 4 (1861), pp. 253–70, 691 (plate).

———. *Oribasii Collectionum Medicarum Reliquae*. Greek text, edited by Johannes Raeder. Leipzig and Berlin, vol. 3 (1931), pp. 253–68.

Saglio, Edmond. *Dictionnaire des Antiquités Grecques et Romaines*, vol. 4, s.v. "nodus."

Scheftelowitz, I. *Das Schlingen- und Netzmotiv im Glauben und Brauch der Völker*. Giessen, 1916.

Wolters, P. "Faden und Knoten als Amulett." *Archiv für Religionswissenschaft*, vol. 8 (1905), Beiheft, pp. 1–22.

Publications Currently Available

Altimiras, J. *Sailing Knots*. New York: Arco Publishing, 1984.

Anonymous. *Samson Rope Manual*. No. 3-83. Third edition. Boston: Samson Ocean Systems, 1982.

———. *Splicing Manual: 1983 Edition*. Boston: Samson Ocean Systems, 1983.

Bigon, Mario, and Regazzoni, Guido. *The Morrow Guide to Knots*. New York: William Morrow & Co., 1982.

Blandford, P. W. *Practical Knots and Ropework*. Blue Ridge Summit, Pa.: TAB Books, 1980.

Hin/Kampa/Hille. *This Is Knotting and Splicing*. Boston: SAIL Books, 1983.

Jarman, Colin. *The Essential Knot Book*. Camden, Maine: International Marine Publishing Co., 1984.

Jarman, Colin, and Beavis, Bill. *Modern Rope Seamanship*. Camden, Maine: International Marine Publishing Co., 1976.

Smith, Hervey Garrett. *The Marlinspike Sailor*. Reprint edition. Clinton Corners, N.Y.: John de Graff, 1981.

Snyder, Paul and Arthur. *Knots and Lines Illustrated*. Clinton Corners, N.Y.: John de Graff, 1970.

Svensson, Sam. *Handbook of Seaman's Ropework*. Reprint edition. New York: Dodd, Mead & Co., 1981. Copyright 1971, Adlard Coles, London.

Toss, Brion. *The Rigger's Apprentice*. Camden, Maine: International Marine Publishing Co., 1984.

Glossary

Becket. An eye in the end of a rope or line.

Belay. To make a line temporarily fast by winding it, figure-eight fashion, round a cleat, a belaying pin, or a pair of bitts.

Belaying Pin. A wooden or metal pin on which to belay a line, particularly the running rigging.

Bend (noun). A knot used to secure a rope to another object or to tie the ends of two ropes together.

Bend (verb). To make fast, to secure, to tie, as "to bend two lines together."

Bight. A curve in a rope or line; the middle of a rope or line. In knotting, the part of the rope or line, between the end and the standing part, on which the knot is formed.

Bitt. A heavy piece of wood or metal set in the deck; used for securing mooring lines, towing lines, and the like. Bitts are often set in pairs.

Block. A device consisting of a sheave within a shell; used for changing the direction of the force or tension exerted on a line.

Bollard. A heavy piece of wood or metal set in the deck of a vessel or on a dock; used for securing lines of various sorts.

Cleat. A piece of wood or metal, bolted or lashed down, on the two arms or horns of which a line may be belayed.

Cross Turns. Frapping turns (q.v.).

Cuckold's Neck. A hitch made in the rope when tying a bowline.

Fiber. The smallest component part of a rope; a threadlike tissue, made of hemp or another plant, which is spun into yarns.

Fid. A piece of wood (lignum vitae or hickory) similar to a marlinespike (but larger) and used for similar purposes.

Frapping Turns. Cross turns; turns taken round, and perpendicular to, the turns of a lashing or seizing.

Hambroline. Small stuff made of three strands of hemp, generally tarred, and laid up right-handed. It weighs about 92 feet to the pound.

Hawser. A rope 5 to 24 inches in circumference, for towing and similar purposes.

Heart. The core of a rope, particularly of a four-strand rope; a small rope running through the center of a hemp or wire rope.

Hitch. A knot used to secure a rope to another object or to another rope or to form a loop or a noose in a rope; a turn with the end under the standing part.

Hockle. A kink in a rope caused by inside yarns that have popped through the cover. Synthetic ropes are especially susceptible to hockling.

Houseline. Small stuff made of three strands of hemp, generally tarred, and laid up left-handed. It is somewhat heavier than marline (about 160 feet to the pound).

Knot. Used to form a knob or stopper in a rope; to enclose or bind an object; to form a loop or a noose; to tie a (small) cord to an object; to tie the ends of two (small) cords together.

Lanyard. Four-stranded tarred hemp, usually less than 4½ inches in circumference.

Lashing. A binding made of small stuff to secure one object to another, such as an eye to a spar or a spar to a spar.

Lay. The direction (right-handed or left-handed, clockwise or counterclockwise) in which the strands of a rope are twisted; also the tightness (soft, medium, common, plain, or hard lay) of the twists. See also p. 20.

Line. A rope serving a particular purpose. The word *line* is more often used by sailors than the word *rope*.

Loop. A loop knot; a fixed loop in a rope or line; a closed or nearly closed curve in a rope or a line.

Marl. To bind, or make secure, with a series of marling hitches.

Marline. Small stuff made of two yarns of hemp, generally tarred, and laid up left-handed. There are three weights: common marline (222 feet to the pound), medium marline (360 feet to the pound), and yacht marline (520 feet to the pound).

Marlinespike. A piece of steel, conical in shape and pointed, for splicing and similar work.

Nettles. Rope yarns, twisted and rubbed smooth, for pointing and similar purposes. They may be twisted in pairs or larger groups, or they may be halved and the two halves twisted into nettles.

Noose. A knot with a loop that binds more closely the more it is drawn; a running knot.

Norman Pin. A pin that is inserted, or manufactured, horizontally through a bitt, a kingpost, or a pair of towing bitts.

Pointing. Any of several methods of working the end of a rope into a rigid conical point.

Pricker. A light piece of metal, with a handle of other material, similar to a marlinespike and used for similar purposes.

Ratline Stuff. Three-stranded tarred hemp, laid up right-handed, of 12, 15, 18, 21, or 24 threads.

Reef Point. One of a number of short pieces of small rope fixed in a sail at regular intervals along a "reef band"; used in reducing sail area.

Reeve. To pass the end of a line through an opening, as through a thimble or a block. The opposite of *to reeve* is *to unreeve.*

Riders. Riding turns (q.v.).

Riding Turns. A second layer of turns put on over the first layer of turns of a seizing.

Rope. A general term denoting any cord over one inch in circumference and made of vegetable or plastic fibers or of metal wires. The component parts of a vegetable-fiber rope are called, from largest to smallest, strands, yarns, and fibers. Ordinarily the fibers are twisted together right-handed, the yarns left-handed, and the strands right-handed. Plain-laid or hawser-laid rope consists of three strands laid up right-handed. Shroud-laid rope consists of four strands laid up right-handed round a heart. Cable-laid rope consists of three plain-laid ropes laid up left-handed.

Roundline. Small stuff made of three strands of hemp, generally tarred, and laid up left-handed. It weighs about 92 feet to the pound.

Round Turn. Two turns. A round turn increases the security of a hitch.

Seize. To put on, or "clap on," a seizing.

Seizing. A small lashing for holding two ropes, or two parts of the same rope, together. Round seizings have riding turns and cross turns. Flat seizings have cross turns but no riding turns. Racking seizings are made with figure-eight turns. There are

also throat seizings, quarter seizings, middle seizings, and end seizings, so named from the part of the rope where the seizing is applied.

Seizing Stuff. Small stuff (q.v.).

Sennit. Braided nettles of small stuff.

Sheave. A grooved roller or pulley that forms part of a block and over which a rope can run. Pronounced "shiv."

Shell. The case or frame of a block within which the sheave is set.

Sling. A strap; a loop for hoisting or lowering a person or any heavy object.

Small Stuff. Seizing stuff; tarred fittings; hambroline, houseline, marline, roundline, spun yarn; hemp cordage, generally tarred, of 2, 3, 4, 6, or 9 threads.

Splice. A method of interweaving the strands of two ropes so as to join them, or the strands of two parts of the same rope so as to form an eye.

Spun Yarn. Small stuff made of hemp of 2, 3, or 4 yarns, tarred, and laid up without being twisted themselves.

Standing Part. In knotting, the main part of the rope as distinguished from the bight and the end.

Stop. To seize or lash, generally temporarily.

Stopper Knot. A knot made at the end of a line to prevent it from unreeving.

Strand. Any of several component parts or cords which, when twisted or laid up together, form a rope. Strands are made of yarns and are laid up in the direction opposite to that in which the yarns are.

Strap. A sling; small stuff marled together, or a rope with the ends spliced together, for slinging heavy objects.

Strop. Strap (q.v.).

Tarred Fittings. Small stuff (q.v.).

Thimble. A grooved piece of metal, circular or pear-shaped, round which an eye may be spliced in hemp or wire rope. Wire-rope thimbles should be pear-shaped and have deep grooves.

Thread. Yarn. Small stuff is sometimes described by specifying the number of threads or yarns it is made of, such as six-thread seizing stuff.

Toggle. A wooden pin, made of lignum vitae or hickory, with an eye spliced round a groove in the middle to fit into a second eye in order to hold two ropes or lines together.

Turn. A loop round an object.

Yarn. Any of the threads which, when twisted or laid up together, form a strand. Yarns are made of fibers.

Index